Paul Andrew

James Conard

Scott Woodgate

Jon Flanders

George Hatoun

Israel Hilerio

Pravin Indurkar

Dennis Pilarinos

Jurgen Willis

PRESENTING
Windows Workflow
Foundation Beta Edition

SAMS   800 East 96th Street, Indianapolis, Indiana 46240 USA

Presenting Windows Workflow Foundation, Beta Edition

International Standard Book Number: 0-672-32848-8

Library of Congress Catalog Card Number: 2005906053

Printed in the United States of America

First Printing: September 2005

08   07   06   05   4   3   2   1

Trademarks

Warning and Disclaimer

Bulk Sales

Sams Publishing offers excellent discounts on this book when ordered in quantity for bulk purchases or special sales. For more information, please contact

> **U.S. Corporate and Government Sales**
> 1-800-382-3419
> corpsales@pearsontechgroup.com

For sales outside of the U.S., please contact

> **International Sales**
> international@pearsoned.com

Publisher
Paul Boger

Acquisitions Editor
Neil Rowe

Development Editor
Mark Renfrow

Managing Editor
Charlotte Clapp

Senior Project Editor
Matthew Purcell

Copy Editor
Kate Givens

Indexer
Aaron Black

Proofreader
Paula Lowell

Technical Editor
Dave Green

Publishing Coordinator
Cindy Teeters

Multimedia Developer
Dan Scherf

Designer
Gary Adair

Page Layout
Brad Chinn

Contents at a Glance

Table of Contents

About the Authors

Paul Andrew is the technical product manager for Windows Workflow Foundation at Microsoft. He is currently responsible for all product management of Windows Workflow Foundation including technical collateral content creation and strategy for events and other marketing activities. His past roles at Microsoft include developer evangelist and as a developer consultant. As part of these roles, he has given talks on developer technologies on many occasions and spent many hours coding in .NET. He holds a Bachelor of Technology in Computer Systems Engineering from Massey University, New Zealand, and has MCSD, MCSE, and MCDBA certifications. He relocated in early 2005 from Microsoft New Zealand to Redmond, Washington, USA but his blog is still at http://blogs.msdn.com/pandrew. Special thanks to Delene and Duncan and to my Mum and Dad.

James Conard is an architect evangelist with Microsoft's Developer & Platform Evangelism (DPE) group. James is responsible for driving the early adoption of Windows Workflow Foundation with key ISVs and customers and for providing support to Microsoft evangelists located throughout the world. He has co-authored several books for Wrox Press and whitepapers on various Microsoft development technologies.

Scott Woodgate is a group product manager responsible for worldwide readiness of business process and integration technologies including BizTalk Server and Windows Workflow Foundation. Scott and his team support the technical community. Scott has previously authored several BizTalk Server books and has been working on these technologies for 5 years.

Jon Flanders is an industry-leading author and instructor of in-depth developer training materials at DevelopMentor. Jon is the author of *Mastering Visual Studio.NET* from O'Reilly and *ASP Internals* from Addison-Wesley. Jon holds a J.D. from Hamline University. He has been working with .NET and ASP.NET since early betas and with BizTalk 2004 since its release in March of 2004.

George Hatoun is a program manager for Workflow in Microsoft Office. He defines Office workflow engine requirements and the integration of Windows Workflow Foundation into Windows SharePoint Services. He works closely with end user customers and IT departments to understand how workflow in SharePoint and Office can improve their business processes. George has been working on collaboration products at Microsoft for nine years, including six years in Office. His previous roles at Microsoft include lead program manager for Outlook Express and MSN Explorer. George holds a B.A. in Computer Science from Rice University. He lives in Redmond, Washington, where he enjoys kayaking, hiking, and snowshoeing in the great Pacific Northwest, and traveling abroad when the weather there is not so great. Thanks to Angela, Mom, Dad, and Teta.

Israel Hilerio is a program manager in the Windows Workflow Foundation team in charge of Forms Integration and Designer Re-hosting. He joined Microsoft on April 2004 as a program manager in the CRM team focusing on Workflow, Activities, and Email Server Connectivity. Israel brings to Microsoft a wealth of knowledge developing software applications having spent more than 15 years developing distributed computing solutions. He has a background in development, supply chain, IT, and manufacturing and a Ph.D. in Computer Science.

Pravin Indurkar is a program manager on the Windows Workflow Foundation team. He has been working on Workflow at Microsoft for three years and is responsible for the state machine workflows in Windows Workflow Foundation. He has worked on several business process modeling assignments and has more than 15 years of industry experience. He holds a bachelor's degree in computer science from Birla Institute of Technology and Science, India.

Dennis Pilarinos is a program manager on the Windows Workflow Service team. His team is responsible for defining and creating the developer tools and parts of the programming model for Windows Workflow Foundation. Dennis holds a Bachelor of Science in Computing Science from Simon Fraser University, Canada. He has been working with Workflow technologies at Microsoft for more than two years.

Jurgen Willis is a program manager with the Windows Workflow Foundation team. He is responsible for the rules technology and condition-driven activities. Prior to joining Microsoft, he spent nine years architecting and building custom applications and implementing BPM solutions for numerous Fortune 500 clients in the telecommunications and financial services industries. He received a B.S. in Engineering and an M.B.A. from the University of Kansas.

We Want to Hear from You!

As the reader of this book, *you* are our most important critic and commentator. We value your opinion and want to know what we're doing right, what we could do better, what areas you'd like to see us publish in, and any other words of wisdom you're willing to pass our way.

As an associate publisher for Sams Publishing, I welcome your comments. You can email or write me directly to let me know what you did or didn't like about this book[md]as well as what we can do to make our books better.

Please note that I cannot help you with technical problems related to the topic of this book. We do have a User Services group, however, where I will forward specific technical questions related to the book.

When you write, please be sure to include this book's title and author as well as your name, email address, and phone number. I will carefully review your comments and share them with the author and editors who worked on the book.

Email: feedback@samspublishing.com

Mail: Paul Boger
         Publisher
         Sams Publishing
         800 East 96th Street
         Indianapolis, IN 46240 USA

For more information about this book or another Sams Publishing title, visit our website at www.samspublishing.com. Type the ISBN (excluding hyphens) or the title of a book in the Search field to find the page you're looking for.

Introduction

Windows Workflow Foundation was announced at the Professional Developers Conference in 2005 and it will be released in mid-2006. This book is written for Beta 1 of the technology and as such it is possible that some parts of the book may be out of date when the technology is released.

The book is intended to give you an introduction to Windows Workflow Foundation and you can read it chapter by chapter, or you can read the first three chapters as an introduction and then skip around to points of interest. You can read it offline (perhaps when you commute to work on the train) or you can work through the examples at your computer. To follow along trying out our examples, you will need Visual Studio 2005 Beta 2 and Windows Workflow Foundation SDK Beta 1. With or without a computer, you should have at least six months of .NET development experience.

This book is not intended to be your reference guide as you develop an application using Windows Workflow Foundation so it doesn't comprehensively cover all the APIs. To find out more, please visit http://msdn.microsoft.com/workflow.

There are nine authors on the book and they represent a combined experience of more than 30 years in Workflow and related technologies. I have the privilege of working with a very experienced and talented team. We are all very excited about bringing this state-of-the-art Workflow engine to the Windows platform. We hope that by using it you can find yourself new opportunities for building all kinds of interesting software.

Someone once told me that Workflow is the happy state you get into when your work just flows. Read this book and perhaps you will agree.

Paul Andrew
Product Manager for Windows Workflow Foundation
Microsoft Corporation

Workflow, Tomorrow's Application Logic

At the professional developer conference in September 2005, Microsoft announced Windows Workflow Foundation as a key component of WinFX in conjunction with Windows Communication Foundation and Windows Presentation Foundation. This chapter describes the motivation behind Windows Workflow Foundation and provides an overview of its features.

> **NOTE**
>
> Windows Workflow Foundation is a beta technology and this book was written before the beta was released. It is very possible that changes to the technology will be made through the beta cycles, which will reflect on the accuracy of information presented in this book.

The Wonder of Flowcharts

Inside classrooms around the planet students often receive their first exposure to computer program design through the concept of a flowchart. The *flowchart* provides a graphical model that is used to formalize the design of program structure—with squares, diamonds, and triangles representing the various steps in the flow such as activities and decisions. Although the flowchart model is an excellent learning tool, the flowchart is not directly represented in running software. The expense of maintaining a flowchart model in software from a CPU-cycles perspective means that the flowchart is nothing more than documentation. After the concepts of flowchart program design are mastered by students, the flowchart model is forgotten and programs are written directly in code.

Although writing programs directly in code has been the main development paradigm for more than 25 years, and many millions of programs have been created, a pure coding approach is not without issues.

- Code written by one developer is often inherently hard to understand by another. Although well-documented or commented code helps, it is often unstructured in approach. Indeed the intellectual property that is the flow of the program often stays in the mind of the original developer and is at risk when that developer moves to a new job or a new role. The flowchart model, if instantiated in code, would certainly provide an additional level of visibility in program design.

- Once compiled and executed, code is inherently opaque. The resulting assembly language or intermediary language running on a CPU natively or through a virtual machine executes a predefined set of op-codes to perform a set of activities but does not provide visibility into how these activities are executed. This has some advantages as it protects the intellectual property of the code itself, but it also creates challenges. As programs become larger, visibility into these programs at runtime becomes more important to troubleshoot errors in context of program execution. The flowchart model, if available at runtime, could provide visibility into the program execution.

- Code is often grouped into procedures or objects. Encapsulation of code, and indeed data, in these formalisms makes program design more componentized and easier to maintain. On the other hand, it poses some interesting challenges. How does data in one procedure or object move to the next procedure or object? There are fundamentally two approaches. The first is to send a message from one object to another such as a method call from one object to another passing state, or an XML message serializing state. Although this design is functional in many cases, it isn't elegant as a state needs to be passed through a chain of many objects all through parameters or XML messages. The second approach centralized the shared state in an object. The state can be retrieved, updated, and persisted to the object when required. Examples of this method include web pages on a site that communicate through shared state held in databases that may be session based or otherwise. However, in each case these state management features were custom-crafted because of the lack of a consistent development framework to manage state. Some of the challenges such a framework would face include scalability challenges in managing state over long time periods. A simple flowchart model has the notion of shared state. A variable is often set in the first step of a flowchart and then referred to later in the thread of execution. If this model for accessing state were more accessible to the programmer in a scalable manner then state management could be more efficient.

Although not part of mainstream development, over the past five years instantiating a flowchart as part of a program runtime has proved so useful in certain scenarios that regardless of the CPU cost it has become the preferred method of interaction. Some of these scenarios are described in the following sections.

Today's Workflow Scenarios

Key scenarios that use the flowchart model, branded as workflow, in software include the following:

- *Document lifecycle management*—Historically, managing the content within documents across multiple users has been ad-hoc and other than versioning tracking within documents themselves the collaboration process required to produce a particular document has not been recorded. More recently, driven either by compliance to regulation, such as Sarbanes-Oxley, or the need to accelerate traditionally paper-based processes, more and more businesses are looking to document lifecycle management. Document lifecycle management includes key workflow aspects such as tracking the people involved, and often enforcing a particular interaction pattern among multiple participants across a piece of content. The most common document lifecycle management scenarios include expense report and absence report submission where a document is submitted to a workflow involving roles, such as the manager role, which approve the content before it flows to another system.

- *Internal application workflow* —Several ERP, CRM, and other LOB vendors implement workflow within their applications to describe specific business processes that are executed within the applications. An example of this is the inventory process inside PeopleSoft. Vendors typically embed workflow to enable their end-users, sometimes developers and sometimes business users, to customize the LOB application. One of the vendor challenges associated with intra-application workflow is that each LOB vendor has to create its own workflow engine and technology rather than using a widely available common technology and as a result customers end up interacting with multiple workflow concepts, styles, and designers across multiple vendor products. Another challenge for customers is that at a business level a workflow may transverse multiple systems, which leads to the requirement to create a workflow that is external to all LOB systems and interacts with them.

- *Business process management (BPM)* —Business process management is the category of products that provide externalized business process and workflow to a set of pre-existing applications. BPM's goal is to drive control back to the business and enable agility in terms of how software responds to changing business requirements and processes. Most often business process management is layered on top of traditional integration technologies that connect prepackaged applications such as SAP and Siebel as well as businesses to other businesses across the Internet to manage the asynchronous stateful aspects of integration.

- *Page flow* —Traversing a user interface often involves navigating across a set of linked pages or views with a subset of the variables shared between the views. Commonly this navigation functionality, or page flow, and the state it requires are intermingled into the user interface layer. By intermingling the navigation functionality with the user interface, there is limited reuse of the navigation functionality and multiple files need to be modified when a navigation change is made. Several vendors have recognized this problem and applied the model-view-controller approach to user interface design separating out the page flow element as a distinct controller element from the user interface. This has been most typically applied to websites with technologies such as the Java struts framework and BEA WebLogic PageFlow, but it is equally applicable in principle to rich user interfaces such as Windows Forms, as demonstrated by the Universal Interface Process block from Microsoft Prescriptive Architecture Group for both WinForms and websites.

All of these scenarios are similar in that by using workflow they achieve greater flexibility for the designer, greater visibility into the running program, and the ability to manage state across multiple steps. Although workflow has been and will continue to be important in these scenarios, workflow has not been generally accepted into program design. Some of the historical challenges with using workflow, such as the expense of an additional layer of abstract in terms of CPU cost, are no longer relevant. Other challenges such as enabling a running workflow to be modified in-flight to provide greater customization have not been well solved in workflow software until today. What if this workflow technology was broadly available for use in all programs?

Introducing Windows Workflow Foundation

Windows Workflow Foundation is a core component of the next generation of the .NET Framework, called WinFX. Windows Workflow Foundation is broadly available to all users of Windows running Windows XP, Server 2003, Windows Vista, and the next generation Windows Server release. Some of the key goals of Windows Workflow Foundation technology are to

- Provide a singular engine for workflow execution for all applications built on the Windows platform.

- Support a wide range of scenarios from a highly people-centric workflow to the highly structured application-centric workflow and a variety of blended rules based on conditional scenarios.

- Bring model-driven workflow development to the entire WinFX development community such that every developer who today is familiar with the .NET Framework application can be immediately productive, building workflow-enabled applications without learning a second parallel set of technologies.

- Enable reuseable workflow component development through strong extensibility points and ensure both developers and ISVs can deeply embed this technology in their applications.

This is a very bold set of goals and Microsoft is achieving these goals by focusing on the core workflow requirements across many scenarios. Windows Workflow Foundation is primarily an engine and a framework—it is not a fully featured product built for a specific scenario. Indeed, although Windows Workflow Foundation is an incredibly important part of all the scenarios described earlier in this chapter, it is insufficient to complete each of these scenarios. For example, in BPM, workflow is supplemented by many features including publish and subscribe messaging, business activity monitoring, and specific development and management tools. Similarly, document lifecycle management requires information worker–centric user interfaces to manipulate the documents and collaboration centers to share them. Nevertheless, developers and ISV can use Windows Workflow Foundation and build all these scenarios around the technology.

Windows Workflow Foundation takes a unique approach to workflow, which is highly extensible. It does not have an inherent language and instead it executes a set of Microsoft and user-created steps. By taking this engine- and framework-based approach, Windows Workflow Foundation is able to address a broad range of scenarios rather than becoming restricted to a singular niche scenario and provide substantial opportunity for partners and ISVs to build a workflow ecosystem around the technology. The next section details the engine architecture for Windows Workflow Foundation.

Windows Workflow Foundation Engine Architecture

Given the breadth of scenarios requiring workflow and the key goal of providing a singular technology layer to support all these scenarios, the workflow technology is a well-factored framework with numerous pluggable interfaces and extensibility as a core design principle. The architecture for Windows Workflow Foundation is depicted in Figure 1.1.

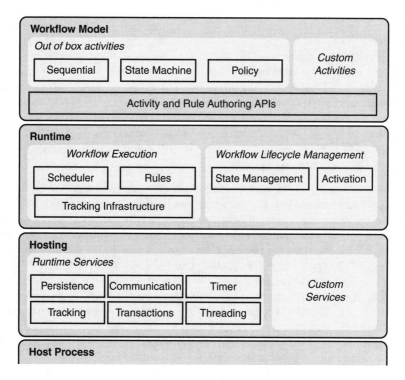

FIGURE 1.1 Windows Workflow Foundation engine architecture.

At the bottom of Figure 1.1 is the *host process*. Windows Workflow Foundation has no inherent execution process. Instead, Windows Workflow Foundation is an in-process engine that runs inside a host process. The host process is responsible for providing a set of services to Windows Workflow Foundation. A wide variety of host processes are available on the Windows platform including console applications, WinForms applications, web applications, web services applications, SharePoint Server, and NT Service applications. Effectively, any executable process can host the Windows Workflow Foundation runtime engine.

This also presents some interesting challenges because the capabilities of each host are often different to another host. SharePoint is a dramatically different environment than a console application. For this reason the Windows Workflow Foundation architecture *hosting layer* provides a set of pluggable interfaces from Windows Workflow Foundation to the host.

Sitting on top of the hosting layer in the Windows Workflow Foundation architecture is the *runtime layer*. The runtime layer is the core of the engine providing both workflow execution and workflow lifecycle management capabilities.

Finally, the workflow model layer is where most developers will interact with Windows Workflow Foundation. The workflow model layer includes the various workflow models, APIs, and the activities. The following sections provide more details on the hosting, runtime, and workflow model layers.

Hosting Layer

The hosting layer provides interfaces between Windows Workflow Foundation and a particular host for the following key services: Communication, Persistence, Tracking, Timer, Threading, and Transaction. The implementations of the former three services that ship with Windows Workflow Foundation are durable while the latter two services are stateless. However, none of the services are necessarily durable if you write your own. By abstracting each of these services Windows Workflow Foundation can take advantage of specific capabilities available in specific hosts. The following sections describe the functions performed by each of these services:

- *Persistence*: Although some workflows may execute for a short period of time, workflow is inherently asynchronous and a particular workflow, such as the Ph.D. thesis approval process, may take many days or months. A workflow engine that retained its state in memory for that period would not scale as each instance of the workflow would consume memory for the duration and eventually the system memory would be exhausted. Instead, a persistent architecture is used where workflow is executed in memory, and should it be required, the workflow state will persist to a store while it waits for a response that might take some time such as the "Ph.D. approved" step in the workflow. Each host application has a specific set of persistence requirements. For example, to persist state, ASP.NET uses a set of Session State objects that has state client providers for in-memory persistence and SQL Server persistence. In contrast, SharePoint persists state in a SharePoint-specific set of tables in SQL Server and your console application may choose to persist state to the file system as XML. With such a large variety of host-specific persistence capabilities, it would not be sensible for a broadly applicable technology such as Windows Workflow Foundation to specify a single persistence provider. The Windows Workflow Foundation hosting layer persistence interface enables Windows Workflow Foundation to work across the full gamut of host persistence architectures.

- *Timer*: Workflows often need to wait for an event to continue. The timer is the supplied clock that is used to manage these delays. For example, an approval workflow may delay and unload from memory until a particular approver completes the necessary approval. The timer implementation in this case might be a durable timer that survives a potential system restart while waiting for approval.

- *Tracking*: A key reason to implement workflow is because the workflow model provides a greater degree of system transparency at runtime than amorphous code. Indeed, all workflows are automatically instrumented without any programming. The tracking instrumentation is consistent across both the event content and the tracking interface. Depending on the host, the target tracking infrastructure is often different. For example, a LOB application often persists workflow tracking information within the LOB database whereas a console application may persist tracking information to an XML file. The tracking interface receives tracking events from the Windows Workflow Foundation runtime and passes them on to the host application.

- *Communications*: Workflows send and receive events or messages from their host. These events trigger workflows, and move the workflow to the next step in the overall flow. There are a wide variety of communications infrastructures available on the Windows platform including web services, .NET calls, loosely coupled messaging, and so on. For this reason, Windows Workflow Foundation does not provide its own proprietary communications layer. Instead, Windows Workflow Foundation provides pluggable interfaces that can be implemented for any communications layer. Of course, there are easy-to-use, prebuilt communication interfaces to and from common targets such as web services and for passing data objects in and out of a workflow—perhaps from a form.

The physical job of development of these interfaces for specific hosts is relatively challenging compared to other aspects of workflow development described shortly. For this reason, ISVs will typically build host layer providers into their host applications so that end-user developers can simply reuse these services. In addition, Windows Workflow Foundation ships prebuilt support for ASP.NET 2.0 and the interfaces shown in Table 1.1.

TABLE 1.1   Prebuilt Host Layer Service Implementations

Host Layer	Service Implementation
Persistence	SQL Server state persistence
Timer	Both an in-memory and SQL Server–based timer
Threading	.NET thread pool
	ASP.NET thread pool
Tracking SQL	Server Tracking Persistence and Event Log recording for termination
Communications	.NET components and web services

Sitting on top of the hosting layer is the runtime layer.

Runtime Layer

The runtime layer is core to Windows Workflow Foundation. In direct comparison to the other layers in the architecture, the runtime layer is not pluggable as it contains the mission-critical services required for workflow. These services include the following:

- *Execution*: The execution service schedules activities and supports common behaviors such as event handling, exceptions, tracking, and transactions.

- *Tracking*: The tracking service creates the tracking events that are serialized through the tracking interface.

- *State management*: The state management service manages states that may be persisted through the persistence interface.

- *Scheduler*: The scheduler service schedules execution of activities.

- *Rules*: The rules service provides policy execution functionality and CodeDOM condition evaluation.

Workflow Model Layer

The workflow model layer is where most application developers will spend the majority of their time writing code for Windows Workflow Foundation. This layer includes support for multiple workflow model types, activities, and the main programming APIs use by most developers.

Windows Workflow Foundation supports two models out of the box:

- *Sequential workflow model*: This model is primarily a structured workflow where a step in the workflow leads to another step in a manner that may be determined often at design-time and can be represented in a flow diagram such as that shown in Figure 1.2.

  Sequential workflows are most often used to represent structured workflows such as system-to-system workflow. These transformational workflows are self-driven once they are initiated, have a highly predictable path through the events, and are often literally sequential in nature.

- *State machine workflow model*: This model uses the paradigm of states and transitions between states to represent the workflow. There is no deterministic path between the steps from a design perspective because the workflow does not execute in a sequential nature. Rather, the workflow is a set of events that are handled in a highly variable order with one event completing and triggering a state that another event may itself trigger from. The state machine model can literally jump from any stage in the workflow to any other stages, and often will do so multiple times before reaching a completed state. The order workflow is a state machine where various messages are received and trigger the workflow to progress to a particular state. Each iteration of this workflow may result in a different path through the model as depicted in Figure 1.3.

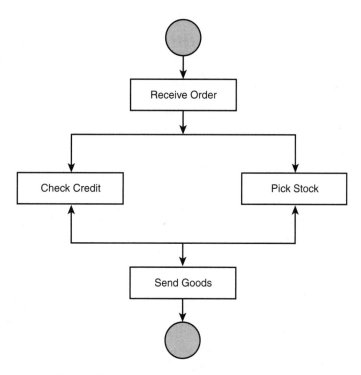

FIGURE 1.2   Sequential workflow.

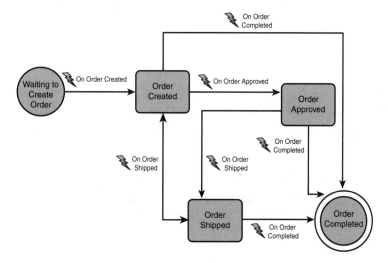

FIGURE 1.3   State machine workflow model.

State Machine Workflows are an effective way of representing highly people-centric work-flows where the workflow thread of execution is not easily represented in a flow. This workflow model is also very useful for scenarios where a high priority event must be processed even though work is already in process or when a large number of events may occur at a particular stage in the workflow. A perfect example is a stage in the order work-flow where an "order cancelled," "order updated," and "order completed" event that may be received at any time and should immediately cancel the entire process.

Although Windows Workflow includes these two models, customers can inherit from them to create their own specific models or create new models.

Regardless of model and sequencing behavior the basic element of execution and reuse is called an *activity*. An example of an activity is "send goods" in the previous sequential workflow example.

There are two types of activities—the simple activity and the composite activities. What makes Windows Workflow Foundation very different from traditional workflow engines is that the engine has no fixed underlying language or grammar. Instead the engine chains a set of activities that are supplied by Microsoft and created by you the developer. Microsoft-supplied constructs include "If," "Code" blocks, activities for web services, and many more. In addition, you can create your own control flow activities such as "do until" but more likely you will be creating higher level activities such as the "Receive Order" activity described previously. By using an activity execution methodology rather than a language, Windows Workflow Foundation is able to support a broad range of scenarios and you can reuse your activities across multiple workflows. Indeed the flow and the state workflow models share a majority of activities with some specific inclusions and exclusions to each model. Activities become the unit of encapsulation in much the same way that ActiveX controls were for Visual Basic 6 applications. It is expected that customers and partners will share activities in the community and generate business from activity creation.

The set of flow control activities that ship with Windows Workflow Foundation include the following:

- Control flow activities: `Sequence`, `Parallel`, `While`, `IfElse`, `Listen`, `EventDriven`, `ConditionedActivityGroup`, `Replicator`, `Delay`

- Transaction and exception activities: `ExceptionHandler`, `Throw`, `Compensate`, `Suspend`, and `Terminate`

- Data/form-centric activities: `UpdateData`, `SelectData`, `WaitForData`, `WaitForQuery`

- Communication activities: `InvokeWebService`, `WebServiceReceive`, `WebServiceResponse`, `InvokeMethod`, and `EventSink`

- The code activity: `Code`

There are three additional activities that are specific for the state machine workflow model: `StateInitalization`, `State`, and `SetState`.

Each activity is derived from the `Activity` base class and includes the code that will execute when the activity and a set of design-time properties for use in the designer is called. Later chapters in this book will go into detail on each of these activities; however, a few activities are worth mentioning here. The data- and form-centric activities enable you to bind data from forms and easily surface that information into a workflow; the web services activities give you the capability to consume and expose web services; more advanced activities such as the conditioned activity group enable policy- or rules-based condition evaluation.

Over time, many activities will become available through the broader activity ecosystem through blogs and shared source as well as through Microsoft partners.

Now that we have addressed activities in detail it is important to point out that the model itself is nothing more than a "root" level activity in the Windows Workflow Foundation infrastructure.

One of the significant features of Windows Workflow Foundation is that it offers you the ability to dynamically create workflow at runtime and dynamically update an existing workflow. This is discussed in more detail later in this book.

Now that you have completed your tour of the Windows Workflow Foundation architecture, it's time to examine the coding and design-time support for you to interact with the engine.

Design-time

Typically, workflow technologies have provided graphical designers that give users the capability to drag and drop shapes to build a workflow. Some tools are targeted at business users while other tools are targeted at developers. Windows Workflow Foundation provides a set of graphical tools inside Visual Studio .NET targeted at developers. The goal of the Visual Studio .NET design experience is to be as familiar as possible to existing .NET developers writing C# and VB.NET applications and building Longhorn applications using Windows Presentation Foundation and Windows Communication Foundation.

After Windows Workflow Foundation is installed, an additional category appears on the Visual Studio .NET File New dialog box called "Workflow," as shown in Figure 1.4.

Most interesting in this introductory chapter are the Sequential Workflow Library and State Machine Workflow Library templates. The Workflow Activity Library is a template for creating custom activities and creates a project with an activity-specific designer, making it easier for you to create activities. The workflow console application and state machine console application are simple host applications for Workflow, and finally, the empty workflow project is an unconfigured workflow project.

When the Sequential Workflow template is chosen, a new project is created and `System.Workflow`, `System.WorkflowActivities`, and `System.WorkflowComponentModel` are all added to the project references. In addition workflow1.cs and workflow1.designer.cs are added to the project. By default, selecting workflow1.designer.cs with the mouse will graphically render the workflow directly inside the Visual Studio designer as shown in Figure 1.5.

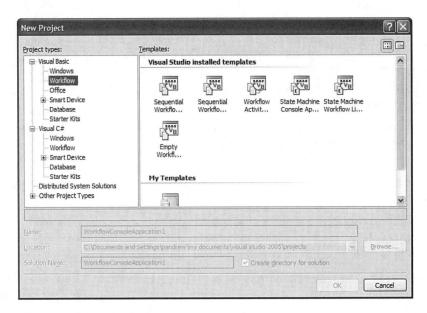

FIGURE 1.4   File New Visual Basic workflow project.

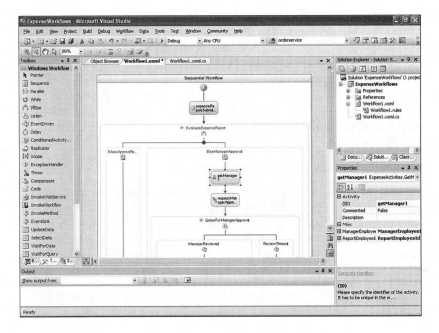

FIGURE 1.5   Visual Studio .NET designer for sequential workflow.

The workflow is described by dragging and dropping shapes from the toolbox. Just like traditional WinForms or ASP.NET development, when a shape has code associated with it, clicking on the shape will open the code-behind where custom code may be entered directly in VB or C#. Any changes to the code-behind file that are relevant to display in the workflow are automatically reflected back in the designer.

In addition you can add a new item to the project that is a workflow with xoml. The xoml file is actually an XML file containing an XML definition of the workflow. That XML is fully accessible to the developer by choosing File, Open With and selecting the XML editor inside Visual Studio .NET. This XML and Visual representation is consistent with the Windows Presentation Framework approach in WinFX as shown in Figure 1.5.

The state machine workflow model is depicted in Figure 1.6.

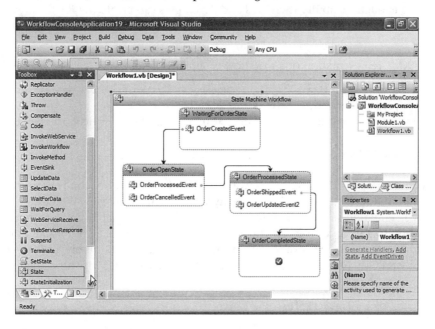

FIGURE 1.6   Visual Studio .NET designer for state machine workflow.

This simple state machine workflow looks similar to a sequential workflow. However, in this case each box represents a state and in most examples the lines in the diagram will not just go in a forward direction as depicted but also backwards—for example an event from the orderprocessedstate may send the state machine back to the orderopenstate. Also notice the state machine–specific activities, such as StateInitialization, in the activity toolbox.

Visual Studio .NET provides "smart tags" to alert the user that properties on specific activities are not properly configured. When the workflow is complete the developer builds the project and the two partial classes that represent the code-beside and the workflow model are compiled and stored in a managed assembly.

Windows Workflow Foundation provides complete support for the familiar F5 debugging experience. Breakpoints can be set on the models at design-time using the mouse or F9 key and when a break-point is triggered, a complete call-stack is available and the debugger allows stepping into and out of the code for the workflow in debug mode.

There is no business user design surface primarily because these surfaces tend to be scenario-specific and Windows Workflow Foundation needs to support a variety of scenarios. The good news is that you can build your own business user design surface on top of Windows Workflow Foundation. The workflow designer can be completely rehosted outside of Visual Studio .NET in your custom application. Further, every aspect of the designer can be reskinned so that the look and feel of the designer control, including the size, color, and geometry of the shapes, matches your application style. By rehosting the designer and providing your customers with specialized activity packages, you can give your end-users the ability to create and modify workflow. If rehosting the designer does not provide enough flexibility then ISVs and developers can create the XML representation of the workflow from a custom tool directly, or better still, build an activity tree in code.

A sample XML representation of a workflow is depicted here:

```
<?Mapping XmlNamespace="Activities" ClrNamespace="System.Workflow.Activities"
Assembly="System.Workflow.Activities" ?>
<SequentialWorkflow x:Class="MyWorkflow" xmlns="Activities" xmlns:x="Definition">
    ...
</SequentialWorkflow>
```

There is another option for generating workflow that is a significant innovation in Windows Workflow Foundation. Unlike many workflow technologies, Windows Workflow Foundation supports a complete coding experience enabling you to create and modify workflows in code. You can choose to use a tool as simple as Notepad and the command-line compiler `wfc.exe` to author workflow. Workflow is simply a class. A sample sequential workflow that executes a single activity called `SendEmail` is shown here:

```
Public Class Workflow1
    Inherits SequentialWorkflow

    Public Sub New()
        MyBase.New()
        InitializeComponent()
    End Sub

    Private Sub InitializeComponent()
        Me.s = New SendEmail
        Me.s.MailFrom = "Paul"
        Me.s.MailTo = "James"
        AddHandler Me.s.OnBeforeSend, AddressOf Me.OnBeforeSend

        Me.Activities.Add(Me.s)
        Me.DynamicUpdateCondition = Nothing
        Me.ID = "Workflow1"
```

```
End Sub

Private WithEvents s As SendEmail

Private Sub OnBeforeSend(ByVal sender As System.Object, ByVal e As _
    System.EventArgs)
    Me.s.MailSubject = "Hello at " & System.DateTime.Now.ToString()
End Sub
```

```
End Class
```

There is a designer for activities inside Visual Studio .NET. However, just like workflows, activities are also simply classes derived from the Activity base class and can be completely created in code. The SendEmail activity skeleton fragment is shown here:

```
<ToolboxItem (GetType(ActivityToolboxItem))> _
Partial Public Class SendEmail
    Inherits System.Workflow.ComponentModel.Activity
    Public Sub New()
        MyBase.New()
        InitializeComponent()
    End Sub

    Public Shared MailToProperty As DependencyProperty = _
      DependencyProperty.Register("MailTo", GetType(System.String), _
      GetType(SendEmail))
    Public Shared MailFromProperty As DependencyProperty = _
      DependencyProperty.Register("MailFrom", GetType(System.String), _
      GetType(SendEmail))
    Public Shared MailSubjectProperty As DependencyProperty = _
      DependencyProperty.Register("MailSubject", GetType(System.String), _
      GetType(SendEmail))

    <DesignerSerializationVisibility(DesignerSerializationVisibility.Visible)> _
        <ValidationVisibility(ValidationVisibility.Optional)> _
            <Browsable(True)> _
                Public Property MailTo() As System.String
        Get
            Return CType(MyBase.GetValue(SendEmail.MailToProperty), String)
        End Get
        Set(ByVal value As System.String)
            MyBase.SetValue(SendEmail.MailToProperty, value)
        End Set
    End Property
```

```
<DesignerSerializationVisibility (DesignerSerializationVisibility.Visible)> _
    <ValidationVisibility (ValidationVisibility.Optional)> _
        <Browsable (True)> _
            Public Property MailFrom() As System.String
    Get
        Return CType(MyBase.GetValue(SendEmail.MailFromProperty), String)

    End Get
    Set(ByVal value As System.String)
        MyBase.SetValue(SendEmail.MailFromProperty, value)

    End Set
End Property

<DesignerSerializationVisibility(DesignerSerializationVisibility.Visible)> _
    <ValidationVisibility(ValidationVisibility.Optional)> _
        <Browsable(True)> _
            Public Property MailSubject() As System.String
    Get
        Return CType(MyBase.GetValue(SendEmail.MailSubjectProperty), String)

    End Get
    Set(ByVal value As System.String)
        MyBase.SetValue(SendEmail.MailSubjectProperty, value)

    End Set
End Property

    Public Event OnBeforeSend As eventhandler
End Class
```

In addition to design-time API workflow generation, dynamic update makes it possible to update running workflows on the fly. The dynamic update functionality opens the door to many interesting scenarios that were not previously possible with traditional workflow engines such as examining the state of the model at runtime and making behavioral changes as a result of variables within the flow.

This section has just touched the surface of activities; you will learn much more about activities later in this book.

In summary, Windows Workflow Foundation provides a complete authoring experience inside Visual Studio .NET with custom designers and debugging support but also provides the flexibility for you to create workflow using code directly or through XML. Now take a quick look at how a sample application uses Windows Workflow Foundation.

Office 12 Workflow

Office is the most popular desktop productivity program on the planet. One of the key feature requests from Office customers is the capability to collaborate on documents using workflow. Office 12 uses the Windows Workflow Foundation engine embedded inside the SharePoint host for workflow. The office client applications, such as Word, can kick off workflow through web services integration with Office. That workflow is executed on SharePoint and as a result a document may be sent through email to a user in Outlook to perform an action. Once the action is performed the workflow continues.

Office also provides a simple design experience in FrontPage and for more complex design, Office has its own specific activity package containing more than 30 custom activities and customers can use this directly in Visual Studio .NET. In addition, the InfoPath designer in Office 12 supports data binding form elements to a workflow. Several prebuilt workflows ship with Office 12 including Review, Approval, and Document Expiration and Office 12 supports custom workflows. Figure 1.7 shows the Review workflow in Microsoft Word.

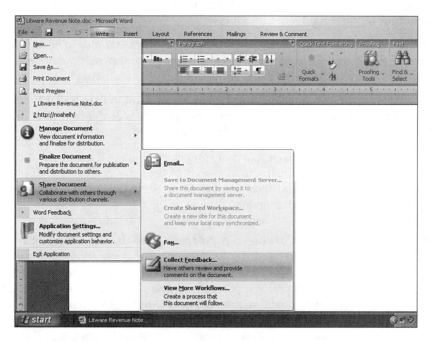

FIGURE 1.7   Microsoft Word showing a Review workflow.

Developers looking to create people-based workflows should first look into customizing Windows Workflow Foundation in the context of the SharePoint host as this strategy will get you access to the Office applications immediately. There is no doubt workflow is a key feature of Office 12 and the Windows Workflow Foundation technology will be used immediately by many information workers around the world.

You have read about the Windows Workflow architecture, design tools, and a brief description of the Office 12 functionality; however, you might be wondering when and why you should use Workflow. Now that you have briefly learned about the capabilities that Windows Workflow Foundation provides, the final section of this chapter addresses the core tenets of workflow. You can think of these as the call to action because these four tenets address key aspects of application design that are fulfilled by workflow.

Call to Action: Core Workflow Tenets

Before we get to the specific tenets, it is appropriate to revise the tenets for service-oriented architecture because often workflow will be coupled in application architecture with web services. As part of the next generation web services effort, several key tenets have been identified. Although these are described in detail elsewhere on the web they have been summarized as follows:

- *Boundaries are explicit*: When compared to objects or remote objects, services have clear boundaries. Calling services is relatively expensive compared to calling code within a service. Choosing where these boundaries exist is an interesting challenge that leads to the second tenet.

- *Services are autonomous*: The key point here is that services, unlike objects, can execute autonomously from other services. The key word here is *can* because of course in many cases one service will call another.

- *Share schema and contract and not class*: In short, the notion here is that loose coupling is good and sharing a schema between services enables a greater degree of loose coupling than sharing explicit class types.

- *Service compatibility is based on policy*: This tenet emphasizes the separation of semantic and structural concerns. Structural aspects of the services are stored in policy files and service compatibility is driven from these, in some cases without modifying the specific business logic of the service.

These tenets focus on boundaries between components, and the point-to-point connections between these components needed to build composite applications. These four tenets in themselves are insufficient for a service-oriented architecture where distributed services are composed into composite applications. What is missing? The key missing pieces are guidance on how to compose these services together, the characteristics of such a system, and the need to involve people as a part of composite application design. To that end, the four core tenets that follow assume the initial set of tenets and expand on them to provide guidance for composite application development:

- *Workflows are long-running and stateful*: Fundamentally, systems are created by the composition of multiple services and, following good design practices, components that perform specific roles should be created as autonomous services. The behavior between these services can be as simple as passing and mapping behaviors or more complex such as sharing transactional semantics and temporal constraints. The temporal aspects of service composition enforce asynchronous requirements on the system. A service that submits a purchase order to other services as part of a composite application waits for two hours for an acknowledgement. This asynchronous controller, or model, should be independently factored as a specialized service component. Hand in hand with the requirement to model asynchrony is the need to include state as part of the model. The service that sent out a purchase order and received an invoice requires information on the purchase order to later update another service. State may be relevant to a single call, relevant across multiple calls, or relevant across an entire asynchronous workflow.

- *Workflows are transparent and dynamic through their lifecycle*: Services and the applications to which they compose should not be, as they are today, like concrete bunkers with no windows. Although policy provides rigor in the definition of how to talk to the service, what the service does—its behavior—is opaque beyond its method call syntax. System behavior should be transparent, enabling the developer to rapidly ascertain the behavior at design-time and make a change in that behavior. Even more importantly, system behavior should be transparent at the runtime level. If the behavior of each service in a composite application were transparent the advantages would be significant. No longer is the service a concrete bunker; rather, it is more analogous to a greenhouse. Troubleshooting, tracking, and understanding the overall composite application behavior becomes dramatically simpler because of the additional visibility into the thread of execution. Entirely new scenarios can be envisioned where the behavior of the system thus far executed can be queried at runtime and used to influence of the future behavior. With access to the system behavior metadata, the thread of execution can analyze the currently completed behavior and make changes to its behavior on the fly on the basis of new program conditions. Having asserted that system behavior should be transparent by default, there are times when the developer will want to decrease the level of transparency. For example, some service behavior may need to be obstructed for intellectual property reasons, or specific service behavior is visible within a bounded set of services but not beyond that. The dial that sets the service transparency should be set through policy and access control rather than the traditional development approach where a transparent system is not a default and developers add small windows to prebuilt concrete bunkers.

- *Workflows coordinate work performed by people and by software*: The original tenets for services make no reference to people and yet people are a vital part of any composite application. Today services typically send messages to people through email and pagers, or receive inputs from people through user interfaces that pass their parameters to and from services. Sometimes a single person provides the information required for the composite application to continue but more often than not an entirely out-of-band interaction occurs between multiple people in a manner that has been historically challenging to model in software before a result is returned to the composite application to continue. People are important; optimizing their behavior as part of the overall system behavior may provide as high a return as optimizing the system behavior itself with some systems having 80% of their cost in exceptions managed by people. The downside of including people from a software engineering perspective is that modeling their behavior is significantly less straight-forward than modeling service behavior. People tend to work in a more ad hoc manner—it is typically more challenging to be imperative with people, and the flow of information between people may not be easily drawn in a flow-based sense because they make choices that may change the workflow at runtime, but is more ad hoc and is better represented as a set of interacting exception conditions.

- *Workflows are based on extensible models:* Every workflow comprises some number of steps, each of which performs a particular part of a complete business process. The set of actions that are used to construct a workflow can be thought of as comprising a model for that particular problem domain. Different problem domains have differ-ent actions, and so a single model isn't appropriate for all workflows. Instead, differ-ent groups of actions—different models—can be created for specific domains. Those actions can then be used to construct workflows supporting various business processes in that domain.

With these tenets you can evaluate when to use workflow in your application. There are many, many applications that could benefit from the use of workflow, yet the lack of availability of a workflow model is highly consistent with the typical programming para-digm. With Windows Workflow Foundation for the first time you get to take advantage of this opportunity; moving forward, it will change the way you think about application development.

Summary

Historically, workflow has been limited in its usage within applications due to the lack of availability of generalized technology. For the first time, Windows Workflow Foundation provides application developers and independent system vendors with a generalized workflow engine for building workflow on the Windows platform. Windows Workflow Foundation can be used by developers to support a broad range of scenarios including, but not limited to, composite application development, document lifecycle management, BPM, IT provisioning, and workflow within LOB applications. Windows Workflow Foundation supports multiple workflow models including sequential and state flow machine. Windows Workflow Foundation's designer, available inside Visual Studio .NET and rehostable in your application, provides a productive environment for developers to build workflow in a manner consistent with familiar ASP.NET, Windows Communication Foundation, Window Presentation Foundation, and WinForm development paradigms. The base unit of a workflow in Windows Workflow Foundation is an activity. Activities are fully extensible and it is expected that developers will build a vast range of activities from generic horizontal activities such as "Send Email" to specialized vertical activities such as "Legal approval" and deliver those to customers and end-users through activity packages. You can use the four tenets of workflow to guide you on using workflow as part of your application development process.

The remaining chapters in this book delve into the details of the various aspects of Workflow Foundation with code examples so that you, the developer, can rapidly build skills with this technology and use it routinely when building next-generation applications on top of WinFX.

In addition to this book, a vibrant workflow community is growing so check out blogs and other community sites—or even post your own experiences and samples.

CHAPTER 2

Developing Your First Workflow

When web services first came out in 2002 I particularly liked the web service new project template, which provided a really simple web service implementation as part of the template. You could either use this as a starter, or you could scoff at those who didn't know that simple stuff by heart, delete it, and start from scratch.

In this chapter I plan to give you the simple stuff for building workflows with Visual Studio 2005. This means an application (or two) that doesn't take much time for you to understand and that you can create from scratch any time you like without documentation reference.

Because Windows Workflow Foundation is part of the Windows platform it can be exposed in any application type supported by the .NET Framework and you have a number of options for achieving this:

- Console application

- Windows forms application

- Web forms application

- Windows service

Chapter 6, "Using Web Services," covers web forms so we'll leave that for now. In this chapter you will walk through a simple console application and a simple Windows forms application, both of which make basic use of a workflow.

Architecture Review

Chapter 1, "Workflow, Tomorrow's Application Logic," introduced you to a number of aspects of the Windows Workflow Foundation architecture. Figure 2.1 shows a summary of the architecture as a review point.

A *workflow* is a defined model that represents some real-world process. The workflow model is constructed out of activities either by code or using a designer. The workflow model may be loaded as a particular workflow instance and that instance is executed on the runtime running on a host process. Many instances of the workflow model can be started and each instance has its own state and execution context.

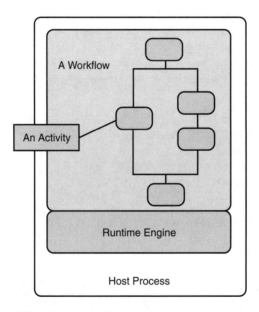

FIGURE 2.1   How a workflow is put together.

What You Need

You can follow along with the code presented in this chapter. To get the most out of this book, you should have some experience with .NET development. Windows Workflow Foundation requires the .NET Framework 2.0 to run. It is also recommended that you have Visual Studio 2005 (any edition) to try any of the samples that are presented in the book. Although .NET Framework 2.0 is required to run Windows Workflow Foundations, you will be able to follow the book if you have experience with .NET Framework 1.1 (or 1.0).

Your First Console Workflow Application

This will be the first of two very simple examples that introduce workflow to common application types.

Workflow Console Application

The workflow console application is a project template that enables you to create one project including a workflow and the host application. It gives you a sequential workflow project item with a console host that is coded to execute that workflow. Of course, you can create an empty workflow project and add items to it, but in that case you would have to write more code.

First create a new project and choose the workflow console application project template. Figure 2.2 shows the available project templates.

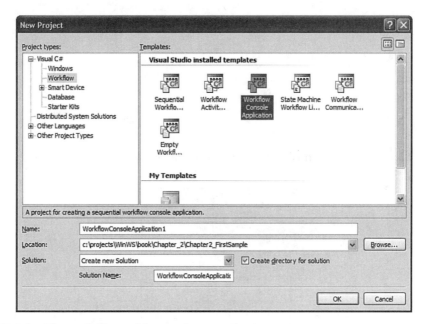

FIGURE 2.2   The available workflow project templates.

Give the project a name and then click OK. Next you will see the blank workflow design surface showing a sequential workflow as in Figure 2.3.

You are ready to drag activities onto the workflow and try them out. Figure 2.4 shows the toolbox and all of the workflow activities.

For now you're only going to use the Code activity. Drag one from the toolbox to the workflow surface.

The new Code activity is called code1 by default. Notice the red circle containing an exclamation point as shown in Figure 2.5. This is a ToolTip to tell you this activity contains an error.

FIGURE 2.3   A blank sequential workflow model in the workflow designer.

FIGURE 2.4   The toolbox in Visual Studio 2005 showing workflow activities.

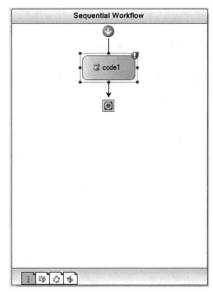

FIGURE 2.5   The Code activity with an error.

If you click on the ToolTip you will see the error as shown in Figure 2.6.

> **NOTE**
>
> Watch out for these ToolTips when building workflows because they show many errors and provide instant feedback so you can avoid compile errors. They also might offer advice on how to fix the problem.

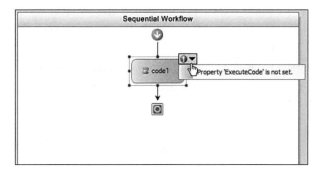

FIGURE 2.6   The error ToolTip on the Code activity.

The ToolTip is telling you that a Code activity must have some code to run and you haven't specified that yet. This workflow uses code-beside, making use of the support for partial classes—a new feature in .NET Framework 2.0. The workflow model is stored in one file that is edited directly by the design surface. All associated code is stored in a separate code-beside file. On compilation, both of these files are compiled as one .NET type that can be executed by the workflow runtime.

> **NOTE**
>
> It is not necessary to use the XML file. There is also support for code-only workflows, which do not require XML.

All you have to do is double-click on the Code activity to get to the code handler (see Figure 2.7).

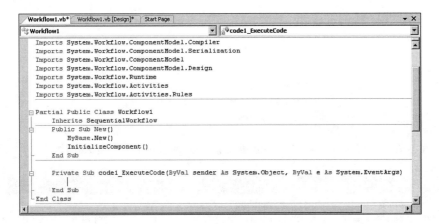

FIGURE 2.7   The code-beside class for the workflow model.

The cursor is now in the code1_ExecuteCode method and you just need to type one line of code to write to the console. The method with the single Console.WriteLine statement is shown here:

```
Private Sub code1_ExecuteCode(ByVal sender As System.Object, _
                              ByVal e As System.EventArgs)
    Console.WriteLine("Hello, World!")
End Sub
```

Now you are done. Run the application and it will output "Hello, World!" to the console.

Adding Input and Output to a Console Application

You've just re-created a program that is classic to computer science students. It doesn't do much though. Next, you will have the workflow output some text that you give it. This next simple walk-through shows you how to use a workflow parameter to get input into a workflow and provide output back to the caller. This is only one of several mechanisms for input/output in a workflow. Others that are available include web services, data activities, local communication services, or workflow message queues.

Describing the Existing Console Host

Start with the sample you created in the previous section. First you will add the parameters to the workflow, next you will access them in the workflow, and finally you will modify the host (found in module1.vb) to set and check the parameters.

This is the main procedure from module1.vb in the WorkflowConsoleApplication default project.

```
Shared Sub Main()
    'fire up the engine
    Dim workflowRuntime As New WorkflowRuntime()
    workflowRuntime.StartRuntime()

    AddHandler workflowRuntime.WorkflowCompleted, AddressOf OnWorkflowCompleted

    'load workflow type
    Dim type As System.Type = GetType(Workflow1)
    workflowRuntime.StartWorkflow(type)

    WaitHandle.WaitOne()

    workflowRuntime.StopRuntime()
End Sub
```

The first two lines create an instance of the WorkflowRuntime, which is the workflow framework runtime engine. Workflow instances are created from it using a factory class pattern for creating workflows. The StartRuntime method allows the engine to initialize some aspects of the runtime. The next line loads the .NET type that holds both the workflow model and the code-beside. The AddHandler line sets up a callback to tell you when the workflow has completed purely so that you can exit the console application.

> **NOTE**
>
> This mechanism for exiting the console application is only suitable if you are running a single workflow instance.

Next is the call to StartWorkflow(), which starts your workflow. Because workflows are executed on threads managed by the workflow runtime, the call to StartWorkflow will return immediately and the workflow will carry on running in parallel. This will be interesting when you look at workflows hosted in Windows Forms applications and other applications. The call to WaitOne() pauses the Main procedure until the event WaitHandle is set. The event is set by the callback once your workflow completes. Finally, the last line of Main() stops the workflow runtime so that you can exit the process.

Adding the Parameters

Parameters are set up for input and output in the StartWorkflow call. To do this you replace the existing StartWorkflow call with this:

```
Dim parameters As Dictionary(Of String, Object) = _
                New Dictionary(Of String, Object)
parameters.Add("MyInputParameter", 42)
parameters.Add("MyOutputParameter", 24)
workflowRuntime.StartWorkflow(type, parameters)
```

The input parameter is passed to the workflow only. After the workflow completes you can get the output parameter back. Make the OnWorkflowCompleted event handler look like this so that you can display it:

```
Shared Sub OnWorkflowCompleted(ByVal sender As Object, _
        ByVal e As WorkflowCompletedEventArgs)
    Console.WriteLine("MyOutputParameter " & _
        e.OutputParameters("MyOutputParameter"))
    WaitHandle.Set()
End Sub
```

Now you need to add the parameter to the workflow model. Return to the Code activity, and choose Properties from the context menu that appears when you right-click the mouse. You will see the dialog shown in Figure 2.8.

FIGURE 2.8   The Workflow Properties dialog.

Click the ... following the Parameters property to show the Workflow Parameters Editor. In the Parameters Editor click Add to add a parameter. Enter two parameters of type System.String, one called MyInputParameter and one called MyOutputParameter. For the second one you must also change the direction to Out. After you have the Parameters set as shown in Figure 2.9, click OK.

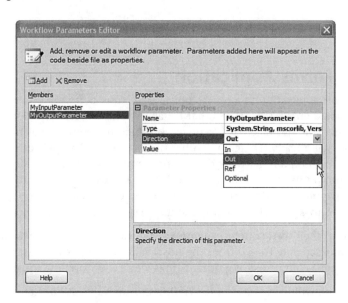

FIGURE 2.9   The Workflow Parameters Editor dialog.

After you've set the parameters, they are added to the workflow definition. Double-click on your Code activity again and change the code to this:

```
Private Sub code1_ExecuteCode(ByVal sender As System.Object, _
                              ByVal e As System.EventArgs)
    Console.WriteLine("MyInputParameter " & _
                      Me.Parameters("MyInputParameter").Value)
    Me.Parameters("MyOutputParameter").Value = "35"
End Sub
```

Now run it again to try it out. You should see the output shown in Figure 2.10. Notice that the input parameter is written out by the workflow and the output parameter was changed by the workflow and written out by the console host.

FIGURE 2.10   Console output from the workflow and host.

Windows Forms Application

A Windows forms application must be responsive to requests from a user such as mouse clicks and keyboard entry. This means that it has to be always ready to do what the user wants. An application also has to do some work, which frequently takes time away from the application being ready. There's a conflict there—should the application be waiting and responsive, or should it get work done? The standard solution for this is to have the user interface run on its own thread of execution on the CPU. However, this introduces complexities to application development and is often done as an afterthought, introducing bugs and not always solving the original user responsiveness problem.

Workflows run in their own context, a context that includes data and execution, so they naturally run in a separate thread from the host. When an application starts a workflow instance, it can also continue doing other things while the workflow runs.

In this section you will look at a simple Windows forms application that uses a workflow to simplify providing user interface responsiveness. It starts a workflow and receives updates back from that workflow at a later time. The user interface for this application is always responsive to the user because starting a workflow and sending messages to workflows takes no noticeable time at all. The interesting part of this sample is looking at how you communicate between the Windows forms application (known as the host for workflow purposes) and the workflow itself, as these are running in different contexts. For this sample you will be using a high-level workflow communications mechanism called *data activities*, which allows for sending and receiving of an instance of a defined data class to and from the workflow. Chapter 5, "Workflow Integration with Data Activities," discusses data activities in detail.

The Windows Forms Application

In the Windows forms application shown in Figure 2.11, the user types his name into the text box and clicks on the Start A Workflow button. The button handler starts a workflow and passes the name to it. The start workflow operation returns immediately and the user interface is responsive to the user who could proceed to enter another name. The workflow runs in the background and it will indirectly add messages to the ListBox over time.

FIGURE 2.11   Windows forms application—form design.

From a workflow point of view the Windows forms application is equivalent to the console host application that you saw earlier in this chapter. This host can communicate with the workflow by updating an instance of a shared data class that contains some number of properties. You can declare the shared data class in whatever way you want and send instances of it back and forth between the workflow and the host. The shared data class, called `MyData`, is defined in the workflow as follows: It contains three property declarations for ID, Name, and Response. Sticking with our "simple stuff" strategy, these properties can be created in Visual Studio 2005 by typing **vbprop** in the code editor and then pressing the Tab key to access the property code snippet. Code snippets are a new feature in Visual Studio 2005. Here is the resulting data class declaration:

```
<SerializableAttribute()> _
<CLSCompliantAttribute(True)> _
Public Class MyData
    ' Declare the variable the property uses.
    Private IDValue As String

    Public Property ID() As String
        Get
            Return IDValue
        End Get
        Set(ByVal value As String)
            IDValue = value
        End Set
    End Property

    ' Declare the variable the property uses.
    Private NameValue As String

    Public Property Name() As String
        Get
```

```
            Return NameValue
        End Get
        Set(ByVal value As String)
            NameValue = value
        End Set
    End Property

    ' Declare the variable the property uses.
    Private ResponseValue As String

    Public Property Response() As String
        Get
            Return ResponseValue
        End Get
        Set(ByVal value As String)
            ResponseValue = value
        End Set
    End Property
End Class
```

The Sample Solution

The solution for this sample contains two projects. The first is a Windows Application project type, which comes with one form by default (see Figure 2.12). The second is a sequential workflow library containing a single code-beside workflow with a data context.

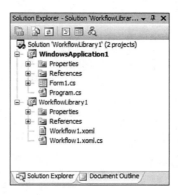

FIGURE 2.12   The Windows forms solution.

Inside the Windows Form Class

Take a look at the code for the form. First there is a declaration and instantiation of the workflow runtime as a member variable of the form class:

```
Public Class Form1
    Dim theWorkflowRuntime As New WorkflowRuntime

    Public Sub New()

        ' This call is required by the Windows Form Designer.
        InitializeComponent()
```

In the constructor you start the workflow runtime and add a service that allows you to use data activities:

```
        theWorkflowRuntime.StartRuntime()
        theWorkflowRuntime.AddService(New DataSourceService(theWorkflowRuntime))
```

This next line sets a delegate in the workflow context to the Windows form instance so that you can call back from the workflow context. This delegate is static and does not refer to a specific instance of the form. You'll see how that is dealt with shortly.

```
        WorkflowLibrary1.MyHandler.PlaceToSendMessage = _
            Form1.StaticMessageReceive


    End Sub

    Private Sub Button1_Click(ByVal sender As System.Object, _
                            ByVal e As System.EventArgs) Handles Button1.Click
```

The button click starts an instance of the workflow.

```
        Dim workflowInstance As WorkflowInstance = _
            theWorkflowRuntime.StartWorkflow(GetType(WorkflowLibrary1.Workflow1))
```

After you have started the workflow instance, you obtain a reference to the data source service that enables you to communicate with the workflow. Here you will use it to send an instance of your data class to the workflow:

```
        Dim service As DataSourceService = _
            CType(theWorkflowRuntime.GetService(GetType(DataSourceService)), _
            DataSourceService)
```

The following three props are added as direction and payload for the data class instance that is being sent to the workflow.

```
        Dim props As Dictionary(Of String, Object) = _
            New Dictionary(Of String, Object)
        props.Add("InstanceId", workflowInstance.InstanceId)
        props.Add("WorkflowType", GetType(WorkflowLibrary1.Workflow1))
        props.Add("DataSource", "newDataSource")
```

To update the data in the workflow you create an instance of the shared data class and populate it with the data you want to send to the workflow. You then call `RaiseDataChanged()` to send the change event to the workflow.

```
Dim message As WorkflowLibrary1.MyData = New WorkflowLibrary1.MyData
message.ID = "1"
message.Name = TextBox1.Text
service.RaiseDataChanged(props, message)
```

Now you have seen how the workflow is started. This provides a mechanism where the user interface passes off a user command to the workflow instance. The workflow instance executes this command in its own data and execution context and sends messages back to the user interface as required.

Next you'll look at how the user interface receives those messages. `ReceiveMessage()` is a method on the form that runs in the user interface execution context to add a new message from the workflow to the listbox control on the form. This is the code from the form class that enables you to receive a message back from the workflow.

```
Public Sub ReceiveMessage(ByVal Message As WorkflowLibrary1.MyData)
    ListBox1.Items.Add(Message.Response)
End Sub
```

This next method is static and it is required for the workflow to call back to in the context of the current form. You can see that this method makes a call using `Form.Invoke()` to the `ReceiveMessage()` method shown in the previous listing. `Form.Invoke()` ensures that the method call enters the user interface thread safely by posting a message on the standard Windows message queue, which all user interface threads must listen for user actions on.

```
Public Shared Sub StaticMessageReceive( _
    ByVal Message As WorkflowLibrary1.MyData)
    Dim theForm As Form1 = Form1.ActiveForm
    Dim PlaceToReceiveMessage As WorkflowLibrary1.MessageDelegate = _
        AddressOf theForm.ReceiveMessage
    theForm.Invoke(PlaceToReceiveMessage, Message)
End Sub
```

Inside the Workflow Class

Recall the shared data class from earlier in this chapter. The shared data class is declared in the workflow file because it must be used by both the workflow and the host. Because the host already has a reference to the workflow you cannot put a reference from the workflow to the host. Hence the shared data class is declared in the workflow to avoid a circular reference. An alternative would be to declare the shared data class in a separate source file.

Next you need to create the interface used to send a message from the workflow to the form. Remember that the workflow executes on a separate thread of execution. This interface is called `IDataHandler` and it is implemented by the host—but not necessarily on the user interface thread that you need for this example.

In the following class declaration first notice the declaration of `PlaceToSendMessage`, which you accessed and set previously in the Windows form code. This is the host's implementation of the `UpdateData` method of `IDataHandler`, which sends the data back into the form.

```
Public Delegate Sub MessageDelegate(ByVal TheParameter As MyData)

Public Class MyHandler
    Implements IDataHandler

    Public Shared PlaceToSendMessage As MessageDelegate

    Public Function SelectData(ByVal message As Object, _
            ByVal dataSourceInfo As DataSourceInfo) As Object _
            Implements IDataHandler.SelectData
        Throw New Exception("The method or operation is not implemented.")
    End Function

    Public Sub UpdateData(ByVal message As Object, _
            ByVal dataSourceInfo As DataSourceInfo) _
            Implements IDataHandler.UpdateData
        PlaceToSendMessage(CType(message, MyData))
    End Sub
```

Next, in this listing, notice the two methods implementing `IDataHandler`. `UpdateData` is used to pass the data class from the workflow to the Windows form. The `SelectData` method is not required.

The last thing to notice in the previous code is that the method `UpdateData` makes the call to the Windows form code by calling the delegate `PlaceToSendMessage`. This calls `StaticMessageReceive` in the Windows form code and then safely adds a line to the ListBox control on the form.

The Workflow Design

The workflow class contains a member variable called `data` that is referred to by all the data activities. This is how the workflow accesses the data that is shared with the host.

```
Partial Public Class Workflow1
    Inherits SequentialWorkflow
    Public Sub New()
        MyBase.New()
```

```
        InitializeComponent()
End Sub
Public data As MyData = New WorkflowLibrary1.MyData
```

In Figure 2.13 you can see the first three activities on the workflow. For more information on how the data activities work see Chapter 5.

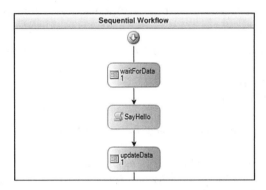

FIGURE 2.13   Top of the workflow design.

The first one is waitForData1, which receives an instance of the shared data class from the host when the workflow is started. The second activity is SayHello, which is a Code activity. The code for this sets the response to a message from the workflow.

```
Private Sub SayHello_ExecuteCode(ByVal sender As System.Object, _
                                 ByVal e As System.EventArgs)
    data.Response = "Hello " & data.Name
End Sub
```

The third activity is updateData1, which sends the shared data class to the host. This is done through the DataHandler class using its UpdateData method. Comparing waitForData1 and updateData1, you should realize that waitForData1 blocks the workflow until data is received from the host and updateData1 proactively pushes the data back to the host. UpdateData closes the loop on the user interface command pattern that I discussed previously. It allows the workflow running in a separate context to send results of the command back to the user interface.

More on the Workflow Design

Because the workflow data and execution context is separate and communication back to the host is so easy, you can have the workflow do as much work as you want without any concern for affecting the user interface responsiveness. You get this opportunity to perform long-running work at no extra charge when you chose workflow as your command pattern.

For illustration purposes I will use a delay to simulate work being done. It's important to understand that the workflow could be doing some long-running financial calculations, or some external slow database operations, or it could be waiting for a response from another user via email. Let's look at the rest of this workflow (see Figure 2.14).

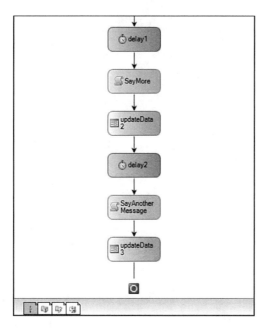

FIGURE 2.14   The rest of the workflow design.

The first Delay activity, delay1, is set to a 10-second delay. Following that is a Code activity, SayMore, which has the following handler to set the Response message up a second time:

```
Private Sub SayMore_ExecuteCode(ByVal sender As System.Object, _
                                ByVal e As System.EventArgs)
    data.Response = data.Name & ", I'm still here"
End Sub
```

The UpdateData activity named updateData2 pushes the data to the host. Next the work-flow will delay again and send another message to the Windows form; here is the last code handler:

```
Private Sub SayAnotherMessage_ExecuteCode(ByVal sender As System.Object, _
                                ByVal e As System.EventArgs)
    data.Response = "I'm going now " & data.Name
End Sub
```

Running the Application

When the application is run you enter a name and click the Start A Workflow button.
The workflow creates a response and sends it back to the user interface as shown in
Figure 2.15.

FIGURE 2.15   The first message back from the workflow.

Entering a second name runs a second workflow and that workflow creates a response as
shown in Figure 2.16.

FIGURE 2.16   Two workflows are running.

With the workflow working in the background and sending results and the user interface
fully responsive, you can create some interesting interactions. The messages in the ListBox
continue to appear as the workflow instances keep executing. You can see in Figure 2.17
there are three messages for each name and they overlap as the multiple workflow
instances are running.

FIGURE 2.17   Three workflow instances have run to completion.

Summary

This chapter provided you with a walk-through of two different and very simple workflow scenarios that can be applied to real-world software problems. This simple stuff provides you with a good level of understanding to progress through the remainder of the book.

March Through the Activities

Activities are the building blocks of a workflow. A number of activities are provided in the Visual Studio 2005 toolbox to create basic workflows. You can also easily create your own activities, which can be added to the toolbox for use in your workflows.

As such, activities are the first point of extensibility for Windows Workflow Foundation. Custom activities can be built that are treated the same as primitive activities that come with Windows Workflow Foundation. Also, custom activities can be built to relate to specific application domains for end-user applications. These custom activities, when targeted at a suitable higher level, could provide a nondeveloper design experience. You can build activities to be used with the workflow application that you build, or you can use activities that come from third-party software.

This chapter introduces you to all the activities that come with Windows Workflow Foundation.

Table of Activities

Table 3.1 provides a reference list of all the activities provided in the toolbox for Windows Workflow Foundation in Visual Studio 2005. This list is the same order as the Visual Studio 2005 toolbox; however, not all of these activities will be present depending on the workflow project template selected.

TABLE 3.1   Activities Provided in the Toolbox for Windows Workflow Foundation in Visual Studio 2005

Activity Name	Description
Sequence	Container for sequentially executed activities
Parallel	Two or more sequences executed in parallel
While	Repeats activities while condition is true
IfElse	Executes activities if a condition is true
Listen	Waits for one of a set of events
EventDriven	Used in a Listen or a workflow event handler to specify the event and contain the executed activities
Delay	Causes the containing branch of the workflow to wait for a timeout
ConditionedActivity Group	A list of activities executed on a variety of conditions
Replicator	Executes multiple copies of a contained activity
TransactionalContext	Contains activities involved in short- or long-term transactions
ExceptionHandler	Contains exception-handling activities
Throw	Throws an exception from a workflow or scope
Compensate	Used in an exception handler body to reference the required compensation
Code	Executes a specified method in the code-beside file
InvokeWebService	Makes a call out to a web service
InvokeWorkflow	Makes a call out to another workflow
UpdateData	Sends an instance of a predefined class of data to the host
SelectData	Requests an instance of a predefined class of data from the host
WaitForData	Accepts an instance of a predefined class of data from the host
WaitForQuery	Accepts a request for an instance of a predefined class of data from the host
WebServiceReceive	Waits for an external web service call to the workflow
WebServiceResponse	Sends a response to an external web service call from the workflow
Suspend	Stops the workflow instance from running; it can be restarted
Terminate	Shuts down this workflow instance
State	Defines a state in a workflow
StateInitialization	Contains activities that are executed on entering a state
SetState	Initiates a state transition in a state machine

Container for Activities

Some activities can act as a container for other activities. This is in addition to the workflows that contain activities. This list shows the main items that can act as containers of activities in the workflow designer:

- Sequential workflow

- State machine workflow

- Exception handlers

- Compensation

- Event handlers

A few activities such as sequential workflows (a workflow is a special kind of activity) and `TransactionalContexts` have complex definitions that are presented as multiple views. These consist of the main sequence, exceptions, events, and compensation. The workflow designer provides access to these views through tabs and the context menu.

Figure 3.1 shows the tabs for the four views. You view each design surface by clicking on the respective tab. A `Scope` activity has the same selections in the context menu, which you access by right-clicking on it.

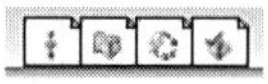

FIGURE 3.1   The tabs in the workflow designer from Visual Studio 2005.

Conditions

Several activities (`While`, `IfElse`, `ConditionedActivityGroup`, and `Replicator`) can have conditions or rules associated with them. Each condition returns either true or false. There are three possible condition types available:

- *Code condition*: A specified method, which the developer writes, that returns true or false. This type of condition is compiled into the workflow.

- *Declarative condition*: A single declarative condition that results in a true or false outcome. The declarative condition is interpreted and this allows it to be modified after the workflow is compiled. This is described in the next section.

- *Policy condition*: A ruleset defined in a policy-derived activity consisting of a collection of conditions and resultant actions.

Any of these types of conditions can operate on shared workflow instance state in the workflow as described by public member variables. In each case a true or false result is fed back into the activity execution.

Declarative Condition

The condition property of an activity must be set to the type of condition being used. You select rules by setting the condition property to `System.Workflow.Activities.Rules.RuleConditionReference`. Once selected, a `[+]` symbol appears next to the condition property. You can click on this symbol to show the condition details. Click on the condition details to show the declarative condition that is associated with your workflow.

You can choose a declarative condition from the list, and add or edit declarative conditions in the list. Figure 3.2 shows the rules editor that displays when you add a declarative condition.

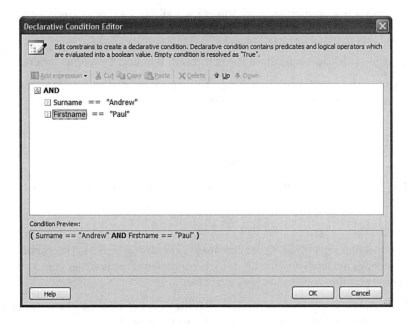

FIGURE 3.2   The Declarative Condition Editor.

In the Declarative Condition Editor you can add logical operators to the condition (AND, OR, and NOT). You can also add predicates. A predicate is a binary operator and two operands. The binary operators supported are ==, >, <, >=, and <=. Supported operands are constant value, arithmetic function, and scoped member, which refers to a workflow instance variable. You can specify the type for the comparison and you can compare to null or an empty string.

Complex conditions can be created based on workflow instance member variables.

Control Flow Activities

Control flow activities help to define the basic structure of a workflow.

Sequence Activity

The Sequence activity (shown in Figure 3.3) is a basic building block activity that expresses the idea of doing one thing, and then another. It executes contained activities sequentially. A sequential workflow is a special kind of sequence.

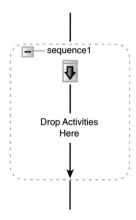

FIGURE 3.3 A Sequence activity.

The sequence is also useful because some activity types that will contain other activities can only contain a single activity. You can only put multiple activities in them if you first add a more general container activity such as a sequence.

The Sequence activity has properties of ID, Description, and Commented. If the Commented property is set to true (see Figure 3.4) the activity will not be part of validation or exception. It also appears a shaded green color in the designer. This is very similar to commenting out code.

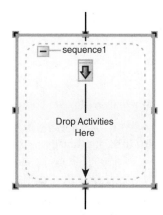

FIGURE 3.4 A commented Sequence activity.

Parallel Activity

Parallel activities (as shown in Figure 3.5) allow multiple activities to execute concurrently. It could be that there are several external requests to be made and they each take several days to respond. Or there may be a collection of short web services to call, each taking two to three seconds to respond. The Parallel activity allows requests to be initiated in parallel and may reduce the overall time it takes to complete them.

When it is initially dragged from the toolbox, the `Parallel` activity contains two paths of execution. You can add more by using the context menu for the `Parallel` activity or using the Add Branch command in the Properties pane.

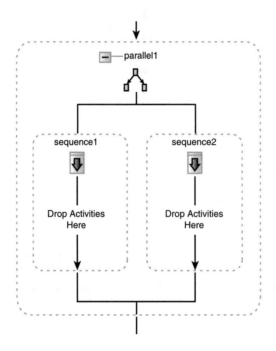

FIGURE 3.5   A `Parallel` activity.

`IfElse` **Activity**

The `IfElse` activity executes contained activities if a condition is true.

In Figure 3.6 there are two branches. The first branch is required to have a condition and the red circle and exclamation point indicate that there is no default condition. It must be added to avoid the error.

The last branch in an `IfElse` is not required to have a condition though if it had one it would be like an `If`-`EndIf` structure that has no `Else`. The `IfElse` activity evaluates the leftmost branch first. If that condition returns true the activities on that branch are executed; otherwise it evaluates the next branch, and so on.

You can add branches to an `IfElse` in much the same way that you can add branches to a `Parallel`.

`While` **Activity**

The `While` activity executes contained activities while the condition is true. A `While` activity can only contain a single child activity, so this is a place where you might use a `Sequence` or a `Parallel` or another multiactivity container.

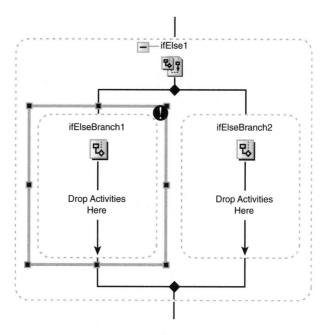

FIGURE 3.6   An IfElse activity.

The designer representation of the While activity in Figure 3.7 gives a good visual as to what it does. The condition is first evaluated; if it is true the contained activity is executed, and then you loop around and the loop repeats until the condition is false.

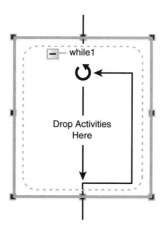

FIGURE 3.7   A While activity.

For-Next **Loop Implemented with a** While **Activity**

The workflow in Figure 3.8 shows how you can use a While activity as a For-Next loop. The While loops around and executes the code1 activity five times.

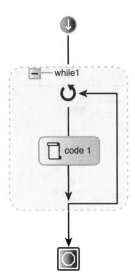

FIGURE 3.8   A workflow showing a `While` activity as a `For-Next` loop.

The `While` activity has a declarative condition, shown in Figure 3.9, that returns true if the `LoopVariable` is less than 5.

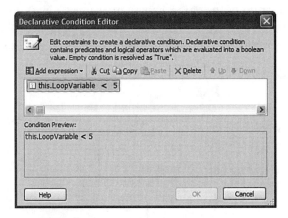

FIGURE 3.9   The Declarative Condition Editor showing a loop.

The class for the workflow contains the declaration for the instance variable and the code-beside method for the `Code` activity. In Listing 3.1, the `Code` activity writes a message and increments the `LoopVariable`.

LISTING 3.1   Implementation Class of a For Loop

```
<RuleConditionsAttribute(GetType(Workflow1))> _
Partial Public Class Workflow1
```

LISTING 3.1   Continued

```
    Inherits SequentialWorkflow

    Public LoopVariable As Integer

    Public Sub New()
        MyBase.New()
        InitializeComponent()

        LoopVariable = 0
    End Sub

    Private Sub code1_ExecuteCode(ByVal sender As System.Object, _
                            ByVal e As System.EventArgs)
        Console.WriteLine("Hello Again")
        LoopVariable = LoopVariable + 1
    End Sub
End Class
```

ConditionedActivityGroup **Activity**

The ConditionedActivityGroup activity (shown in Figure 3.10) loops through a collection of activities, executing them until an Until condition is true. Each activity in the collection is executed according to a When condition and an Unless condition. These three types of conditions default so that each activity is executed once only.

FIGURE 3.10   A ConditionedActivityGroup activity.

For more information on the ConditionedActivityGroup activity see Chapter 8, "Advanced Activities and Activity Behaviors."

Replicator **Activity**

The Replicator activity, shown in Figure 3.11, contains a single activity. At runtime it executes multiple copies of that activity. It is particularly useful for a human-based workflow where a number of approvers are required, the exact number is not known until runtime.

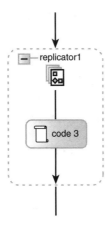

FIGURE 3.11 A Replicator activity.

For more information on the Replicator activity see Chapter 8.

Delay **Activity**

The Delay activity causes the containing branch of the workflow to wait for a specified amount of time. The workflow may be dehydrated during the delay if it becomes completely idle and rehydrated when the time expires.

> **NOTE**
>
> *Dehydrated* is a term used to describe how an idle workflow instance can be unloaded from memory and written to persistent store. A workflow instance is idle when all branches are waiting for long-running actions or other external response. *Rehydration* describes the workflow state being loaded back from persistent store and assigned a processing thread to be executed on. The dehydration/rehydration mechanism allows a workflow instance to survive machine reboots because it can be reloaded by the host after the reboot. It also allows scalability of the workflow engine.

Delay has a property called TimeoutDuration that is a TimeSpan with a default value of 00:00:00. You can either specify a value for TimeoutDuration or you can implement the InitializeTimeoutDuration() handler, which is called to set the TimeoutDuration property.

You can use a Delay activity to delay until a specific time if you calculate the TimeSpan between now and then yourself. For example, if you wanted to delay until

2:30 a.m. tomorrow morning you could use the code in Listing 3.2 in your InitializeTimeoutDuration().

LISTING 3.2 InitializeTimeout to Wait Until a Set Time

```
Public Sub delay1_InitializeTimeoutDuration(ByVal sender As Object, _
                                    ByVal e As EventArgs)
    ' find time today
    Dim NextStop As DateTime = DateTime.Today
    NextStop = NextStop.AddHours(2).AddMinutes(30)

    ' if time past today then wait until tomorrow
    If (NextStop <= DateTime.Now) Then
        NextStop = NextStop.AddDays(1)
    End If

    CType(sender,Delay).TimeoutDuration = NextStop.Subtract(DateTime.Now)
End Sub
```

You might use a Delay activity to

- Set a timeout while waiting for a response from external systems or people
- Run a scheduled job at a specified time
- Poll something at an interval

Workflow Lifetime Activities

Activities that affect the lifetime of a workflow are known as *workflow lifetime activities*, described in the following sections.

InvokeWorkflow **Activity**

The InvokeWorkflow activity (see Figure 3.12) is used to execute another workflow asynchronously. The InvokeWorkflow activity completes immediately (before the launched workflow starts executing) and the next activity in the branch is executed.

Suspend **Activity**

The Suspend activity (shown in Figure 3.13) temporarily stops the execution of the current workflow. It can pass an error message back to the host, which can be specified through the Error property in the Suspend activity. The Error property can refer to a string literal, a field or property reference, or an activity reference.

Suspended workflow instances can still receive messages that are queued up until the workflow is restarted. The workflow can only be restarted by the host by calling Resume() on the WorkflowInstance class.

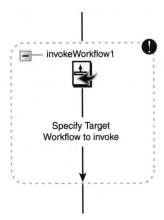

FIGURE 3.12   An `InvokeWorkflow` activity.

FIGURE 3.13   A Suspend activity.

`Terminate` **Activity**

A workflow normally completes after all activity branches are finished. If something unexpected occurs in the workflow an exception can be thrown. But an exception can be caught and handled which, depending on the problem, may not be desirable. The `Terminate` activity (shown in Figure 3.14) guarantees that no other activity will run after this one. As with the suspend activity you can pass an error message back to the host.

Event Waiting Activities

Some activities wait for an event, as the following sections illustrate.

`EventDriven` **Activity**

The `EventDriven` activity is a special kind of sequence where the first activity in the sequence must be an activity that waits for an event. This includes activities such as `WaitForData`, `WaitForQuery`, `WebServiceReceive`, `Delay`, or a custom-built event-sink activity in a Local Communications Service project. The `EventDriven` activity can only be used in two specific places:

- In a `Listen` activity. The `Listen` activity has two `EventDriven` activities in it when you add it to the workflow. You can drag additional `EventDriven` activities into a `Listen`, or you can use the context menu or the Add Branch action in the properties page.

- In the Events tab of the workflow (see Figure 3.15). You can drag the `EventDriven` activity to where it says Drop EventDriven Activity Here. The Workflow Events page appears when you click the third icon from the left in the bottom-left tabs.

FIGURE 3.14   A `Terminate` activity.

Listen **Activity**

The `Listen` activity (shown in Figure 3.16) waits on multiple events at once. The `Listen` activity contains multiple `EventDriven` activities to achieve this. Only one event waiting activity (the first to receive an event) ever gets run in each execution of a `Listen`. When the event is received the subsequent activities in that sequence are executed as in a regular sequence.

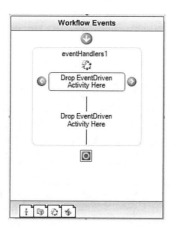

FIGURE 3.15   The Workflow Events design surface.

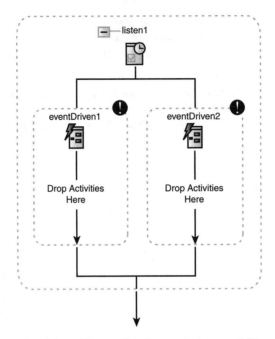

FIGURE 3.16   A Listen activity with contained EventDriven activities.

Typically one of the paths in a Listen contains a Delay. The Delay activity is implemented as an event that occurs after a timeout.

The Listen activity in Figure 3.17 contains two EventDriven paths. The first one waits for a web service call into the workflow. The second one is a Delay. If the Delay timeout occurs first then the web service receive will stop and the workflow will continue with activities following the Delay.

Transaction and Exception Activities

Transactions apply to workflows and to transactional/context activities. If a transactional/ context is used, the workflow can continue after any exception has occurred. If an exception is caught at the workflow level it can be handled but the workflow cannot continue.

TransactionalContext Activity

The TransactionalContext activity provides short- and long-term transaction support, exception-handling support, and event-handling support. It defines the transaction boundary and contains all the activities that are to be part of the transaction. This section focuses on catching transaction exceptions at the workflow level.

The TransactionalContext activity actually refers to a set of behaviors that are described in Chapter 8.

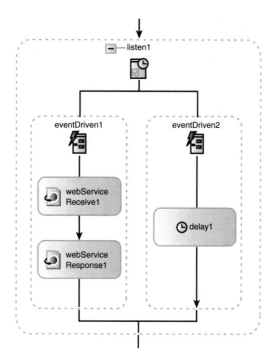

FIGURE 3.17   A Listen activity with a Delay path and a Web Service path.

Throw **Activity**

An exception may be thrown using the Throw activity (shown in Figure 3.18) from within a workflow or within a transactional/context. An exception may also be thrown by another activity on an error condition. Workflows use the second tab on the lower-left of the design surface as shown in Figure 3.1 for accessing the exceptions views. For the exception view of a Transactional/context use the context menu in a Scope to access the exception view.

FIGURE 3.18   A Throw activity.

When an exception is thrown it will terminate the workflow immediately unless it is caught. To catch an exception in the workflow click on the View Exceptions tab to show the Exceptions view. The Exceptions view is where you can drag and drop exception handlers.

ExceptionHandler **Activity**

Exception handlers can only be dragged and dropped to the Exceptions view. Figure 3.19 shows the Exceptions view with no exception handlers. The Scope exceptions view behaves in a similar way.

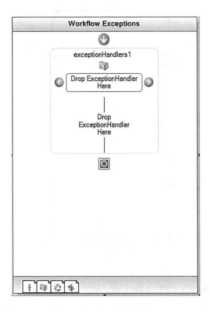

FIGURE 3.19   The Workflow exceptions design surface.

To catch an exception, you must drag and drop an exception handler from the toolbox and have properties configured. You can drag and drop any number of exception handlers to handle different kinds of exceptions in different ways. In this way, an ExceptionHandler activity functions just like a catch block in code. Figure 3.20 shows the exceptions view with one exception handler and a Code activity added to the body of the exception handler.

In Figure 3.20 the code2 activity will be executed if the exception handler catches an exception. The Code activity has access to the specific exception through a variable specified in the Variable property of the exception handler. The Type property specifies what exceptions will be caught by this exception handler. If the Type property is set to System.Exception, all exceptions will be caught by this exception handler.

For a long-running transaction a Compensate activity is added to the exception handler body.

Compensate **Activity**

The Compensate activity (shown in Figure 3.21) can only be added to the body of an exception handler. It is used to point to compensation logic that is required to roll back any long-running transaction that has failed. Failure of a long-running transaction is identified by an exception being raised. This figure shows a `Compensate` activity in the body of an exception handler. For more detail see Chapter 8.

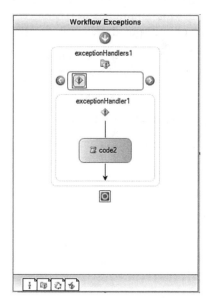

FIGURE 3.20   The Workflow exceptions design surface with one exception handler.

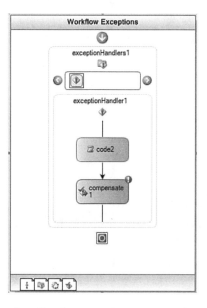

FIGURE 3.21   An exception handler that contains a `Code` and a `Compensate`.

Data-Centric Activities

The data-centric (or form-centric) activities are a simple mechanism for workflow to host communication and vice versa. This communication centers around a data class that defines the structure of the communicated data.

There are four activities in this group and among them they allow for both proactive and reactive, requests and submits of data, to and from the workflow and host.

In other words, to look at things from the workflow point of view, looking at the host:

- It is possible to request data from the host or to send data to the host.
- It is also possible to suspend and wait for a data query from the host, and it's possible to suspend and wait for data to arrive from the host.

And from the host point of view, looking at the workflow:

- It is possible to send data to the workflow or to send a request for data.
- It is also possible to implement an interface that can be called at any time to receive data from the workflow or to receive a request for data.

A data source is created in the workflow. The data source refers to the data class and a class that implements the host interface `IDataHandler`. Think of this as the interface class. An `ID` property in the data class is used as part of correlating a data update from the host with a `WaitForData` or `WaitForQuery`.

Chapter 5, "Workflow Integration with Data Activitites," has more detail on these four activities:

- `UpdateData`
- `SelectData`
- `WaitForData`
- `WaitForQuery`

Web Services Activities

Windows Workflow Foundation has built-in support for calling web services and for publishing a workflow as a web service.

See Chapter 6, "Using Web Services," for a detailed discussion of these activities:

- `InvokeWebService`
- `WebServiceReceive`
- `WebServiceResponse`

The Code Activity

The code activity stands alone. It permits quick adding of a code handler anywhere in the workflow.

A Code activity (shown in Figure 3.22) enables you to add some C# or Visual Basic .NET code into any part of a workflow just by dragging it in and double-clicking on it. This is a very simple form of a custom activity. The code entered in this way lives in the code-beside file that is compiled with the workflow.

FIGURE 3.22 A Code activity.

State Workflow Activities

A finite state machine is a standard programming pattern in which behavior responds to events differently depending on a recorded state. Action occurs on state transitions that are triggered by events.

These activities are all specific to the State Machine workflow style and they only appear on the toolbox when you are using the State Machine workflow designer.

State Activity

The State activity (shown in Figure 3.23) represents one state that the state machine can be in. When you create a new state machine workflow you always start with one state on the design surface.

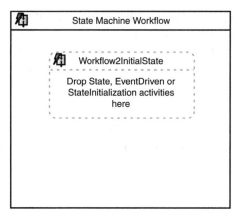

FIGURE 3.23 The Workflow1 initial state.

`StateInitialization` **Activity**

Each state activity must either contain an `EventDriven` activity or a `StateInitialization` activity. The `StateInitialization` activity can have action activities dragged into it to execute on the change to the state.

`SetState` **Activity**

The `SetState` activity (shown in Figure 3.24) is dragged into the view of a `StateTransitionHandler` to specify a new state to change to. It can also appear at the end of an `EventDriven` sequence.

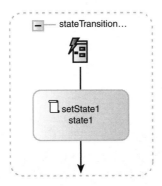

FIGURE 3.24   A `SetState` activity.

Custom Activities

Most of the provided activities for Windows Workflow Foundation are related to the structure of a workflow, communications with a workflow, or the lifetime of a workflow. The really important activities are ones related to the application domain of the software you are building. These are all created with custom activities.

`InvokeMethod` **Activity in Communications Library**

A workflow communications library project type can be built to create activities that either invoke or handle events. Once built, these appear on the toolbox and can be used to communicate between the workflow and an external system.

The `InvokeMethod` activity calls out from the workflow to an external system.

`EventSink` **in Communications Library Activity**

The `EventSink` activity waits for an event from outside the workflow. These events arrive via the host process. The `EventSink` activity can be correlated with a related `InvokeMethod` call.

There is a discussion of `InvokeMethod` and `EventSink` in Chapter 9.

Composite Activity in Activity Library

If you build an Activity Library project template in Visual Studio 2005 you can build an activity yourself easily. You can build an activity using the activity designer (see Figure 3.25), which creates a composite activity from a sequence of pre-existing activities.

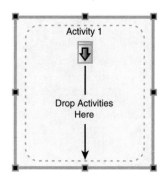

FIGURE 3.25   The composite activity designer.

Coded Activity in Activity Library

In the same Activity Library project type you can code an activity in C# or Visual Basic .NET. To do this you change the base class property for the activity from `System.Workflow.Activities.Sequence` to `System.Workflow.ComponentModel.Activity`.

See Chapter 7 for more details about creating custom activities.

Summary

This chapter provided you with an overview of all the Workflow activities that appear on the toolbox in Visual Studio 2005 when you are editing a workflow.

CHAPTER 4

Workflow in Microsoft Office System

This chapter introduces the Office Workflow vision. It talks about the user experience of Workflow in Office, discusses the architecture of Workflow in Office, and gives an overview of designing workflows in Office.

Workflow in the next version of the Microsoft Office System came about as part of a larger document lifecycle effort, which covers a range of scenarios from inception to expiration of documents and similar content. Document lifecycle and, by extension, workflow are focused on providing end-to-end solutions for knowledge workers.

In evaluating how to fulfill these scenarios, the Office team first gathered feedback from customers on the workflow usage patterns that were common in their organizations, and the characteristics of current and desired workflow systems in enterprises. Analyzing that customer research helped Office create a vision for how workflow should be represented to end users. It also yielded a set of technical requirements for a robust workflow development platform.

Key Vision Elements

The key components of the Office workflow experience are to provide the following:

- Structure for associating business process logic with documents and items in Microsoft SharePoint Products and Technologies.

- Out-of-the-box value to information workers in the form of solutions and self-service tools, which can be used to create common workflows and track their results without specific IT involvement.

- Extensibility by enabling rich workflow solutions to be built using FrontPage and the Windows Workflow Foundation designer.

A Workflow Engine for Office

Early on, the Office product team realized that building its own limited purpose workflow engine could meet many of the requirements of the out-of-the-box workflow solutions that were planned, but it would not meet the needs of third-party developers who wanted to author more complex workflow for use in Office, nor would it provide an appropriate toolset or development experience consistent with other Microsoft workflow applications. These realizations helped with the selection of the then nascent Windows Workflow Foundation engine as the cornerstone of workflow in the next version of Office.

The workflow system created for the next version of Office is centered on documents (and list items) stored on a SharePoint Products and Technologies server. In this system, the "truth" of the current workflow state resides on the server, and clients synchronize their representations of human workflow to that truth in order to provide a rich workflow user experience in the familiar Microsoft Office interface.

In this chapter, you'll first explore the end user experience of workflow in the next version of Office to help explain how workflow concepts are surfaced to user interface elements. Next, you'll learn how Office hosted the Windows Workflow Foundation engine in SharePoint Products and Technologies in order to achieve this user experience. Finally, we'll present information about the unique aspects of authoring workflows for Office, as compared to a base Windows Workflow Foundation host.

Where Humans Meet Workflow— The Office Workflow Experience

Let's meet the actors involved in an Office workflow and their roles, and then walk through key elements of the Office workflow user experience.

Workflow Actors

There are many actors in the Office workflow system. These are illustrated in Figure 4.1.

Let's look at the major actors in more detail:

- A *workflow designer* is a person who creates a workflow, its forms, resources, and metadata. The designer is either a *professional developer* using a tool such as Visual Studio to create a code-based workflow, or a *knowledge worker* using a no-code authoring environment such as FrontPage to stitch together predeployed activities into a new workflow. The major difference between professional developer-designed workflows and knowledge worker-designed workflows is the flexibility that professional developers have to include new activities and code behind the workflow model. On the other hand, workflows that do not contain new code have the advantage of being more easily deployable because they do not require a SharePoint server administrator (usually an IT worker) to review and deploy the new workflow.

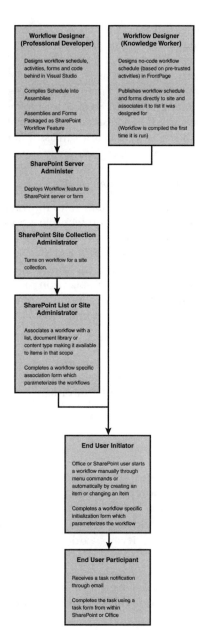

FIGURE 4.1   The workflow designer, administrator, and end user are the principal workflow actors in the Microsoft Office System.

- There are several types of *administrators* who play a part in workflow. *Server administrators* deploy new code-based workflows that have been packaged as a SharePoint

Products and Technologies feature. (A *feature* is a new SharePoint Products and Technologies concept that makes it easier to deploy related functionality and meta-data, either to a single server or across a farm.) *Site collection administrators* manage the set of features that are available to users of a site collection, and must turn on a workflow before it is available for use. Finally, a workflow must be associated (added) to a list or document library in SharePoint Products and Technologies before it is available to end users. A *list administrator* can associate a workflow with a document library or list, and a site administrator can associate a workflow with a content type. When a workflow is associated, the administrator completes an association form that partially parameterizes the workflow, and this could include setting customization options that were provided by the workflow designer.

- *End users* of course play the most important roles in workflows because they do the real work! A *workflow initiator* is the person who starts a workflow or causes it to be started. A workflow can be started manually through menu commands in Share-Point Products and Technologies or Office; it can also be automatically started based on document creation or modification. If the workflow is manually started, the initiator may be required to fill out an initialization form that was created by the workflow designer; similar to the association form, this partially parameterizes the workflow and may allow for flow customizations. *Workflow participants* are people who have work assigned to them in a workflow. A participant can be any member of a SharePoint Products and Technologies site, or even an external partici-pant whose participation is proxied by a site member. The most common mecha-nism by which a workflow participant interacts with a workflow is the workflow task, which was also created by the workflow designer (and can be unique to each workflow).

Workflow User Experience

To understand how these roles behave and interact, you'll explore each of the major concepts of the Office System workflow user experience. You'll learn how to configure and start workflows, and how users in both SharePoint Products and Technologies and the Microsoft Office System interact with workflows, including receiving notifications of workflow tasks, completing tasks, and viewing workflow status.

Workflow Association

Workflow association is the process of adding a workflow to a document library, list, or content type in SharePoint. This is done through the customization page of the document library, list, or content type.

NOTE

The next version of SharePoint Products and Technologies has a new template concept called *content types*. Content types can include schema elements such as column templates and also settings such as workflow associations. Content types are not useful by themselves; they must be added to a list; when this is done, its settings are added to the list. The main benefit of using content types instead of modifying list schema and settings directly is reusability; a content type can be added to multiple lists and managed centrally.

Figure 4.2 shows a typical customization page for a SharePoint Products and Technologies document library. Here the document library administrator would click on Workflow Settings to access the workflow settings pages.

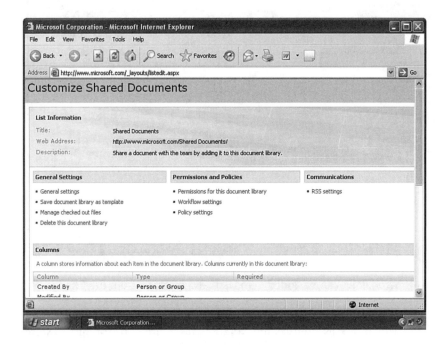

FIGURE 4.2   This page is the starting point for customizing a SharePoint Products and Technologies document library or list.

The next page displays the workflows that have already been associated with this document library with options to add and remove them. There is no limit to the number of workflows that can be added to a document library, list, or content type in SharePoint Products and Technologies. The same workflow can be added multiple times with different parameters. Figure 4.3 shows a document library with one review workflow and one approval workflow associated to it.

Clicking on the Add a Workflow link takes the administrator to the first of two workflow association pages, as shown in Figure 4.4. The user is asked to select a workflow to use; the choice is from the list of workflows that have been installed and turned on for this site collection, as described earlier in this chapter.

The administrator is required to supply a friendly name for the workflow; this is subsequently used to identify the workflow association on the Change Workflow Settings page (see Figure 4.3) and also to the end user when starting a workflow (Figures 4.7 and 4.9).

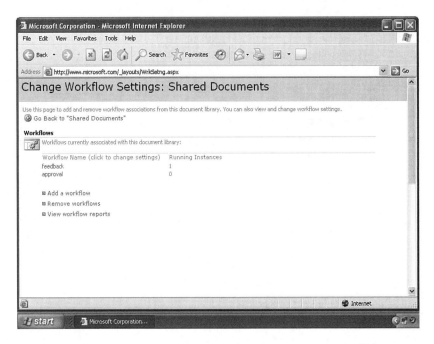

FIGURE 4.3   Workflows can be added, removed, and modified from the Change Workflow Settings page.

He can select which task list to use store workflow tasks, and a history list to store workflow history events. Tasks in an Office workflow are the way that "ToDos" for humans in the workflow are represented. The workflow history list is a SharePoint Products and Technologies list that can be used by a running workflow as a log for information that can later be reported on.

Finally, on this page (see Figure 4.4) the user can select between start options, allowing the workflow to be started manually, when an item changes, or when an item is created. It might make sense for a workflow that controls the expiration of a document (for example, after a number of months or when a certain condition is met) to start immediately upon document creation.

After completing the first workflow association page, which contains general settings applicable to every workflow, the administrator is navigated to a second workflow association page, which actually loads a workflow instance specific form that was designed, packaged, and deployed alongside the workflow. This *workflow association form*, shown in Figure 4.5, is completely customizable by each workflow, and the settings created on this form are stored in SharePoint Products and Technologies and made available to the workflow when it starts. This allows a workflow designer to be able to create a single flexible workflow and have it reused for many purposes through customizations set on the association form. For example, the form may have an option as to whether the workflow is serial or parallel or how the workflow should respond if one approver rejects the document for review.

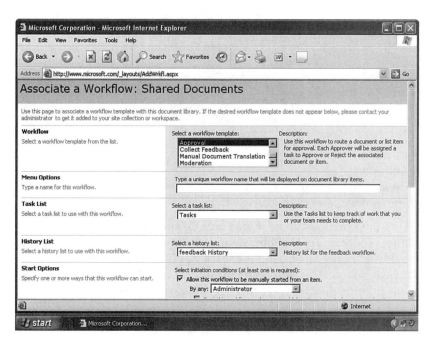

FIGURE 4.4   The first (general) workflow association page allows the user to pick a workflow template and options that are common to all Office workflows.

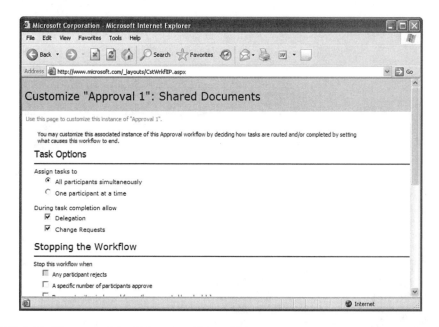

FIGURE 4.5   The second (workflow-specific) workflow association page displays a workflow defined customization form.

> **NOTE**
>
> Associating a workflow in SharePoint Products and Services does not actually start any workflow instance (that is, Windows Workflow Foundation engine has not run up to this point)—it simply enables workflows to be started subsequently. The workflow association information is stored in an internal SQL table in SharePoint Products and Technologies until such time as the workflow initiation conditions are met. At that point, the association form data (along with the initiation form data, if any) is used to parameterize a new workflow instance.

Workflow Initiation

Now that the workflow is associated to a document library, an end user will see a number of entry points where the workflow can be started:

- In Office, the workflow can be started on a document saved to that library or any of the Office authoring applications. Figure 4.6 shows the Share Document menu where the out-of-the-box Collect Feedback workflow can be immediately started, and there is a View More Workflows menu item that displays all the workflows available from the library where this document is saved (see Figure 4.7).

- In SharePoint Products and Technologies, a workflow can be started in a document library, list, or content type through a workflow context menu item (see Figure 4.8) or a similar entry point on the toolbar of a list item's edit form. Clicking on either of these menu items displays the Workflows page, shown in Figure 4.9, and the list of workflows that can be started on the document or item.

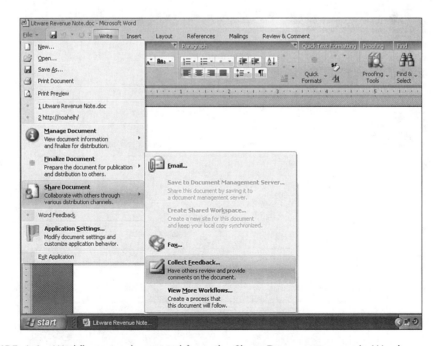

FIGURE 4.6   Workflows can be started from the Share Document menu in Word.

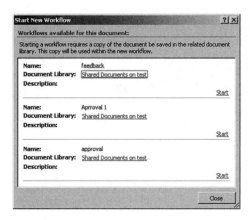

FIGURE 4.7   Word displays the list of workflows available from the location where the document is saved.

Regardless of which entry point is selected (from an Office client or SharePoint Products and Technologies) the workflow host checks to see whether a Workflow Initiation form is present and, if so, displays that form to the user. For workflows using InfoPath forms, a single form can be designed once and is displayed symmetrically in SharePoint Products and Technologies (see Figure 4.8) and the Office client shown in Figure 4.9, so that regardless of whether the user is starting from the client or the server, the experience is symmetric. Workflows using ASPX forms (instead of InfoPath forms) cannot be started form Microsoft Office applications, but can be initiated form the server.

INFOPATH CLIENT NOT REQUIRED TO DISPLAY FORMS

Workflow forms can be designed in InfoPath Designer, but do not require that end users have the InfoPath client installed on their machines. This is because a new server technology, InfoPath Forms Server, includes the ability to render InfoPath forms into web pages. Also, in the next version of Office, InfoPath technologies can be used to display workflow forms within the core authoring applications (Microsoft Office Word, Microsoft Office PowerPoint, Microsoft Office Excel) without the full InfoPath client being installed or loaded. As shown in Figure 4.8 and Figure 4.9, the fact that InfoPath forms are used is largely hidden to the end user. The user experience is similar to that of interacting with a native ASPX form inside of SharePoint Products and Technologies or a dialog box inside Word, respectively.

When a workflow is started in an Office client application, such as Word, the initiation form is displayed in a dialog using InfoPath technologies, but the InfoPath client is not actually required. After the end user completes the Workflow Initiation form, the data from this form and the workflow association form are used to start a new workflow instance.

NOTE

If no initiation form is supplied by the workflow designer, no additional form is displayed and the workflow instance is started immediately.

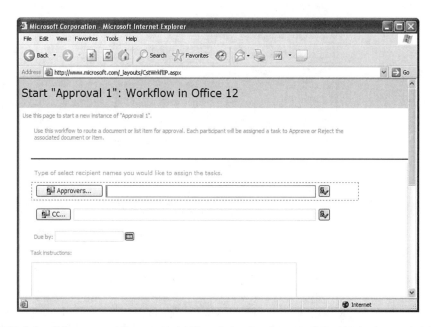

FIGURE 4.8   When a workflow starts in SharePoint Products and Technologies, an initiation form is typically displayed; this form can be either an ASPX form or, as shown here, an InfoPath form rendered as an ASPX form using InfoPath Forms Server controls.

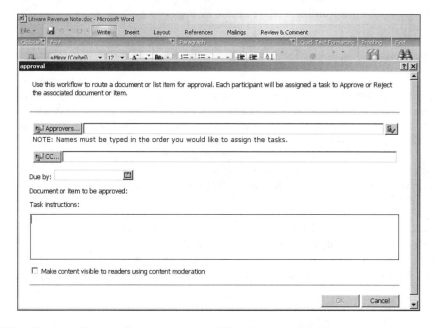

FIGURE 4.9   A workflow being started in an Office client application.

Workflow Notification

Most workflows designed for the Office System will be human-centric, and will require actions by human users at particular points in the workflow. These workflow actions, or ToDos, are represented as workflow tasks in SharePoint Products and Technologies, as will be discussed presently. To inform users that *workflow tasks* have been assigned to them, the workflow model sends a workflow notification to the user in the form of an email message.

The workflow notification email contains a link to the task as well as the document or item around which the workflow is occurring. The email can be displayed in any mail client, but if it is displayed in the next version of Outlook, there is additional integration in the form of an Edit this task button, as shown in Figure 4.10. This allows the user to complete the task directly from within Outlook without having to change contexts.

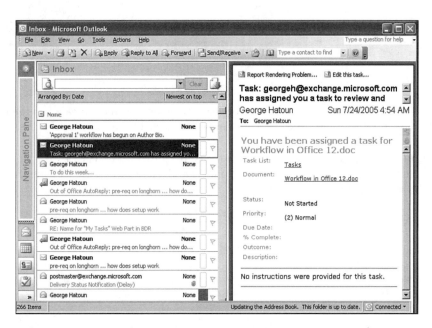

FIGURE 4.10   Workflows notifying end users of a task.

Workflow Tasks and Task Completion

In addition to receiving task notifications inside of Outlook, users of the Office clients will get a notification when they are viewing a document that is involved in a workflow, and there is an active workflow task assigned to them. As shown in Figure 4.11, the notification in Word appears as a yellow bar above the document window. PowerPoint, Excel, and InfoPath will all show similar notifications. Clicking on the bar opens the task in a window in Word.

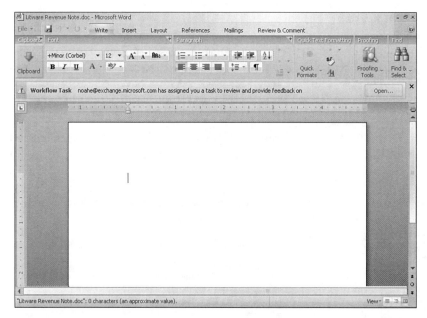

FIGURE 4.11   A Word user is shown a yellow bar above the document area when there is a workflow task assigned to her. The yellow bar provides access to the ToDo task for the user.

In addition to being able to access workflow tasks in Word, end users can view workflow tasks directly on the server in SharePoint Products and Technologies by viewing the task list, as shown in Figure 4.12.

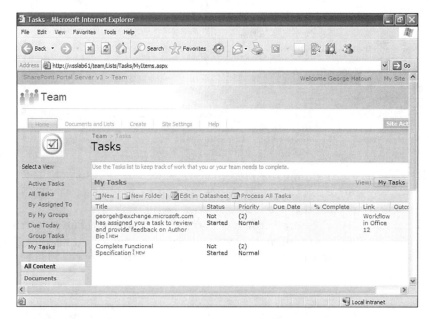

FIGURE 4.12   The SharePoint task list can contain both workflow and non-workflow tasks.

WORKFLOW TASK VERSUS TASK

Workflow tasks can be created in the same SharePoint Products and Technologies task lists that non-workflow tasks have been created in. Alternatively, the list administrator can choose to segregate workflow tasks into their own task list. The main differences between an ordinary task and a workflow task are:

- The additional schema elements that are used by the workflow host to correlate it with both the item and the workflow instance.

- The use of a different task edit form, which displays different (workflow-specific) fields than are shown on an ordinary task edit form. These edit forms can either be specified as ASPX forms or InfoPath forms (in which case they are rendered into ASPX forms on the server using InfoPath Forms Server technologies).

Regardless of whether a workflow task is accessed on the client or the server, the task completion experience is similar. When the user goes to edit a workflow task, a form is displayed. Similar to workflow association and workflow initiation forms, either ASPX or InfoPath forms can be used for workflow task completion. Figures 4.13 and 4.14 show the task completion experience in the Office client and server, respectively.

NOTE

Some workflow tasks, such as creating a digital signature, require that the task only be completed in a client application. A workflow designer can specify this requirement in workflow metadata when creating a workflow template, and the task will not be editable on the server.

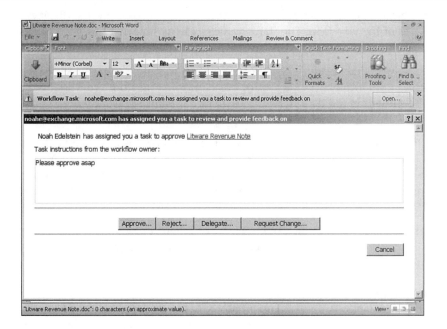

FIGURE 4.13   Workflow tasks can be completed in the Office clients.

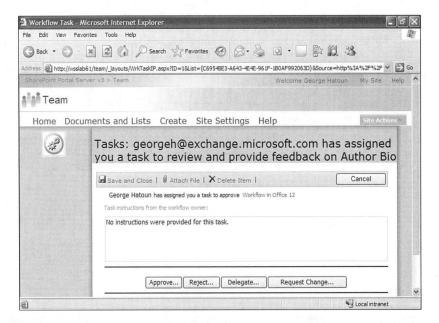

FIGURE 4.14   Workflow tasks can be completed directly on the SharePoint Products and Technologies server.

Workflow Status

Each workflow association to a list creates a workflow status column that displays the current status of the workflow. The status value is a hyperlink that navigates the user to the workflow status page.

Each running workflow instance has a corresponding workflow status page (see Figure 4.15) that is automatically generated using basic information from the workflow such as the workflow initiator and date started, plus a view of all of the workflow tasks created to date as part of this workflow.

The workflow status page is also the place where a workflow instance can be deleted or modified. Running workflows can be deleted by list administrators. Modifications to running workflows are triggered by the initiator of the workflow completing a workflow modification form, which is created by the workflow designer. The available workflow modification forms are listed links on the workflow status page.

The Workflow Status page can be used to view the progress of workflow tasks, delete the current workflow instance, or make modifications to a running workflow (using the modification form links).

Workflow Reporting

Business process managers implement workflows not just for their value in managing processes, but also for reporting on those business processes so that they can analyze metrics to identify trends, problem areas, and resource bottlenecks. A built-in report facility (see Figure 4.16) allows business process owners to view reports installed by the workflow template.

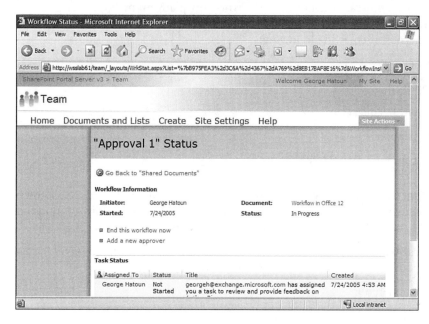

FIGURE 4.15   The workflow status page.

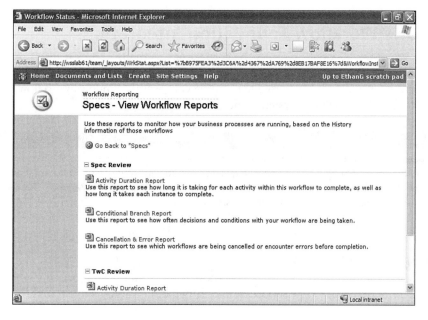

FIGURE 4.16   The workflow reporting page.

Out-of-the-Box Office Workflows

A key part of the Office System workflow experience is a set of out-of-the box workflow solutions that showcase the power of the workflow platform by implementing the most common workflow in use today. These templates will address a number of document-based scenarios, such as the following:

- Review

- Approval

- Signature collection

- Translation

- Custom multistep workflow

In addition, there will be a variation of the approval workflow that addresses the market requirements of the East Asian region, and an issue-tracking workflow solution designed around the issues list in SharePoint Products and Technologies is also planned.

There are also a few workflows planned for the next version of Office Server System that will integrate with these SharePoint Products and Technologies features:

- List moderation

- Publishing process

- Document expiration

Windows Workflow Foundation Integration

Windows Workflow Foundation forms the cornerstone of the workflow features provided by the Office System. The integration of Windows Workflow Foundation was achieved by implementing a number of host providers and by connecting Windows Workflow Foundation concepts to Office System concepts.

> **CAUTION**
>
> One important caveat: The hosting model is presented here as a description of one workflow host implementation, but not prescriptive guidance on how to write a host implementation. Some design decisions were driven by the specific scale-out architecture of Windows SharePoint Services and may not generalize to other hosts.

Topology and Persistence

To understand the hosting of Windows Workflow Foundation, it's important to understand that Windows SharePoint Services scales in two dimensions as illustrated in

Figure 4.17. Incoming requests are load-balancing across multiple stateless front-end web servers running the Windows SharePoint Services process, so the number of these servers can be increased as expected load increases. In addition, the number of back-end database servers can also be increased as the number of site collections increases.

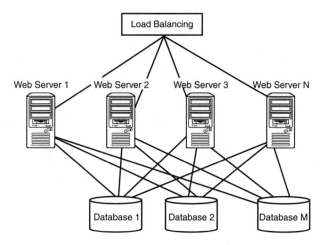

FIGURE 4.17   Windows SharePoint Services scales out in two dimensions.

Workflow integrates with Windows SharePoint Services on both the front-end and back-end machines. On the front-end machines, the Windows Workflow Foundation engine is loaded in the same process as Windows SharePoint Services, such that every front-end machine is potentially running its own copy of Windows Workflow Foundation.

The back-end machines are used for storing state for both workflow templates and for running workflows. Dedicated SQL tables are used to manage workflow associations and workflow instance data. In addition, workflow instances are correlated to items in workflows and workflow tasks through metadata stored on those items. The Windows Workflow Foundation engine does not run on the back-end SQL machines though workflow instances are stored there as described next.

Workflow Dehydration Model

Human workflows are inherently long running because even in ideal circumstances, humans take a relatively long time to complete work compared to machines. In many Office scenarios, workflow will typically last for days, but it's not uncommon for a workflow to last weeks, months, or even years. Due to the scale goals of the Office System, it's not feasible to keep all "running" workflows in memory for a long period of time; very soon the resources required by accumulated long-running workflows would bring the system to a halt.

For this reason, Windows SharePoint Services dehydrates any workflows that are paused waiting for user input (for example, task completion). The workflows are sent from the front-end web servers to the back-end databases until such time as they are reactivated by an event.

Event Delivery

Events play a key role in both the initiation and reactivation of Office workflows. Workflows can be automatically initiated on a "new item" or "item changed" event in SharePoint Products and Technologies. For example, a workflow can be configured (through workflow association) to start a new instance whenever a document is created in a library.

Events are also the trigger for reactivating dehydrated workflows. For example, a workflow can subscribe to "item changed" events the item it is running on and tasks it has created, so that if either of these items is modified, the workflow is notified. Because the workflow is likely dehydrated at this point, the workflow host layer keeps track of the various event subscriptions and will enqueue the events, rehydrate the relevant instance to a front-end machine, and deliver these events to the instance.

The Workflow Timer Provider

To support the Windows Workflow Foundation delay activity (for example, to send out a reminder or to end a workflow when it is past its due date), Windows SharePoint Services implements a workflow timer provider that accepts delays from workflows, tracks them in a SQL table, and rehydrates the workflow instance with the delay-specified event at the appropriate time.

Object Model and Web Services

To allow workflow operations such as starting a workflow or completing a task to be automated, Windows SharePoint Services exposes an extensive workflow object model that you can read about in the Windows SharePoint Services Software Development Kit (SDK). In addition, the Office Server product implements a SOAP web service that wraps the portion of the workflow object model needed for Office to start workflows, get status of workflow tasks, and complete tasks.

History and Reporting

Windows Workflow Foundation supports hosts implementing a tracking provider. Office does not implement this because SharePoint is always the source of the events driving the workflow, and it therefore makes sense to track them at the source where the data is richest. For workflow history, relevant events are persisted to a SharePoint Products and Technologies–based workflow history list, which can in turn be reported in a number of clients that connect to list data sources, such as Microsoft Office Access, Visio, and Excel. A number of out-of-the-box Excel and Visio reports are being provided to complement the out-of-the-box Office workflows.

Designing Workflows for Office

Designing workflows for Office is fundamentally similar to designing workflows for other Windows Workflow Foundation hosts, including the default host that is provided with Windows Workflow Foundation. However, there are subtle but important differences. What follows is a high-level overview of the tools and process of designing workflows for Office.

Workflow Model and Forms Authoring

The targeted design tools for Office workflows are

- FrontPage, a soup-to-nuts workflow design tool for knowledge workers.

- Windows Workflow Foundation plug-in to Visual Studio 2005, a workflow-authoring environment for professional developers. This plug-in comes with the Windows Workflow Foundation SDK. An Office workflow developer can make use of the custom activity set that comes with Office.

- InfoPath Designer, a forms authoring environment for both knowledge workers and professional developers (InfoPath Designer integrates with Visual Studio 2005).

Workflow model authoring in FrontPage is facilitated by a wizard-driven user interface that lets a knowledge worker stitch together a number of predeployed workflow activities rapidly into a new workflow model without writing code (see Figure 4.18). Because no new code is created, FrontPage also provides a streamlined deployment of workflows without administrator actions.

Workflows authored using the Windows Workflow Foundation graphical design environment offer the richest possibilities for customization because almost any code that calls into web services or Windows SharePoint Services object model can be added.

In addition, InfoPath Designer provides a design canvas for creating databound forms for workflow association, initiation, task completion, and workflow modifications, and these forms can be integrated with workflow schedules.

Office Activities

Workflow activities are fundamental building blocks for creating workflows. Windows Workflow Foundation ships a number of broadly useful activities, most of which can be used in Office workflows. In addition, Office will ship a number of Office-specific activities to facilitate development of custom workflows that integrate with Office System features. These will include activities around task management (such as create task, delete task), items (such as item update, on item change), and interacting with other elements of the workflow host environment described previously (such as writing to the workflow history list).

FIGURE 4.18   FrontPage provides a wizard-driven interface for workflow design against predeployed workflow activities.

Metadata, Packaging, and Deployment

In order for a new workflow to be associated to a list in SharePoint Products and Technologies, it is necessary to package that workflow along with its forms and resources into a single deployable .wsp file (similar in structure to .cab files). The files in the workflow are cataloged in an XML-based manifest file, so that the server knows where each file should be installed. The manifest file can be created by the workflow designer in any XML editor.

In addition, the developer has the ability to define metadata on the workflow that restricts the usage of the workflow in various ways. For example, metadata can be specified such that a workflow only runs on a document library, or items of a particular content type, or the workflow can only support manual initiation (versus automatic initiation) because form input is required by the end user. The metadata file is also packaged into the .wsp deployment file.

The developer can hand off the workflow to a server admin who will deploy the workflow on a front-end server, and if necessary it will be replicated across a farm. At this point, a new workflow template is available.

Finally, a site collection administrator must enable the workflow template for a particular site collection before it can be used.

Summary

Workflow in the next version of Office is centered on human workflow scenarios such as document review. Office will ship a number of out-of-the-box workflows that are designed for large classes of knowledge workers. Workflows are deeply integrated with familiar task and item concepts in the Office system.

Developing workflows for Office can be done rapidly using a wizard interface in FrontPage, or professional developers can take advantage of the richness and flexibility of the Visual Studio development environment, specifically the Windows Workflow Foundation and InfoPath plug-ins.

Workflow Integration with Data Activities

This chapter describes how workflows could be integrated with XML document WebForms to capture information that will be used to drive workflow logic. The key to understanding this integration lies in the data activities and interaction patterns modeled in the workflow.

What You Need

The required software, hardware, and knowledge required and in some cases recommended to set and work with Windows Workflow Foundation are:

- Required software—.NET Framework 2.0 SDK and Windows Workflow Foundation

- Recommended software—Visual Studio .NET 2005 (Any edition)

- Recommended hardware—Any PC that meets .NET Framework 2.0 SDK minimum requirements

- Recommended skills—C# 1.1 familiarity

Workflow Integration with XML Documents at a Glance

This chapter uses data activities as the mechanism for interacting with XML documents. The information that will be covered includes the following:

- Why data activities?—Their purpose and advantage

- The four types of data activities

- Data Sources and their usage

- Data Source Service and its purpose

- Data exchanges—A look at the relationship between data activities

- InfoPath Data Exchange Application—A single form application with Workflow backend

What Are Data Activities?

Data activities provide a standard communication mechanism for exchanging data between the workflow and the application executing the workflow. When using these activities, developers only define the characteristics of the data that is going to be exchanged and don't worry about the communication mechanism used to exchange the data.

Why Data Activities?

Workflows exchange data with the applications executing the workflow (that is, the host application) using queues and messages. Workflow queues provide a reliable message foundation for exchanging data. If a host application is interested in sending information to the workflow, it is responsible for placing that data in a workflow queue. Data placed in queues is retrieved by activity listeners that monitor specific queues. Queue interactions provide the lowest level of communication available to the workflow to receive data from the host application. Workflows communicate with host applications by invoking method calls on specific interfaces registered with the host. These methods act as event handlers, which are triggered directly by the workflow. One abstraction layer that exists on top of the queue service is the *Local Communication Service*, or *LCS* (Chapter 9, "Workflow Communication with .NET," provides a detailed explanation of this service).

This abstraction layer allows workflows and host applications to exchange information by simply defining an interface and without worrying about the existence of queues. The information used to define these interfaces implicitly creates queues using the information defined in the correlation values. LCS interfaces define events that are used to send information to the workflow and methods that are used by the workflow to communicate with host applications. These interfaces act as a communication contract between the workflow and the host. To simplify this approach, data activities were built.

Data activities provide an abstraction layer on top of LCS (see Figure 5.1). They use a predefined interface for exchanging data between the workflow and the host application executing the workflow. They are targeted for developers who are interested in exchanging data between the workflow and the host application in a predefined fashion and who want to define the payload of that exchange.

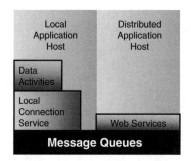

FIGURE 5.1 Windows Workflow Foundation communication stack.

Data activities provide a mechanism for defining the characteristics of the data that will be exchanged between the workflow and the host application. They shield developers from having to know the protocol used to exchange that data between the workflow and the host (see Figure 5.2). They provide an out-of-the-box mechanism for sending and querying data from the workflow to the host and vice versa. Data exchanges between host applications and workflows require knowledge of data sources, data handlers, and unique keys, not message protocols. *Data sources* describe the makeup of the data that will be exchanged between the workflow and the host application. *Data handlers* provide a mechanism for managing data that was sent by the workflow to the host. *Unique keys* specify the tokens in the information that makes the data exchange between the workflow and host application self-contained. The host application service that enables the communications to take place without exposing the protocol semantics is the Data Source Service. The Data Source Service is responsible for allowing the host application to send and query data from the workflow and managing the incoming requests that come from the workflow to the host application. This service lives as part of the workflow runtime services.

Data Activities Types

There are four types of data activities: `WaitForData` (Figure 5.3), `WaitForQuery` (Figure 5.4), `UpdateData` (Figure 5.5), and `SelectData` (Figure 5.6). `WaitForData` receives information being submitted by the host to the workflow.

All of these activities are configured using the concept of data sources. *Data sources* define, from the point of view of the workflow, a channel of communication for exchanging data between the workflow and the host application.

`WaitForQuery` processes a query request submitted by the host and returns the information associated with the data source back to the host (see Figure 5.4). From the host perspective, `WaitForQuery` behaves in a synchronous fashion.

`UpdateData` is the mechanism used by the workflow to send information to the host (see Figure 5.5). Information submitted to the host is received by the `DataSourceService` and dispatched to the data handler associated with the activity.

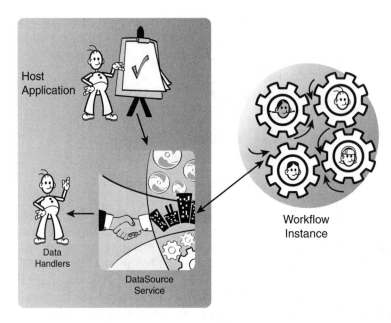

FIGURE 5.2   Data activity communications.

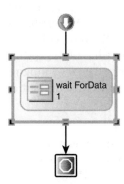

FIGURE 5.3   Activity used for receiving data from the host application, `WaitForData` activity.

`SelectData` sends a query request to the host (see Figure 5.6). The query submitted to the host is received by the `DataSourceService` and dispatched to the data handler associated with the activity to return information back to the workflow. From the workflow perspective, `SelectData` behaves in a synchronous fashion.

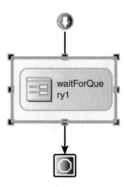

FIGURE 5.4   Activity used for receiving a query request from the host application, `WaitForQuery` activity.

FIGURE 5.5   Activity used for sending information to the host application, `UpdateData` activity.

FIGURE 5.6   Activity used for sending query requests to the host application, `SelectData` activity.

Data Sources

As mentioned earlier, data activities are configured using data sources (see Figure 5.7). Data sources define a homogenous channel where information flows between the workflow and the host. This channel is used to ensure that the same type of data being sent by the workflow is expected to be received by the workflow. Data sources define the following:

- Data being exchanged between the workflow and the host application

- Unique properties of the data being exchanged

- Data handlers used to receive information and process query requests being submitted by the workflow to the host

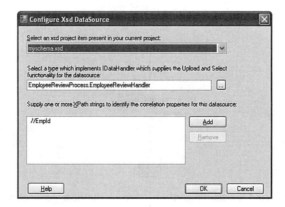

FIGURE 5.7   Data Source Configuration dialog.

Types

There are two types of data sources—object and XSD (see Figure 5.8). *Object data sources* are used to define payloads that are instances of .NET classes or types. They are configured by pointing to a type in the code-beside of the workflow or by pointing to an assembly. This data source is ideal when using predefined classes contained in third-party SDKs. XSD data sources map their payload to an XSD file. The assumption is that the information you are going to be exchanging between the workflow and host application is going to represent an XML document. This doesn't mean that the information is passed over the wire as XML. XSD data sources take an XSD file and autogenerate a .NET class. Once created, this type is available to the code-beside to program against. The class is used by the workflow to exchange data with the host application. The host application uses this class to serialize objects of this type into XML documents and deserialize XML documents into objects of this type to communicate back to the workflow. This data source is ideal when there is a requirement to store information in XML documents (for example InfoPath documents). All payload classes must be attributed as serializable classes.

FIGURE 5.8   The Create New Data Source dialog.

Unique Keys

Multiple payloads are constantly being exchanged between the workflow and the host application. In many cases, payloads are created from a common Type. To distinguish between the various payloads, Windows Workflow Foundation introduces the concept of a *unique key*. Each payload definition, whether specified using a class or XSD, requires a unique identifier or key that is used to differentiate information that is handled by a data source. This information is used to route the payload to the correct activity awaiting data in the workflow and is used by the host to differentiate between data that is published to it via the Data Source Service. XSDDataSources define unique keys using XPath expressions.

Data Handlers

Data published from the workflow to the host is processed by data handlers. Data handlers implement the `IDataHandler` interface located in `System.Workflow.ComponentModel`.

```
Public Interface IDataHandler
  Function SelectData(ByVal message As Object, ByVal dataSourceInfo As _
    DataSourceInfo) As Object
  Sub UpdateData(ByVal message As Object, ByVal dataSourceInfo As DataSourceInfo)
End Interface
```

Class definitions for data handlers are not required to be defined inside the workflow code. They could be defined in a separate assembly. Because data handlers are stateless, any required state needs to be kept outside of the instance. Singleton objects could be used to preserve state between multiple data handler instances. Data handlers receive information from two data activities, `UpdateData` and `SelectData`.

UpdateData   The `UpdateData` activity sends or publishes information from the workflow to the host. The data being published is processed by the `UpdateData` method. The object parameter represents the data object being published by the workflow. This data object is of the same Type specified in the Data Source definition when it was configured. The `DataSourceInfo` parameter gives the handler the context for this data transfer.

```
Public Class DataSourceInfo
    Public Property DataObjectTypeName As String
    End Property
    Public Property DataSourceType As Type
    End Property
    Public Property Name As String
    End Property
    Public Property Properties As String
    End Property
End Class
```

The object's `DataObjectTypeName` property returns the name of the type of the payload. When using an `XSDDataSource`, this value represents the type of the proxy class generated at design time to represent the XSD. The `DataSourceType` property returns the type of the data source, either `ObjectDataSource` or `XSDDataSource`. The `Name` property returns the name of the data source. The `Properties` property returns a list of semicolon-separated unique keys.

SelectData   The `SelectData` activity sends a query request to the host. The query request is processed by the `SelectData` method in the host and returns the query result that will be consumed by the workflow. The object parameter passes a data object that represents the object being queried. The data object being passed as part of the query is partially populated. It is the responsibility of the host to fill it up and return it. The only required value is the unique identifier of the object. These values are used by the `SelectData` method to query its data context and return a unique data object back to the workflow.

DataSourceService

The `DataSourceService` is the glue that ties together the data activities in the workflow side with the host. It is a service that is registered with the workflow runtime. The `DataSourceService` sits between the publishing data activities (that is, `UploadData` and `SelectData`) and the workflow. It intercepts messages sent to the host and dispatches the data handlers associated with each data activity. The `DataSourceService` knows which data handlers to dispatch by using the data source definition contained in the publishing information. A subset of this information is passed to the data handler in the form of a `DataSourceInfo` object.

Messages are sent to the workflow instance via the `DataSourceService`. The `DataSourceService` provides two methods that can be used to send data to and query data from the workflow.

```
Public Class DataSourceService
    Inherits System.Workflow.Activities.IDataSourceService

    'There is some code before this one
    Public Sub RaiseDataChanged(ByVal contextProperties As IDictionary, _
        ByVal msg As Object)
```

```
    End Sub

    Public Function RaiseDataQueried(ByVal contextProperties As IDictionary, _
        ByVal msg As Object) As Object
    End Function

End Class
```

The `RaiseDataChanged` method sends data from the host to a `WaitForData` activity contained by the workflow. The `RaiseDataQueried` method sends a query request from the host to a `WaitForQuery` activity contained by the workflow. The `WaitForQuery` activity will internally match the query request against the data object associated with it and if the unique keys and types match it will return that data object back to the host as the result value of the call.

There are four different types of Dictionary values that could be placed in the `contextProperties`:

```
Dim properties As Dictionary = New Dictionary
properties.Add("InstanceId", instanceId)
properties.Add("WorkflowType", GetType(Workflow1))
properties.Add("DataSource", "dataSource1")
properties.Add("Activation", true)
```

`InstanceId` holds the ID of the current workflow instance. Workflow instance IDs are defined using GUIDs. `WorkflowType` is the class of the workflow that is being executed. `DataSource` is the name of the data source used inside the workflow when configuring the data activities. This name has to exactly match the name of the data source property contained by the data activity. The `Activation` property is optional. If not present, it is assumed to be false. It signals the workflow that the data being passed will start the execution of the workflow.

The payload or message in the `RaiseDataChanged` and `RaiseDataQueried` methods need to match the .NET type specified in the data source. This data object is internally cast to its original type to allow access to its unique identifier values. These values together with the data source name are used to locate internal queues, which are used as the delivery vehicle to exchange data between the host and the workflow.

Data Exchanges

There is an implicit order that must be followed by data activities in order for them to work properly over the same data source. The first data activity used in the same data source initializes the communications. After that, the other data activities become followers. This means the unique keys used to receive or send information between the workflow and the host must remain unchanged throughout the lifetime of the data source.

Think of it as a phone conversation; once you dial and establish communications with a second party, no additional dialing is required. The configuration information for the call stays in place until you hang up.

Imagine you have a payload of Type command:

```
<SerializableAttribute()>  _
Public Class Command

    Private _id As String

    Private _value As String

    'Unique ID Property
    Public Property ID As String
        Get
            Return Me._id
        End Get
        Set
            Me._id = value
        End Set
    End Property

    Public Property Value As String
        Get
            Return Me._value
        End Get
        Set
            Me._value = value
        End Set
    End Property
End Class
```

Let's say the host application wants to send a message to the workflow and the first activity in the workflow is a WaitForData.

```
Dim dService As DataSourceService = _
CType(workflowRuntime.GetService(GetType(DataSourceService)),DataSourceService)
Dim properties As Dictionary = New Dictionary
properties.Add("InstanceId", instanceId)
properties.Add("WorkflowType", GetType(Workflow1))
properties.Add("DataSource", "dataSource1")
properties.Add("Activation", true)

Dim data As Command = New Command
```

```
data.ID = "ChangeUser"
data.Value = "pedrot"

dService.RaiseDataChanged(properties, data)
```

After the `WaitForData` activity receives the data, any subsequent message the workflow wants to publish to the host on `"dataSource1"` has to have the `"ChangeUser"` ID. This is required because communications between the workflow and the host are established using data source names and unique key values. In a similar fashion, if the host application ever wanted to query the data object associated with `"dataSource1"`, it would have to initialize the data object to contain the `"ChangeUser"` ID, as shown in the following code:

```
Dim properties As Dictionary = New Dictionary
properties.Add("InstanceId", instanceId)
properties.Add("WorkflowType", GetType(Workflow1))
properties.Add("DataSource", "dataSource1")

Dim data As Command = New Command
data.ID = "ChangeUser"
Dim data2 As Command = dService.RaiseDataChanged(properties, data)
```

There are other scenarios where order is important when placing the data activities inside workflows. For example, if a receiving data activity is placed inside a loop (`Replicator`, `ConditionedActivityGroup`, `Listen`, or `While` loop), `IfElse` activity, it would be difficult for the activity position itself as both a communication initializer and a follower. To solve this problem, an initializing `UpdateData` activity will need to be placed before the loop, listen, or condition activity to ensure the initialization of the communications (see Figure 5.9). The purpose of the initializing activity is to open the communication channel before information can be transmitted through it.

InfoPath Data Exchange Application

Write a WinForm application that takes advantage of data activities to exchange InfoPath data between the workflow and the application. First, start by designing an InfoPath Form. Identify the fields you would like to capture in your form and exchange between the workflow and the host application. Second, create a workflow application that will be packaged as an assembly. Last, integrate the InfoPath form with the workflow using data activities and create a WinForm application that acts as a bridge between the InfoPath form and the workflow.

Sample Scenario

The goal of this application is to develop an employee review form whose initial data will be populated by the workflow. The InfoPath form will be completed offline by a manager. Once completed, the form will be synced back into the system to complete the process. The data that will be autopopulated when the form is initialized are employee first name, last name, level, and ID. The employee ID will be entered by the manager in the WinForm application when requesting the employee review form and will be written to the form directly. After the employee ID is submitted to the system, the system will retrieve the first name, last name, and employee level from a back end system and populate the XML object that represents the InfoPath document. The workflow will exchange this information with the WinForm. The WinForm application will serialize this XML object into an XML file and will place it in a directory together with the InfoPath document. The XML file will be opened using the InfoPath document. The manager will enter its comments into the review area of the forms and will save the form's output. The output of the form will overwrite the previous XML document contained by the directory. Once the form is completed and the InfoPath document is closed, the WinForm application will be notified and it will retrieve the XML document, deserialize into an XML object, and send it to the workflow. The workflow will receive the document and finish the process. Employee IDs will be used as the unique key in the process.

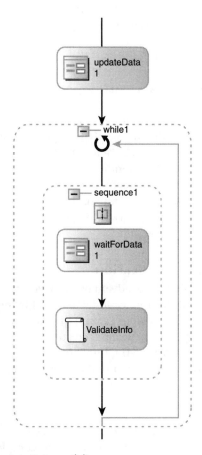

FIGURE 5.9   Initializing UpdateData activity.

Workflow Development   Start this exercise by creating an InfoPath form that contains the following fields: employee ID, employee first name, employee last name, employee level, manager ID, manager first name, manager last name, and a review comments section (see Figure 5.10).

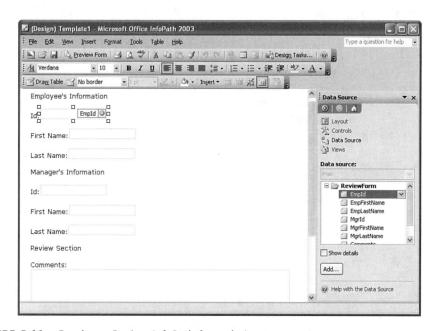

FIGURE 5.10   Employee Review InfoPath form designer.

Continue by extracting the XSD definition out of the InfoPath document. To perform this step go to the File tab and select the Extract Form Files menu item. This will display a dialog box where you specify the destination for the extraction (see Figure 5.11). The extraction directory will contain the XSD file you are interested in.

Workflow Development   Start this exercise by creating a workflow application (see Figure 5.12). The workflow application will be used to define the Employee Review process.

To facilitate the exchange of Review document XML data between the Infopath document and the workflow, the XSD file you extracted will be added as an existing project item and configured to autogenerate a .NET proxy class. The .NET proxy class provides a Type representation of the XSD. The configuration for this autogeneration takes place by specifying the `WorkflowXSDGenerator` class name in the Custom Tool property of the XSD file, `myschema.xsd` (see Figure 5.13). The autogenerated class definition for your InfoPath document will look like this:

```
Namespace EmployeeReviewProcess
```

```vb
<System.SerializableAttribute(), _
System.Xml.Serialization.XmlTypeAttribute( _
AnonymousType:=true, Namespace:= _
"http://schemas.microsoft.com/office/infopath/2003/myXSD/2005-07-22T14:16:46"), _
System.Xml.Serialization.XmlRootAttribute(Namespace:= _
"http://schemas.microsoft.com/office/infopath/2003/myXSD/2005-07-22T14:16:46", _
IsNullable:=false)>

    Public Class ReviewForm

        Private empIdField As String

        Private empFirstNameField As String

        Private empLastNameField As String

        Private mgrIdField As String

        Private mgrFirstNameField As String

        Private mgrLastNameField As String

        Private commentsField As String

        Private anyAttrField() As System.Xml.XmlAttribute

        Public Property EmpId As String
            Get
                Return Me.empIdField
            End Get
            Set
                Me.empIdField = value
            End Set
        End Property

        Public Property EmpFirstName As String
            Get
                Return Me.empFirstNameField
            End Get
            Set
                Me.empFirstNameField = value
            End Set
        End Property

        Public Property EmpLastName As String
```

```
      Get
            Return Me.empLastNameField
      End Get
      Set
            Me.empLastNameField = value
      End Set
End Property


Public Property MgrId As String
      Get
            Return Me.mgrIdField
      End Get
      Set
            Me.mgrIdField = value
      End Set
End Property


Public Property MgrFirstName As String
      Get
            Return Me.mgrFirstNameField
      End Get
      Set
            Me.mgrFirstNameField = value
      End Set
End Property


Public Property MgrLastName As String
      Get
            Return Me.mgrLastNameField
      End Get
      Set
            Me.mgrLastNameField = value
      End Set
End Property


Public Property Comments As String
      Get
            Return Me.commentsField
      End Get
      Set
            Me.commentsField = value
      End Set
End Property


<System.Xml.Serialization.XmlAnyAttributeAttribute()>  _
```

```
    Public Property AnyAttr As System.Xml.XmlAttribute()
        Get
            Return Me.anyAttrField
        End Get
        Set
            Me.anyAttrField = value
        End Set
    End Property
    End Class
End Namespace
```

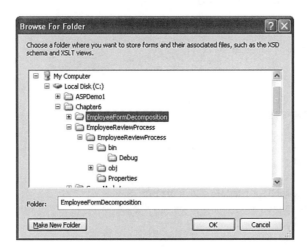

FIGURE 5.11   Dialog for extracting InfoPath Files.

Next, define a class that implements the IDataHandler interface. There are two methods in the IDataHandler interface. The method of interest for this sample is UpdateData. This method will be used to send data from the workflow to the host via the Data Source Service. The operation you want to perform in the UpdateData method is to serialize the content of the data object into an XML document. The code for the IDataHandlers implementation follows:

```
Public Class EmployeeReviewHandler
    Inherits IDataHandler

    Function IDataHandler_SelectData(ByVal message As Object, _
            ByVal dataSourceInfo As DataSourceInfo) _
            As Object Implements IDataHandler.SelectData
        Return Nothing
    End Function
```

```vbnet
Sub IDataHandler_UpdateData(ByVal message As Object, _
        ByVal dataSourceInfo As DataSourceInfo) _
        Implements IDataHandler.UpdateData
    Dim xmlRoot As XmlRootAttribute = Nothing
    Dim t As Type = message.GetType
    Dim attributes() As Object = t.GetCustomAttributes(false)
    For Each attribute As Object In attributes
        If attribute.GetType.Name.Contains("XmlRootAttribute") Then
            xmlRoot = CType(attribute,XmlRootAttribute)
        End If
    Next
    Dim tokens() As String = dataSourceInfo.DataObjectTypeName.Split( _
        Microsoft.VisualBasic.ChrW(46))
    Dim fileName As String = tokens((tokens.Length - 1))
    Dim fileLocation As String = (dirLocation _
            + (fileName + ".xml"))
    Dim writer As TextWriter = New StreamWriter(fileLocation)
    Dim serializer As XmlSerializer = New XmlSerializer( _
        message.GetType, xmlRoot)
    serializer.Serialize(writer, message)
    writer.Close
End Sub
End Class
```

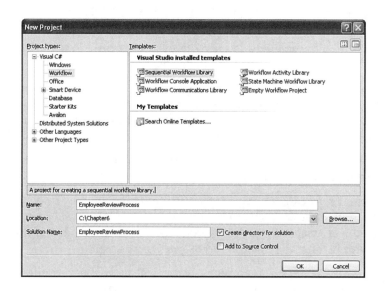

FIGURE 5.12   Dialog for creating a new Workflow project.

FIGURE 5.13   Property dialog for InfoPath XSD document with populated Custom Tool property.

When the data handler executes, it will serialize the data object associated with the UpdateData activity into an XML file. This code will also reside on the code-beside of the workflow application. Putting this information on the code-beside of the workflow is done merely for packaging purposes. The code can reside on any external assembly.

After the data handler is executed, the manager can go to the directory where the WinForm application is executing and open the InfoPath form. Inside the InfoPath form the manager loads the newly generated XML document and fills out the review.

At this point, you have all the information required to configure the data activities. Continue by placing an UpdateData activity into the Workflow Designer Surface (see Figure 5.14). This activity will be responsible for sending initial document information to the WinForm application for serialization.

Configure the DataSource property of this activity by clicking on the .... This will display the Data Source configuration dialog (see Figure 5.15).

Using this dialog, a new data source will be created to represent your Employee Review form. The data source you are going to be creating is of type XSDDataSource. The reason for this is that the original source of your information is derived from an XSD. The name of the data source is going to be ReviewFormDS (see Figure 5.16).

Selecting OK on the Create New Data Source dialog will allow you to configure the data source. The XSD from the InfoPath document, myschema.xsd, will be used to populate the structure of the data or payload. The EmployeeReviewHandler will be used to populate the IDataHandler implementation. The unique key used to identify this payload will be the employee ID. After the data source is configured, it is ready to be used (see Figure 5.17).

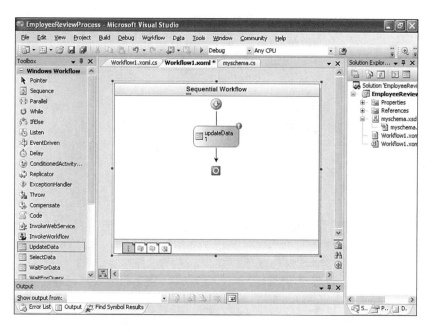

FIGURE 5.14 Employee review process with `UpdateData` activity.

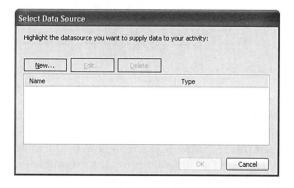

FIGURE 5.15 Data Source picker.

Back at the `UpdateData` activity, the `DataObject` property is the next value that needs to be configured. Enter a variable name and press Enter. This will automatically create a new variable of the proxy class specified in the `DataSource` property. This variable will be used to store the instance data associated with this data source. For this example, use a variable name called `ReviewInfoObj` (see Figure 5.18).

FIGURE 5.16   Create ReviewFormDS dialog.

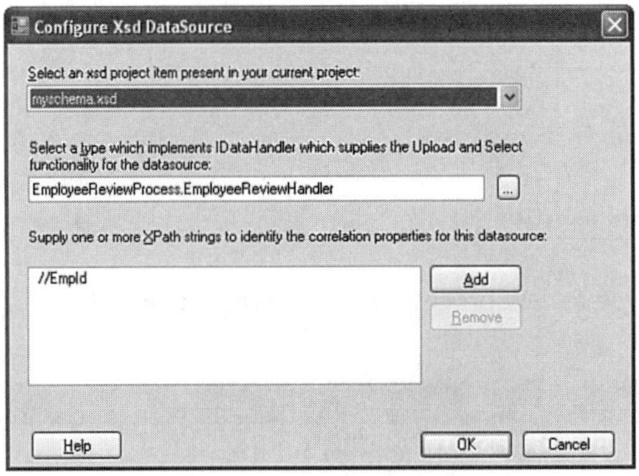

FIGURE 5.17   ReviewFormDS Configuration dialog.

After the `UpdateData` activity is fully configured, a workflow input parameter needs to be defined. This parameter will be used to pass the employee ID when the workflow is started. To define workflow parameters using the workflow designer, select the Sequential Workflow label and open the properties of the workflow. In the properties window select the ... on the parameters property. This will display the Workflow Parameters Editor window (see Figure 5.19). In the editor window, define the name of your property, the .NET type, direction, and value. The value field is used to create a code-beside variable that you can use to bind information against it:

```
Public Class Workflow3DataContext Inherits DataContext

    Public ReviewInfoObj As ReviewForm = New EmployeeReviewProcess.ReviewForm
    Public employeeId As String

End Class
```

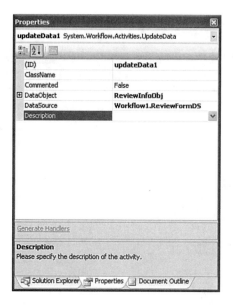

FIGURE 5.18 DataObject definition for ReviewFormDS.

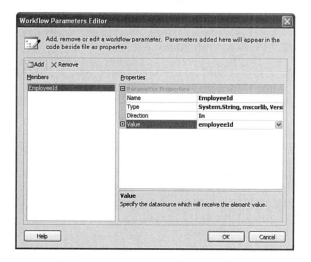

FIGURE 5.19 Workflow Parameters Editor with Employee Id Parameter.

Next, a code shape should be added before the UpdateData activity to transfer the value stored in the employeeId variable to the ReviewInfoObj.EmpId member (see Figure 5.20). The code handler for the Code activity property looks like this:

```
Public Sub TransferVariables(ByVal sender As Object, ByVal e As EventArgs)
     ReviewInfoObj.EmpId = Me.employeeId
End Sub
```

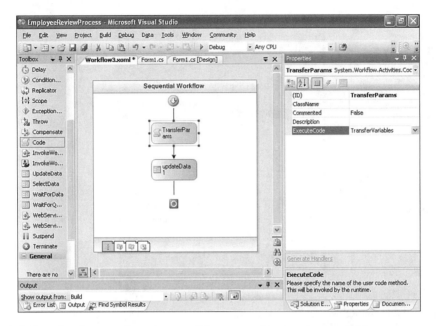

FIGURE 5.20   Employee review process with `Code` and `UpdateData` activities.

Using this code handler it is possible to assign other values in the `ReviewInfoObj`. Doing this results in an XML document with additional fields.

The last step in the workflow should be a `WaitForData` activity. This activity will be responsible for receiving the updated `ReviewInfoObj` back from the WinForm application after the InfoPath information has been transformed back into an object. Configure the `WaitForData` activity using the same values as the `UpdateData` activity (see Figure 5.21).

At this point, you are ready to build the workflow application. Building the workflow application generates an assembly that can be used inside a WinForm application. The imports for the application should look like this:

```
Imports System
Imports System.Workflow.Runtime
Imports System.Workflow.ComponentModel
Imports System.Workflow.Activities
Imports System.Workflow.Activities.Rules
Imports System.Windows.Forms
```

The references for the workflow application should contain the assemblies shown in Figure 5.22.

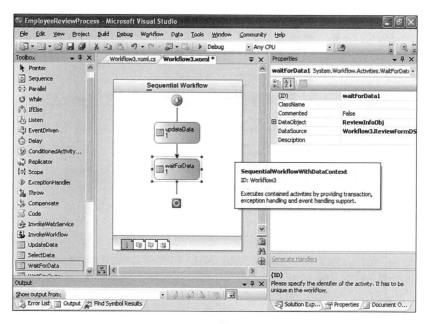

FIGURE 5.21   Employee Review Process with WaitForData activity.

FIGURE 5.22   Workflow project required references.

Windows Application Development   Next you are ready to create a Windows application project (see Figure 5.23). The new project will live in the same solution as the Workflow Application. This will allow you to treat the WinForm and the Workflow as a unit and build them together.

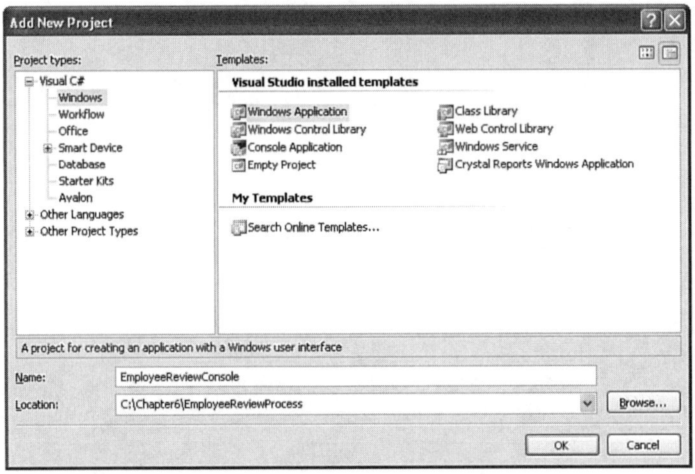

FIGURE 5.23   New Windows Application Project creation.

The WinForm that is used to collect the customer information contains two buttons (see Figure 5.24). The first button is used to start the employee review process. The second button is used to submit the finalized review form.

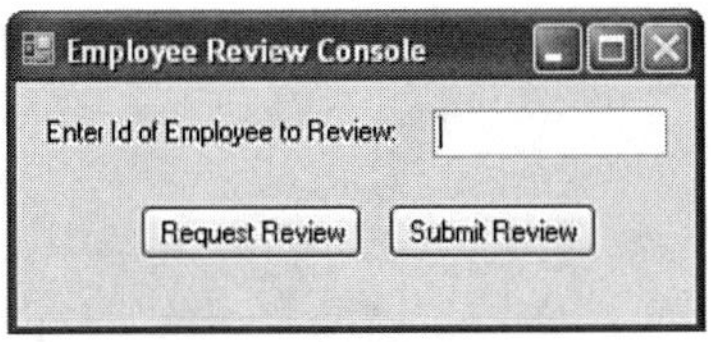

FIGURE 5.24   WinForm controls layout.

The code used to initialize the workflow runtime environment will be placed inside the Form constructor after the `InitializeComponent` method:

```
Public Class Form1 Inherits Form
    Private workflowRuntime As WorkflowRuntime
    Private dsService As DataSourceService
```

```
        Private workflowInstanceId As Guid
        Private workflowType As Type

        Public Sub New()
            MyBase.New
            InitializeComponent
            workflowType = GetType(EmployeeReviewProcess.Workflow3)
            workflowRuntime = New WorkflowRuntime
            workflowRuntime.AddService(New DataSourceService(workflowRuntime))
            dsService = CType(workflowRuntime.GetService(GetType(DataSourceService)), _
                    DataSourceService)
            workflowRuntime.StartRuntime
        End Sub
End Class
```

The workflow start logic will be placed on the event handler of the Request Review button. After the button is clicked the workflow will receive the employeeId as a workflow parameter:

```
Private Sub button1_Click(ByVal sender As Object, ByVal e As EventArgs)
        Dim parameters As Dictionary = New Dictionary
        parameters("EmployeeId") = Me.textBox1.Text
        workflowInstanceId = Guid.NewGuid
        workflowRuntime.StartWorkflow(workflowType, workflowInstanceId, parameters)
End Sub
```

At this point, let's build the application and test the first button click. Before the application builds you will have to add the following imports to the Windows application:

```
Imports System
Imports System.Workflow.ComponentModel
Imports System.Workflow.Runtime
Imports System.Workflow.Activities
Imports System.Workflow.Activities.Rules
Imports System.Xml.Serialization
Imports System.IO
Imports System.Windows.Forms
```

In addition, you will have to add theses references outlined in Figure 5.25.

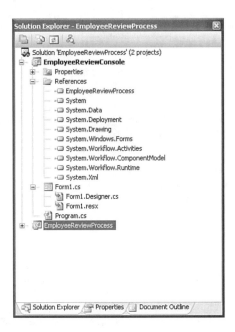

FIGURE 5.25   Windows application project required references.

Executing the application and selecting the Request Review button passes the Employee ID information to the workflow as a parameter. Also, start the execution of the workflow activities where the `Code` activity copies the `EmployeeId` parameter to the `ReviewInfoObj.EmpId` and the `UpdateData` activity sends the `ReviewInfoObj` to the WinForm application. The `DataSourceService` receives the call from the `UpdateData` activity and triggers the execution of the `DataHandler` implementation registered in the `DataSource` definition. The `void IDataHandler.UpdateData(object message, DataSourceInfo dataSourceInfo)` method, inside the `DataHandler` class, serializes the message object into an XML file. This XML file is created in the same directory where the Windows application executable lives.

The next step is to configure the InfoPath document to data bind against the created XML. To enable this, the InfoPath document needs to be configured to receive information from a DataConnection. Open the InfoPath document in Design mode, and then select the Data Connections ... item in the Tools menu. This will open the Data Connections dialog (see Figure 5.26).

Use this dialog to add a new data connection, follow the Data Connection Wizard to configure the connection to receive data, and define that the data will come from an XML file. Browse to the directory where the XML file you generated is located and select it. Finishing the wizard steps creates a secondary data source (see Figure 5.27).

FIGURE 5.26   InfoPath Data Connections dialog.

FIGURE 5.27   InfoPath data source controls.

After configuring the data source, rebind the Employee ID field to the EmpId field contained in the secondary data source. Save, close, and reopen the form. You will notice that the information contained in the XML file that was generated by the application is displayed. Return to the InfoPath form and add a button control. Inside this button define a new rule that always executes. Create an action inside that rule whose purpose is to synchronize the EmpId from the secondary data source to the EmpId contained in the main data source (see Figure 5.28).

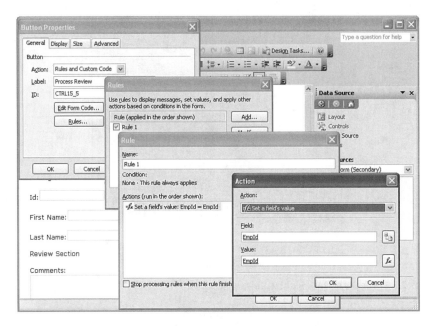

FIGURE 5.28   InfoPath Rule and Action for synchronizing EmpId from secondary data source to main data source.

Why are we doing all of this? At the beginning of this scenario you generated a .NET type using the InfoPath XSD as the baseline. This allowed you to create a class that is serializable into an XML document and define a DataSource channel in which data will be exchanged between the workflow and the host with a payload used by the InfoPath document. When the application executes, it takes information from the workflow and creates an XML document. The information in this document is used against the element in the main data source. However, when the document is saved, it will generate an XML document that will export the information contained in the main data source. The important thing to remember is that this information will deserialize into the .NET type you are using to define your DataSource. What that means is that you would be able to reconstruct an object directly from the XML document and pass that object to the workflow. The reason we created the actions in the rules was to ensure the main data source was completely populated. This provides a complete InfoPath data source from which a fully populated object is created. However, this requires that after the manager enters all of the information in the InfoPath document, the button needs to be clicked before the document is saved.

The last piece of code required to read the InfoPath document XML, convert it into an object, and send it to the workflow is missing. This code will be triggered using the second button in the application, Submit Review. Inside this event handler is where the Data Source Service will be used to send information to the workflow:

```
Private Sub button2_Click(ByVal sender As Object, ByVal e As EventArgs)
        Dim payload As Object = createObjectFromXML
        Dim properties As Dictionary = New Dictionary
        properties.Add("InstanceId", workflowInstanceId)
        properties.Add("WorkflowType", workflowType)
        properties.Add("DataSource", "Workflow3.ReviewFormDS")
        dsService.RaiseDataChanged(properties, payload)
End Sub
```

The `createObjectFromXML` method reads an XML file, generated using InfoPath Form's editor, and creates an object whose type matches the class defined in the `ReviewFormDS` data source, ReviewForm. The file being read is stored in the same location as the XML file that was used as the input to the InfoPath form. See the following code for the implementation details of the `createObjectFromXML` method:

```
Private Function createObjectFromXML() As Object
        Dim fileLocation As String = _
"C:\Chapter6\EmployeeReviewProcess\EmployeeReviewConsole\"& _
"bin\Debug\FormReviewed.xml"

        Dim xmlDoc As TextReader = New StreamReader(fileLocation)
        Dim docData As String = xmlDoc.ReadToEnd
        xmlDoc.Close

        ' Remove an XML attribute that messes up serialization.
        Dim startTag As Integer = docData.IndexOf("xml:lang")
        Dim endTag As Integer = docData.IndexOf("en-us", startTag)
        Dim newData As String = docData.Remove(startTag, ((endTag - startTag) _
                    + 6))
        Dim t As Type = GetType(EmployeeReviewProcess.ReviewForm)
        Dim attributes() As Object = t.GetCustomAttributes(false)
        Dim xmlRoot As XmlRootAttribute = Nothing
        For Each attribute As Object In attributes
            If attribute.GetType.Name.Contains("XmlRootAttribute") Then
                xmlRoot = CType(attribute,XmlRootAttribute)
            End If
        Next
        Dim data As String = newData
        Dim reader As StringReader = New StringReader(data)
        Dim serializer As XmlSerializer = New XmlSerializer(t, xmlRoot)
        Dim xmlReader As XmlReader = New XmlTextReader(reader)
        Dim dataObject As Object = serializer.Deserialize(xmlReader)
        reader.Close
        Return dataObject
    End Function
```

After the object is created you initialize the data source communication channel by defining the various dictionary parameters required to send the payload back to the workflow using the predefined data source definition, `ReviewFormDS`. This information is received by the `WaitForData` activity and once executed, it marks the workflow as executed.

Summary

The data activities provide an out-of-the-box mechanism for exchanging data between the workflow and the host application. They are configured using data sources and provide a simple mechanism to bind data to form applications. They are specially suited for manipulating InfoPath documents or other XML Schema–based documents.

CHAPTER **6**

Using Web Services

Using Web Services with Windows Workflow Foundation

When building applications today the call of using web services is strong. Web services provide an easy way to build distributed applications because of their use of open protocols and data formats (generally HTTP and XML).

Service Oriented Architecture (SOA) is a new way of thinking about how to build distributed applications in this new web services world. The ideas of SOA are actually fairly simple and straightforward. They are based around four basic tenets:

- Boundaries are explicit.

- Services are autonomous.

- Services share schema and contract, not class.

- Service compatibility is based on policy.

Some say that SOA is missing one importance piece: Workflow. This chapter will explain how you can integrate Windows Workflow Foundation into both your web services client and your web services themselves. Because this is a book about Workflow and not SOA we'll concentrate on the implementation details of adding Workflow to your SOA designs, not on the SOA designs themselves.

Calling a Web Service

Calling a web service from .NET code is fairly straightforward. The .NET framework provides the `SoapHttpClientProcotol` class (found in the `System.Web.Services.Protocols` namespace). This class knows how to invoke web services. It is able to turn a .NET call stack into a SOAP Envelope that can be sent to a web service using HTTP, and receive a corresponding response SOAP Envelope, deserialize the response, and return it to the caller as a .NET type.

When you want to call a web service from a .NET project you are writing, you can add a Web Reference to your project. Adding a Reference to your project adds a .NET assembly-level reference to whatever assembly you specify.

Adding a Web Reference causes VS.NET to generate code that allows you to call to a web service the same way you would call into any .NET object referenced from an external assembly. The Add Web Reference command in VS.NET is a code generation tool that is available from the Project menu, or from the context menu if you right-click on the project node in the Solution Explorer. The code it generates allows you to call a web service that uses the definition provided by a Web Service Description Language (WSDL) file. When the Add Web Reference command is used, a dialog appears and you can type an URL in the address bar. This can either be an URL to a WSDL file (which can either live on your local machine or on the network) or the URL to an ASMX web service. After you click the OK button, this functionality takes care of generating a new class that can invoke a web service that implements the document you specify (this is done by running code that lives in an SDK tool named WSDL.exe—so you can do this from a command line as well).

The code generated by the Web Reference is a class that derives from the `SoapHttpClientProtocol` class. This class is expressly generated to know how to call the web service specified by the WSDL. The metadata in the WSDL is used to generate strongly typed methods that wrap the loosely typed methods of the base class. This allows you to call a method named `Add` versus calling the `Invoke` method of `SoapHttpClientProtocol`.

`SoapHttpClientProtocol` is a class that is programmed to call any basic web service. The derived class that is created from the Add Web Reference is generated to facilitate the ease of calling the web service by creating a set of wrapper methods that closely mimic the operation(s) that the WSDL defines. This base class knows how to turn the call stack from the .NET method that you call to (like `Add`) into the appropriate SOAP call to the web service. It uses the `XmlSerializer` class and other classes in the `System.Xml` namespace to accomplish this. See *Applied SOAP: Implementing .NET Web Services* for more information about programming web services in general.

Using Web References is the general way of programming against web services from any .NET-based project in VS.NET.

Calling a Web Service from a Workflow

When you want to call from a workflow into a web service, you can add the `InvokeWebService` activity to your workflow. The `InvokeWebService` activity allows you to do this by building on top of this typical .NET facility for calling a web service (again, the `SoapHttpClientProtocol` class).

To add this activity, drag and drop it from the toolbox onto the Workflow design surface. This spawns the Add Web Reference dialog in Visual Studio. You can either specify the URL in this dialog, or you can click Cancel. If you don't cancel, but do specify the URL to the WSDL for which you would like to create a Web Reference, some of the InvokeWebService activity properties will be set for you automatically.

In order for the InvokeWebService activity to compile, the properties that must be set are the ProxyClassName, the MethodName, and the URL. ProxyClassName and URL are the properties set for you automatically if you use the Add Web Reference dialog that appears when you drag and drop the InvokeWebService activity onto your workflow. The ProxyClassName property is the name of the SoapHttpClientProcotol-derived class that you want to use to invoke the web service.

The MethodName is the name of the method on the ProxyClassName type that you want to call for a particular InvokeWebService activity. You'll have more than one MethodName to choose from if the web service has multiple operations (as the proxy class will have multiple methods). The MethodName property will be a combo box that will display only the methods available on the proxy class you specified using the ProxyClassName property.

After you have selected the MethodName on the proxy class that you want to invoke with this activity (which eventually will be calling the operation on the web service), you will have to supply the parameters (it is possible that there will be no parameters if the web service operation is a One-Way Message Exchange Pattern (MEP) that has no message parameters).

After the MethodName is specified on the proxy class, the property grid in the designer for your InvokeWebService activity will expand to include a Properties section. This section enables you to associate available variables for initializing the input parameters that will be sent to the web service, and for the return value (again, if the MEP is One-Way there won't be any return value parameter to set).

When executed, the InvokeWebService activity is going to call the method you specify on an instance of the proxy class. The call will pass as input parameters whatever the values of the variables you've picked as input parameters at the time of the call, and setting the value of the variable you've picked as the return value with the return of the web service operation.

Using Web Services: An Example

Imagine the middle of a workflow that is doing order processing for a particular product (we'll call them mega-widgets). During the processing of the workflow you need to call a web service to provide more data about the mega-widget order (data necessary for the workflow to continue). Assume the workflow has the primary key of the mega-widget order, and the service will return the order detail information to your workflow.

In the client workflow application, drag and drop the InvokeWebService activity from the toolbox onto the design surface. When you do that, the Add Web Reference dialog shown in Figure 6.1 appears.

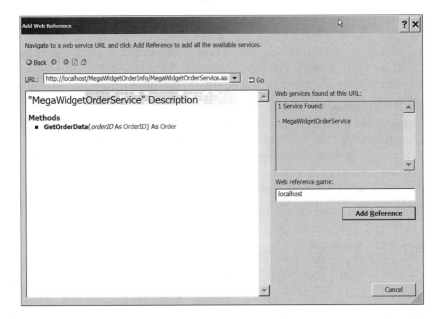

FIGURE 6.1   The Add Web Reference dialog.

Specify the URL to the WSDL of the web service you would like to invoke, which in this case is http://localhost/MegaWidgetOrderInfo/MegaWidgetOrderService.asmx?WSDL. After the Methods (Operations) appear in the browser window of this dialog, click the Add Reference button and VS.NET will generate the necessary files (most importantly, the proxy class) for the workflow to call this web service.

After the Add Web Reference wizard is done, the InvokeWebService activity has been added to the workflow design surface, and the URL and ProxyClassName properties have been filled in (see Figure 6.2).

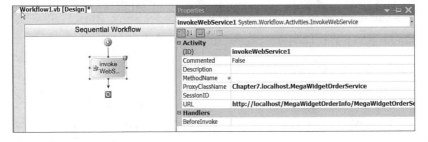

FIGURE 6.2   InvokeWebService properties grid.

Then you need to go the properties of the activity and set the MethodName property to the name of the method or operation on the web service that you want this InvokeWebService activity to invoke. In this example, pick GetOrderData from the combo box in the property grid.

After you select the `MethodName`, the properties in the grid for this activity expand to include the Parameters category. The method you've chosen has one input parameter—an instance of a type named OrderID, and one output parameter—an instance of a type named Order. Both of these types were generated by the Add Web Reference wizard (to be technical, wsdl.exe) based upon the message types specified by the WSDL from the MegaWidgetOrderInfo Service.

Put in the name of a property associated with your workflow—or, like all such properties in Windows Workflow Foundation, you can specify a property name and then a Path (a subproperty or field on the property specified as the property name itself). In this case, just type in two variable names—_orderData for the (`ReturnValue`) property and _orderInfo for the `orderID` property (the `orderID` property name is the name given to the element in the schema specified by the WSDL document). You can see these properties set in Figure 6.3 and the designer-generated code in Listing 6.1.

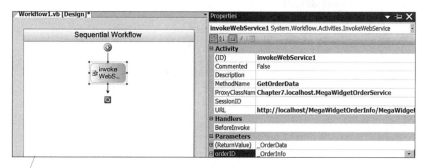

FIGURE 6.3   Completed `InvokeWebService` properties.

LISTING 6.1   Designer-Generated Code

```
Partial Public Class Workflow1
    Inherits SequentialWorkflow
    Public _orderDataAs MegaWidgetWorkflowClient.localhost.Order = _
        New MegaWidgetWorkflowClient.localhost.Order
    Public _orderInfo As MegaWidgetWorkflowClient.localhost.OrderID = _
        New MegaWidgetWorkflowClient.localhost.OrderID
    Public Sub New()
        MyBase.New()
        InitializeComponent()
    End Sub
End Class
```

The _orderData and _orderInfo fields were added when you typed those names into the property grid. Now you have to add some additional code to make sure that the _orderInfo instance is initialized correctly for your particular workflow before the InvokeWebServices activity is executed.

You could do this in many different ways, but for this example, create a parameter for the workflow itself that is the primary key of the order you are working with. Use that parameter to set the ID property of the _orderInfo instance before the InvokeWebServices activity is executed. Drag and drop a code activity into your workflow right before the InvokeWebServices activity, and when you double-click on it, add the code shown in Listing 6.2. (I specified the parameter to initialize the _ID field on my DataContext class when I created the parameter on the workflow itself).

LISTING 6.2   Code to Set the Web Service Parameter Values

```
Public Sub setWSParams_ExecuteCode(ByVal sender As Object, ByVal e As EventArgs)
    _orderInfo.ID = _ID
End Sub
```

You can see the workflow design in Figure 6.4.

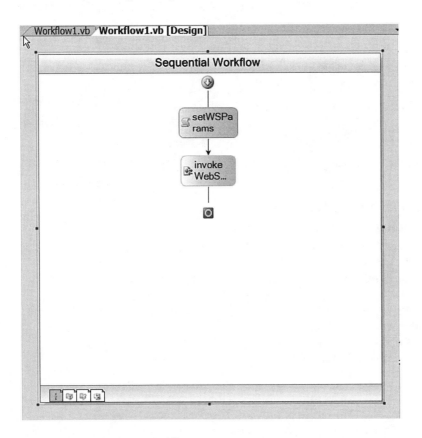

FIGURE 6.4   InvokeWebService workflow.

Now all you need to do is to execute the workflow, passing in the correct parameters. The MegaWidgetWorkflowClient project is a Workflow Console application, so modify the Main method to accept an input from the Console, and then invoke the workflow, passing in the Console input as the ID parameter. You can see that code in Listing 6.3.

LISTING 6.3   Executing the Workflow

```
Public Sub setWSParams_ExecuteCode(ByVal sender As Object, ByVal e As EventArgs)
     _orderInfo.ID = _ID
   End Sub
```

For completeness, add another Code activity after the InvokeWebServices activity in the workflow, which will print to the Console the data returned from the web service call. You can see that code in Listing 6.4 and the final workflow design in Figure 6.5.

LISTING 6.4   Code to Display the Web Service Return Value

```
Public Sub displayWSReturn_ExecuteCode(ByVal sender As Object, _
   ByVal e As EventArgs)
      Console.WriteLine("The Web Service returned {0}", _
         orderData.Data.ToString())
   End Sub
```

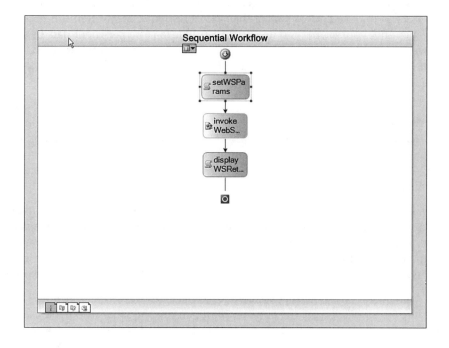

FIGURE 6.5   Final InvokeWebService design.

Although this is a simple example, this is how you work with the data that has been returned from the web service, by adding activities after the `InvokeWebService` activity in your workflow. Assuming the call to the web service was successful, the field or property you specified to hold the `ReturnValue` property from the web service will be initialized with whatever value the proxy class returned (which will be a deserialized version of the XML message that the web service returned to the proxy class).

This will be the basic set of steps you will follow whenever you use the `InvokeWebService` activity:

1. Add the activity to your workflow, specifying the URL to the WSDL of the web service you would like to invoke.

2. Specify the `MethodName`, and then specify the field or property name(s) for the parameters to that method.

3. Add the code or activity before the `InvokeWebService` activity that will ensure that the input parameters will be initialized with the correct values.

4. Add the code or activity after the `InvokeWebService` activity that will harvest the return value and execute the appropriate code for your workflow.

Sessions

Many web services today use HTTP as their transport protocol. If that is the case, oftentimes they send HTTP cookies as part of their HTTP response. Most often this cookie uniquely identifies your client, and uses that identifier to store per-client data in the web service (web applications, of course, have been using this functionality for years). To make this work, your web service client must send the cookie(s) back to the web service on every request.

If you build your web service in .NET, the ASMX infrastructure supports this out-of-the-box. When you add the `WebMethod` attribute to a method in your ASMX class, you can set the `EnableSession` property to true. The ASP.NET infrastructure will then send an HTTP cookie back to the web service client when the client makes a call into this method. Your web service code can use the `HttpContext.Session` property to store per-client state, to keep track of any per-client data you want.

The `InvokeWebService` activity in Windows Workflow Foundation supports the use of cookies across multiple invocations to the same server during the execution of a single workflow. To make this work, you set the `SessionID` property of the `InvokeWebService` activity in your workflow that you'd like to start the "session" with the web service. The property is a string value; you just want to set it to something unique for your workflow.

On each subsequent `InvokeWebService` activity in your workflow that you would like to use the same "session," you set the `SessionID` property to the same string you used on the `InvokeWebService` activity that started the session. Any `InvokeWebService` activities that come after the initializing activity will send the same cookie value back to the web service, ensuring that the web service will be able to keep track of the per-user state.

You can see such a workflow and the `InvokeWebService` activities properties in Figure 6.6. Notice that the two `InvokeWebService` activities will have the same value for the `SessionID` property, and so the web service (assuming it supports sessions using HTTP cookies) will be able to keep session state for the workflow between those two invocations.

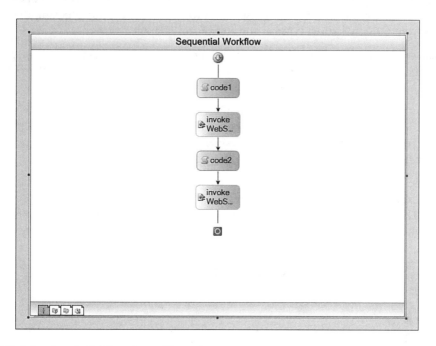

FIGURE 6.6   `InvokeWebService` with sessions.

Adding the Web Reference Manually

If you click the Cancel button on the Add Web Reference dialog when it appears, none of the required properties on the activity are set for you automatically. To get the activity to compile and function, you must set the required properties manually. This means you must have already added the web reference to your project manually or you have to add it manually before the `InvokeWebService` activity will pass validation.

This is useful if you have one web service you want to call multiple times; there is no need to add the web reference more than once (only one `SoapHttpClientProtocol` class is needed). You can then use the same class associating it with multiple `InvokeWebService` activities whether you are calling the same method multiple times, or calling multiple methods.

Exposing a Workflow via a Web Service

If, instead of calling a web service, you would like to use a workflow to implement a web service, you can do that as well. The workflow runtime has been extended to work inside of the typical web service context inside of .NET—namely the ASMX context. After you are done integrating your workflow with web services you will end up with an ASMX web service that clients can call to activate and execute your workflow.

To create this web service from your workflow, add the `WebServiceReceive` activity as the top activity in your workflow. Assuming a sequential workflow, the activate property on the `WebServiceReceive` activity must also be set to true. We'll discuss exposing web services from other workflow types at the end of this chapter.

The `WebServiceReceive` shape allows generation of a `System.Web.WebService`-derived class that can be called by any web service client. When the client calls into the web service, the workflow will activate.

To create the web service, you need an interface definition. The generation of the actual `WebService`-derived class is done dynamically when you compile your workflow project. The web service definition will be based upon an interface definition that you create or reference (more on the implementation details of this later).

When you add the `WebServiceReceive` activity to your workflow, specify the interface you want to expose. Do this by setting the `InterfaceName` property on the `WebServiceReceive` activity. The `InterfaceName` property has a type editor that opens the .NET Type browser dialog, which has been filtered to only show interfaces. You can see this in Figure 6.7.

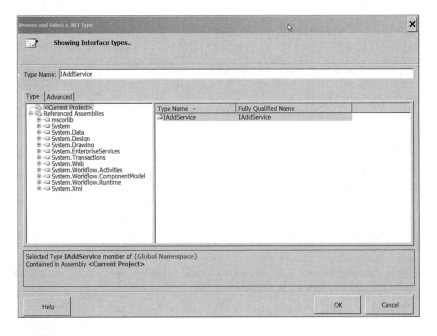

FIGURE 6.7   Interface picker dialog.

After you pick the interface, you also specify the method from that interface that you would like your `WebMethod` to be modeled after. This is the `MethodName` property on the

WebServiceReceive activity. After you've picked the interface, the MethodName property in the property grid will be a combo box populated with the methods from the interface. The signature of the method you pick will determine the signature of your web service.

If the method has any parameters, you have to reference properties that will be populated when the web service is invoked by a client. As always, the properties must be the right type and either on your DataContext or on another activity. After you pick a method that has parameters, the property grid will expand and you will have to either pick existing variables for those properties or type in new variable names. If you type a variable name into the property grid, the designer will create a new field for you of the correct type inside of the designer class for the workflow. If you want to use a property as the store for the parameters you must define the property and then type the parameter names into the property grid.

The method you pick ends up being the method on the WebService-derived class, and ends up defining the operation in the WSDL that will be generated for your web service. If the method you pick has a return value, the MEP of the operation will be request-response; if your method has no return value, the MEP will be One-Way.

If the method does have a return value, your web service operation will be request-response, which means through your workflow you need to designate a variable to be the value that gets returned to the web service client. This is what the WebServiceResponse activity is for.

You add the WebServiceResponse activity to your workflow at whatever point the response for the WebService client will be ready—after whatever other activities have executed necessary to generate the right response. The WebServiceResponse has a ReceiveActivityId property that specifies the particular WebServiceReceive activity that it is associated with. After you pick the right WebServiceReceive activity, the property grid of the WebServiceResponse activity will expand and show the (ReturnValue) property. You specify this property, and its value (at the time the WebServiceResponse activity executes) will be sent back to the web service client.

Let's walk through a simple example of exposing a web service from a sequential work-flow, taking the canonical example of a web service that performs simple mathematical calculations. Assume you have an interface that looks like the one in Listing 6.5.

LISTING 6.5   IAddService Interface

```
Public Interface IAddService
    Function Add(ByVal x As Integer, ByVal y As Integer) As Integer
End Interface
```

For this project, create a new empty workflow project and add a new sequential workflow with code separation. To the top of the workflow, add the WebServiceReceive activity, name it AddReceive, and set its Activate property to true. Next, pick what interface and method you would like to use as the signature for the web service. To do this, go to the InterfaceName property. The editor button on this property opens the .NET type-picker dialog, which you use to select the `IAddService` interface. This interface can be defined in a code file in the same project, but more likely it will have been defined in a separate assembly. If it were in a separate assembly, you would have to reference that separate assembly to get the interface to appear on the .NET type-picker dialog.

After you pick the `IAddService` interface, you can then go to the `MethodName` property and pick the `Add` method from the list of interface methods (easy in this case because the interface has only one method). After you pick the `Add` method, two parameters (the parameters defined on the `IAddService.Add` method itself) appear under the Parameters category in the property pane for the `AddReceive` activity. You can either link those properties to already defined variables, or you can type in variable names and fields will be created in the designer-generated code. For names, select _x and _y respectively and the designer will drop a field definition of the right type into the `Workflow`-derived class for you.

When the workflow gets hooked up to the web service, the workflow infrastructure will set the values of the _x and _y fields based upon the data that will come in from the web service. After the `AddReceive` activity has executed, those variables will be filled in with the values passed in via the web service, and other activities can then access the values to actually provide the implementation of the algorithm (which in this case is pretty easy: Just add the values together).

Now that you've taken care of the incoming parameters, you need to deal with the return value. Because the `Add` method has a return value, the web service will have an operation with the name of Add that has a request-response MEP. This means you need a response, so after the `WebServiceReceive` activity you have to add a `WebServiceResponse` activity. Drop that activity onto the workflow after the `WebServiceReceive` activity shape (if the chosen method had no return value, you wouldn't need a `WebServiceResponse` activity).

Set the ID property of the `WebServiceResponse` activity to `AddResponse`, and set its `ReceiveActivityId` property to `AddReceive`—the ID of the `WebServiceReceive` activity you created a moment ago. After you link the `WebServiceResponse` activity to its `WebServiceReceive` activity, the designer adds the (`ReturnValue`) property to the Parameters category in the property grid for the `WebServiceResponse` activity (because this is a request-response MEP). Then set the name of the variable that the workflow runtime will send back through its web service infrastructure, which in the end will get sent back to the web service client. In this case, name the variable _ret by typing that name into the property grid; a field of type `System.Int32` is added to the `workflow` class.

To actually implement this service, between the `AddReceive` and the `AddResponse` activities, the workflow has to run some code that actually adds the two incoming parameters and sets the return variable to the correct value. At the point of the `AddResponse` activity, the return value must have been initialized to a correct value or else an incorrect value will be returned to the web service client (whatever the value of the `ReturnValue` property is at the time of the `WebServiceResponse` activity is what is returned via the web service).

This is an implementation decision on the part of the workflow implementation itself. One option is to add additional activities of some sort between the `WebServiceReceive` activity and the `WebServiceResponse` activity. These activities will execute and can actually implement the algorithm necessary to fulfill the service's implementation. For this simple example, the `Code` activity could be used. If a `Code` activity is added between the `AddReceive` and the `AddResponse` activity shapes in your workflow, you could implement the service in the method the `Code` activity will execute for you.

Another option is to use the events of either the `WebServiceReceive` or `WebServiceResponse` activities. The `WebServiceReceive` has an event named `AfterWebServiceReceive` that fires after the activity itself executes. You can add an event handler for this event and you can implement all or part of your service's logic in that method. In this simple example it would be trivial to just do that necessary addition logic in that event handler method. To add the event handler, all you need to do is type a name into the property grid next to the event, and the event handler code will be generated for you automatically.

The `WebServiceResponse` activity also has an event; logically it fires right before the activity itself is about to execute and is named `BeforeWebServiceResponse`. This would allow you to do any processing that still needs to be done for the `ReturnValue` to be returned successfully. Again, in this simple example, your service's algorithm could also be implemented in the event handler for this event. In a more complicated service, it might be necessary to put some code in the `AfterWebServiceReceive` event handler, have additional activities between the `WebServiceReceive` activity and the `WebServiceResponse` activity, and put a final piece of code in the event handler for the `BeforeWebServiceResponse` event.

Implement the `Add` algorithm in a `Code` activity named `AddImplementation`. You can see the complicated code in Listing 6.6 inside of the final `DataContext` implementation and the final workflow in Figure 6.8.

LISTING 6.6   `DataContext` Class for Add Service Workflow

```
Imports System
Imports System.Workflow.ComponentModel
Imports System.Workflow.Runtime
Imports System.Workflow.Activities
Imports Microsoft.Workflow.DeclarativeRules

Partial Public Class AddServiceWorkflow
    Inherits SequentialWorkflow

    Public _x As System.Int32 = Nothing
    Public _y As System.Int32 = Nothing
    Public _ret As System.Int32 = Nothing
    Public Sub New()
        MyBase.New()
        InitializeComponent()
    End Sub
```

LISTING 6.6   Continued

```
Public Sub AddImplementation_ExecuteCode(ByVal sender As Object, _
   ByVal e As EventArgs)
     _ret = _x + _y
End Sub

End Class
```

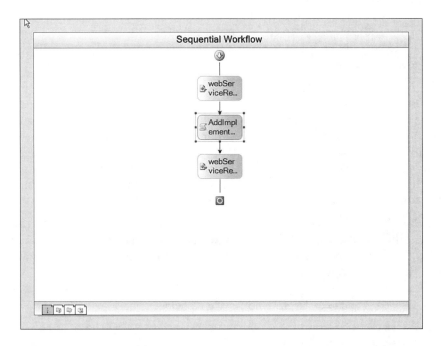

FIGURE 6.8   Web service workflow.

Hooking Up the Workflow-generated WebService

Now that you have finished the web service workflow, you need to actually get it to work inside of an ASP.NET web service context. To do this, you first need a web service project. You can add a new web service project to your existing solution by right-clicking on the solution node in the Solution Explorer and selecting Add from the context menu and New Web Site from the Add submenu. I prefer the HTTP option for web services (versus FTP or File System) because this option uses IIS as the HTTP Host for the web service, and therefore the URL will stay stable during development.

Add a web service project and specify AddWorkflowWebService as the name of the website. Next you need a reference to all the assemblies you'll need—first and foremost the work-flow assembly you just created, because that is a project in the same solution for which you can create a project-level reference. You also need a reference to the System.Workflow.Runtime assembly.

The `System.Workflow.Runtime` assembly contains the types that initialize and run the workflow runtime inside of the ASP.NET worker process. Without this initialization your workflow web service cannot run.

Inside of this assembly is a type named `WorkflowWebHostingModule` that implements the standard `IHttpModule` interface and that can be plugged in as an ASP.NET module. It is this module that allows the workflow runtime to be initialized correctly. The first step is to modify the `web.config` for this application and configure this type as a module. It also needs the `web.config` to be modified to allow for its custom configuration section handler. See Listing 6.7 for the contents of the `web.config`.

LISTING 6.7 Workflow-Enabled `Web.Config`

```
<?xml version="1.0"?>
<configuration xmlns="http://schemas.microsoft.com/.NetConfiguration/v2.0">
    <configSections>
        <section name="WorkflowRuntime" _
            type="System.Workflow.Runtime.Configuration.WorkflowRuntimeSection, _
            System.Workflow.Runtime,Version=1.0.0.0,
 Culture=neutral,PublicKeyToken=31bf3856ad364e35"/>
    </configSections>
    <WorkflowRuntime/>
    <system.web>
<httpModules>
        <add type="System.Workflow.Runtime.Hosting.WorkflowWebHostingModule, _
            System.Workflow.Runtime, Version=1.0.00000.0, Culture=neutral, _
            PublicKeyToken=31bf3856ad364e35" name="WorkflowHost"/>

        <compilation debug="true">
            <assemblies>
                <add assembly="System.Workflow.Runtime, _
                    Version=1.0.0.0, Culture=neutral,
PublicKeyToken=31bf3856ad364e35"/>
            </assemblies>
        </compilation>
        <authentication mode="Windows"/>
    </system.web>
</configuration>
```

The next step is to get the `WebService`-derived class that was created from the workflow definition (again, this is only created when you have the `WebServiceReceive` shape configured correctly). The class will have the same name as the name of the workflow class with a `_WebService` added. The workflow in this project was named `AddWebServiceWorkflow.AddServiceWorkflow` (the namespace qualified name), so the `WebService` class will be named `AddWebServiceWorkflow.AddServiceWorkflow_WebService`. When VS.NET created the web service project, it created an ASMX web service named `Service.asmx`. My preference is to leave that file alone and modify the base class, which can be found (in this case) in the `App_Code` folder in a code file named `Service.vb`. I can modify the class in that file to derive from `AddWebServiceWorkflow.AddServiceWorkflow_WebService` instead of directly from the `WebService` base class. See Listing 6.8.

LISTING 6.8   The New Web Service Code File

```
Imports System.Web
Imports System.Web.Services
Imports System.Web.Services.Protocols

<WebService(Namespace:="http://workflowrus.com/WebServices/")> _
<WebServiceBinding(ConformsTo:=WsiProfiles.BasicProfile1_1, _
    EmitConformanceClaims:=True)> _
Public Class Service
    Inherits AddWebServiceWorkflow.AddServiceWorkflow_WebService

End Class
```

Because the `AddServiceWorkflow_WebService` class derives from `WebService`, this all works just fine. At this point you have a fully functional web service that can be called by any web service client. You can easily build a client in .NET by adding a web reference to any .NET project (as you've seen earlier this could even be called by a workflow through web services) to the WSDL generated for this web service (which in this case could be found at http://localhost/AddWorkflowWebService/Service.asmx?WSDL).

For this example I've created a simple Windows Forms client in VB.NET. You can see the form in Figure 6.9, and the code listing in Listing 6.9.

LISTING 6.9   The Web Service Client Code

```
Imports AddWebServiceClient.localhost
Public Class Form1
    Private Sub Add_Click(ByVal sender As System.Object, _
        ByVal e As System.EventArgs) Handles Add.Click
        Dim ws As New Service
        Dim res As Integer = ws.Add(Int32.Parse(_x.Text), Int32.Parse(_y.Text))
        result.Text = res.ToString()
    End Sub
End Class
```

FIGURE 6.9   Web service client.

You can create the web service project described in this section by right-clicking on the project node in the Solution Explorer and selecting Publish as Web Service. You can also find this command on the Project menu when you have the project selected in the Solution Explorer. Using this command is the preferable way to get the web service needed to run a workflow-based web service, but it can be created by hand if needed (or added to an existing web service).

State Machine Workflows and Web Services

Another design that would dictate a slightly different implementation would be if you wanted to use a state machine workflow to expose a web service. The state machine workflow is designed so it can be used to expose a web service. See Chapter 10, "State Machine Workflow," for more information about creating state machine workflows.

Summary

Web services are the typical implementation of SOA today. You've seen in this chapter that Windows Workflow Foundation has a rich integration story with web services, allowing you to invoke web services directly from your workflow using the `InvokeWebService` activity, as well as giving you implementation options for exposing your workflows via web services using the `WebServiceReceive` and `WebServiceReponse` activities.

CHAPTER 7

Developing Activities

A workflow in Windows Workflow Foundation is defined as a singly rooted hierarchical organization (a tree) of components called activities. Activities are the basic unit of reuse and execution within a workflow. An activity could be thought of as a step in a workflow.

Activities are ideal for intraprocess functional composition within a given workflow. In this chapter, you'll learn how to create your own custom activities using the Windows Workflow Service Activity Component Model as it applies to the various components that compose an activity.

Activity Component Model

At the highest level, activities can be separated into two categories: basic and composite. *Basic activities* have their functional behavior predefined and only expose properties, handlers, events, and conditions for further configuration. *Composite activities* can also expose properties, events, and conditions just like basic activities. Composite activities can be further extended by acting as a container for additional activities including both basic and other composites. As a special case of this, the root node of the workflow is an activity itself.

Windows Workflow Foundation ships a default set of root, composite, and basic activities to support the rapid development of useful workflows by application developers. Examples of basic activities that Windows Workflow Foundation provides include the `Terminate`, `Suspend`, and `Code` activities. Composite activities include `While`, `Sequence`, `Parallel`, and the `IfElse` conditional activity. The two roots that Windows Workflow Foundation provides are based are the Sequential root and the State Machine root.

Perhaps more importantly for those interested in extending the framework, Windows Workflow Foundation includes a public activity component model (API) that supports the development of brand-new root, composite, and basic activities. These new activities can be used on their own, or in conjunction with the default set, to extend the ways in which workflows are modeled and executed. The possibilities for such extensions are essentially unbounded, and are limited only by the fundamentals of the activity component model. In other words, Windows Workflow Foundation aims to provide a framework for authoring and executing different classes of workflows (not just the ones we know about today). An activity designer is provided with Windows Workflow Foundation that can be used to create composite activities without using code. All activity types can be created in code.

Anatomy of an Activity

When creating custom activities, you are authoring a set of related classes that use the Windows Workflow Foundation activity component model. This framework provides a component model–based architecture where each of these components is responsible for encapsulating a specific piece of functionality. More often than not, each component maps to a class.

The list of activity components that are part of the framework are as follows:

- Activity Definition—required
- Activity Executor
- Activity Validator
- Activity Designer
- Activity Toolbox item

> **NOTE**
>
> Although a subset of these components logically composes an activity, often the definition class is referred to as "the activity" as it is the centerpiece to which these other classes are associated.

The only mandatory classes that an activity writer must provide are the Activity Definition. A separate Activity Executor will be created only when creating a custom composite activity. Table 7.1 provides a quick overview of each activity component.

TABLE 7.1   Activity Components

Component	Definition
Definition	Used at design-time and runtime to access the properties and handlers of an activity.
Executor	Instantiated and managed by the runtime, in order to execute a workflow instance containing the activity.

Component	Definition
Validator	Used at design-time and runtime to validate the values of the properties and handlers of an activity.
Designer	Used within a designer such as Visual Studio 2005 to render the activity on the design surface.
Toolbox item	Used within a designer such as Visual Studio 2005 to display the activity in the toolbox and initialize the activity definition component when it is dragged from the toolbox to the design surface.

Activity Definition

The activity definition component of an activity defines the properties and events to be exposed for use at design-time and runtime by workflow authors. Within Visual Studio 2005, think of these as the properties that appear in the Property Browser window.

The definition class of a basic activity must inherit from the `System.Workflow.Component Model.Activity` (or derived) type. Likewise, custom composite activities must inherit from the `System.Workflow.ComponentModel.CompositeActivity` (or derived) type.

The following code sample shows the definition class of a new custom activity called "CreateCustomer". This activity is defined with a single named property called "CustomerFirstName".

```
Namespace CustomerManagmentLibrary
    Imports System
    Imports System.ComponentModel
    Imports System.ComponentModel.Design
    Imports System.Collections
    Imports System.Workflow.ComponentModel
    Imports System.Workflow.ComponentModel.Design
    Imports System.Workflow.Runtime
    Imports System.Workflow.Activities

    Public Class CreateCustomer
        Inherits Activity

        Public Shared CustomerFirstNameProperty As DependencyProperty = _
            DependencyProperty.Register("CustomerFirstName", _
            GetType(System.String), _
                GetType(CustomerManagmentLibrary.CreateCustomer))

        Public Sub New()
            MyBase.New
            InitializeComponent
```

```
        End Sub

        Public Property CustomerFirstName As String
            Get
                Return CType( _
                    MyBase.GetValueCreateCustomer.CustomerFirstNameProperty, _
                    String)
            End Get
            Set
                MyBase.SetValue(CreateCustomer.CustomerFirstNameProperty, value)
            End Set
        End Property
    End Class
End Namespace
```

You'll notice the definition of a `CustomerFirstNameProperty DependencyProperty`. *The DependencyProperty type* is an abstraction that provide two important capabilities in the context of the programmability of the activity's state:

- They provide a centralized repository of the user's workflow state. This provides a way to intercept the state changes. For example, Windows Workflow Foundation will automatically detect and throw an exception if an attempt is made to change the value of a metaproperty.

- Usage of dependency properties increases the performance of runtime state serialization versus using properties or fields.

Two types of properties exist within the activity definition. The first are properties that are instance-state–specific, for example, the value of the `CustomerFirstName` property in the previous example. The second type of properties are those that are workflow instance-state independent; these are called *metadata properties*, and their values are consistent across workflow instances. Developers should use metadata properties when they do not want the values of the properties modified beyond the `InitializeComponent()` method. An example of a metadata property would be the ID of any of the activities that compose a workflow. The ID properties do not need to change; however, an instance property like the To property on a `SendEmail` activity would probably be different for each workflow instance. Metadata properties are defined by the `<DependencyPropertyOptions (DependencyPropertyOptions.Metadata)>` attribute.

Component References

The activity definition component is the class by which all the other components are related. Thus, references to other components that compose this activity are defined as attributes on the definition class. As an example, if you wanted to Associate a Validator and Designer component with the `CreateCustomer` activity defined previously, the attribute's code would look like this:

```
Namespace CustomerManagementLibrary
    <Designer(GetType(CreateCustomer), Designer), _
     Unknown(), _
     Validator(GetType(CreateCustomerValidator))> _
    Public Class CreateCustomer
        Inherits Activity
    End Class
End Namespace
```

Activity Executor

The executor component of an activity is a stateless component that defines execution logic for the activity. Because the activity framework is a component model and not a formalized language, the Windows Workflow Foundation runtime itself does not and cannot enforce the semantics of any particular activity—for example, the runtime does not know that the children of a `Parallel` activity should be executed concurrently; it is the `Parallel` activity executor that knows this and that asks the runtime to execute its children concurrently. The runtime itself therefore provides the services through which an activity can achieve its execution objectives.

How does an activity within a workflow get executed? Three entities interact during the normal execution of an activity:

- The activity A itself

- A's parent (composite) activity P (in the case of the root activity, which has no parent activity, the host is the "parent" entity that requests execution of the activity; this effectively corresponds to the creation of a new workflow instance)

- The Windows Workflows Foundation runtime

Each entity has a different function, and only by working together and conforming to agreed-upon contracts that define acceptable interaction will all entities agree upon the outcome of the activity's execution.

When a workflow instance is created, the runtime initializes the root activity, and the root propagates the `Initialize()` method call to all its children. Usually the kind of logic defined in the `Initialize()` method performs operations like setting up message and queue subscriptions.

The runtime core scheduler then calls the `Execute()` method on the activity. This is the centerpiece of the executor where the logic describing the execution of the activity is performed.

After execution, an activity can close itself by returning `Status.Closed`. This indicates to the runtime that it has finished executing. However, if the parent of the activity is cancelled before execution completes, the `Cancel()` method is called on the activity. The logic defined in the `Cancel()` method usually deals with releasing any runtime resources acquired during execution or initialization. The activity can again return Status.Closed from the canceling state and arrive into the Closed state.

Finally, from the Closed state, the runtime can request rollback of any work performed by the activity by invoking the Compensate() method. Again, after compensation is finished, the activity can return Status.Closed. It should be noted, that an Compensate() is called only if the activity supports transactions, a topic covered in Chapter 8, "Advanced Activities and Activity Behaviors".

All this being said, for simple activities developers can overwrite the Execute() method provided on the System.Workflow.ComponentModel.Activity class to define the execution semantics of their custom activity. "Simple" in this case is defined by activities that don't require any of the richness of initialization, compensation, or cancellation; generally, basic activities or activities that do not require any further execution beyond the scope of the Execute() method. For example, if you were creating a SendEmail activity that exposed the expected To, From, Subject, and Body properties, its Activity class definition would look like the following code. Notice that the definition includes DependencyProperty items, and has an override of the Execute method.

```
Public NotInheritable Class SendMail
    Inherits Activity

    Public Shared ToProperty As DependencyProperty
    Public Shared FromProperty As DependencyProperty
    Public Shared SubjectProperty As DependencyProperty
    Public Shared MessageProperty As DependencyProperty
    Public Shared BeforeSendEvent As DependencyProperty

    Public Sub New()
        MyBase.New
    End Sub

    Public Property To As String
        Get
            Return CType(MyBase.GetValue(ToProperty),String)
        End Get
        Set
            MyBase.SetValue(ToProperty, value)
        End Set
    End Property

    Public Property From As String
        Get
            Return CType(MyBase.GetValue(FromProperty),String)
        End Get
```

```
        Set
            MyBase.SetValue(FromProperty, value)
        End Set
    End Property

    Public Property Subject As String
        Get
            Return CType(MyBase.GetValue(SubjectProperty),String)
        End Get
        Set
            MyBase.SetValue(SubjectProperty, value)
        End Set
    End Property

    Public Property Message As String
        Get
            Return CType(MyBase.GetValue(MessageProperty),String)
        End Get
        Set
            MyBase.SetValue(MessageProperty, value)
        End Set
    End Property

    Protected Overridable Function Execute( _
        ByVal c As ActivityExecutionContext) As Status
        MyBase.FireEvent(SendMail.BeforeSendEvent, Me, EventArgs.Empty)
        'Send the email out
        Dim mailHost As SmtpClient = New SmtpClient
        Dim msg As MailMessage = New MailMessage(From, To, Subject, Message)
        mailHost.Host = "SMTPHOST"
        mailHost.Send(msg)
        Return Status.Closed
    End Function
End Class
```

Activity Validator

The validator component of an activity provides validation logic, both design-time and runtime, for an activity to ensure that its structure is configured correctly.

Before drilling into how this is accomplished, developers usually will want to provide validation of an activity's properties. This can be accomplished via the <Validation VisibilityAttribute>. This attribute needs to be defined on the properties of the activity. The developer can select from the following three values and associated validation:

- `Optional`—The property can accept null values.

- `Required`—Values must be specified for property and you automatically check to see that this is the case.

- `Hidden`—No automatic validation.

If `Required` is selected, upon use within a workflow, the custom activity will require that the property be configured via the familiar configuration errors (the red exclamation points on the activity).

```
<ValidationVisibility (ValidationVisibility.Required)>  _
Public Property Name As String
    Get
        Return CType(MyBase.GetValue(NameProperty),String)
    End Get
    Set
        MyBase.SetValue(NameProperty, value)
    End Set
End Property
```

Your custom validator class should inherit from either
`System.Workflow.ComponentModel.ActivityValidator` or `System.Workflow.Component`
`Model.CompositeActivityValidator`, depending upon whether your activity is basic or composite, in order to guarantee the execution of fundamental validation checks that are performed by these base classes.

At design-time, validation occurs automatically during the compilation of a workflow and is explicitly called when an activity is dropped onto the design surface. This allows developers to employ a *correct-by-construction* paradigm if they choose. For example, the following code requires that the first activity within the composite is a `Code` activity.

```
Public Class MyValidator
    Inherits SequenceValidator

    Public Overrides Function Validate(ByVal manager As ValidationManager, _
            ByVal obj As Object) As ValidationErrorCollection
        Dim validationErrors As ValidationErrorCollection = _
            New ValidationErrorCollection(MyBase.Validate(manager, obj))
        Dim myActivity As Activity1 = CType(obj,Activity1)
        If (Not (myActivity) Is Nothing) Then
            If ((myActivity.Activities.Count >= 1)  _
                    AndAlso Not (myActivity.Activities(0) = Code)) Then
                Dim CustomActivityValidationError As ValidationError = _
                    New ValidationError( _
                    "This activity cannont cannot contain code", 2)
```

```
                validationErrors.Add(CustomActivityValidationError)
            End If
        End If
        Return validationErrors
    End Function
End Class
```

At runtime, validation occurs on a workflow instance when a dynamic update is performed. This validation might be different than (and is often a superset of) the validation performed at compile-time, in order to ensure the safety of a runtime operation such as the addition or replacement of an activity in the activity tree of a running workflow instance.

Activity Designer

The designer component of an activity defines the visual representation of the activity in the Workflow & Custom Activity Designer. This component is responsible for defining how a developer interacts with the activity.

The `System.Workflow.ComponentModel.Design.ActivityDesigner` class is inherited by designers that require only a very lightweight rendering implementation. All the standard Windows Workflow Foundation basic activities inherit directly from `ActivityDesigner` as they don't have any children or an organized hierarchy.

The `ActivityDesigner` type offers most of the functionality required by all activities and thus is the root in the Windows Workflow Foundation designer derivation chain.

The features offered by the `ActivityDesigner` are

- Basic layout logic
- Rendering support by drawing icons, description, border, interior, and background
- Rendering help text
- Default adornments required by designers
- Context menu through DesignerVerbs
- Filtering of design-time–specific properties
- Default event generation
- Default hit testing
- Triggering validation
- ToolTip support
- Participation in keyboard navigation

Activity Designers that derive from `CompositeActivityDesigner` are those activities that require children. The features offered by `CompositeActivityDesigner` are

- Expanding/collapsing of the designers
- Drag-and-drop indicators
- Layout of container and children
- Drawing of container and children
- Hit testing of the children
- Keyboard navigation

In the next section, the following topics will be discussed in the text and in the code:

- The inheritance hierarchy available to create a custom designer
- Designer layout
- Designer sizing
- Connector drawing

In this example, our activity designer derives from `CompositeActivityDesigner`. We are creating a designer for a composite activity.

```
NotInheritable Class MyActivityDesigner
    Inherits StructuredCompositeActivityDesigner
```

The constructor for this class is empty but required.

```
Public Sub New()
    MyBase.New
End Sub
```

Note: This area hasn't been implemented but exposed to provide the readers knowledge that they can override these methods:

```
Public Overrides ReadOnly Property FirstSelectableObject As Object
    Get
        Throw New System.NotImplementedException
    End Get
End Property

Public Overrides ReadOnly Property LastSelectableObject As Object
    Get
        Throw New System.NotImplementedException
```

```
        End Get
    End Property
```

The `OnPaint()` method is called when the designer for the component will be drawn on the design surface. In this example, we are doing most of the drawing logic in the `DrawConnectors()` method. This method is described in further detail later in this chapter.

```
    Protected Overrides Sub OnPaint(ByVal e As ActivityDesignerPaintEventArgs)
        MyBase.OnPaint(e)
        If Expanded Then
            DrawConnectors(e.Graphics)
        End If
    End Sub

    Protected Overrides Function GetDropTargets(ByVal dropPoint As Point) _
        As Rectangle()
        Throw New NotImplementedException
    End Function

    Public Overrides Function GetNextSelectableObject(ByVal current As Object,
_
            ByVal direction As DesignerNavigationDirection) As Object
        Throw New NotImplementedException
    End Function
```

The `OnLayoutSize()` method calculates the layout for the designer and children within the composite activity. In this case, we have three children activity designers.

```
    Protected Overrides Sub OnLayoutSize( _
        ByVal e As ActivityDesignerLayoutEventArgs)
        MyBase.OnLayoutSize(e)
        Dim containerSize As Size = Size.Empty
```

This gets the collection of the activity designers which this activity comprises.

```
        Dim activityDesigners As ReadOnlyCollection = ContainedDesigners
```

Next, we set the outer container height by calculating the children activity designers and appropriate padding:

```
        containerSize.Height = (15 _
            + (Math.Max(activityDesigners(0).Size.Height, _
                activityDesigners(1).Size.Height) + (15 _
            + (activityDesigners(2).Size.Height + 60))))
```

Next, we set the outer container width by calculating the children activity designers and appropriate padding:

```
containerSize.Width = (containerSize.Width + (10 _
    + (activityDesigners(0).Size.Width + (10 _
    + (activityDesigners(1).Size.Width + 10))))))
```

This `for` loop does a bit of logic to see whether another activity is placed in either of the two parallel children and thus grows the sibling activity height accordingly. This is purely cosmetic to prevent a lopsided activity designer. In order to grow either the first or second designer, we need to figure out which one is bigger.

```
Dim i As Integer = 0
Do While (i < 2)
    Dim BigSize As Integer = _
        Math.Max(activityDesigners(0).Size.Height, _
        activityDesigners(1).Size.Height)
    activityDesigners(i).Size = _
        New Size(activityDesigners(i).Size.Width, BigSize)
    i = (i + 1)
Loop
Size = containerSize
End Sub
```

The `OnLayoutPosition()` method determines where within the parent container, each of the children activities will be positioned.

```
Protected Overrides Sub OnLayoutPosition( _
    ByVal e As ActivityDesignerLayoutEventArgs)
    Dim bounds As Rectangle = Bounds
```

Again, we get an array of all the activity designers.

```
Dim activityDesigner As ReadOnlyCollection = ContainedDesigners
Dim width As Integer = 0
Dim height As Integer = 0
```

There are three children activities, and they are numbered from left to right (the 0 and the first elements in the array) and finally one below (the second element in the array) the two siblings.

The location of the 0 and first designers are determined first. We add a padding of 10 pixels horizontally and 15 pixels between the top of the outer container and the bottom activity.

```
        Dim i As Integer = 0
        Do While (i < 2)
            width = (width + 10)
            Dim designerSize As Size = activityDesigner(i).Size
            activityDesigner(i).Location = New Point((Location.X + width), _
                (Location.Y + (height + 15)))
            width = (width + designerSize.Width)
            i = (i + 1)
        Loop
```

Next, we calculate the max height of the first or second activity so that the third is placed below either one of them. We also set the location of the third activity centered between the first and second and offset vertically by 30 pixels.

```
        height = Math.Max(activityDesigner(0).Size.Height, _
            activityDesigner(1).Size.Height)
        Me.ContainedDesigners(2).Location = New Point((Location.X  _
            + ((Me.Size.Width - activityDesigner(2).Size.Width)  _
            / 2)), (Location.Y + (height + 30)))
        MyBase.OnLayoutPosition(e)
    End Sub
```

In this method, we draw the connections between all three activities. The majority of this code is simply getting the connection points between designers, figuring out x and y coordinates and calling the DrawConnectors() method with the defined coordinates.

```
    Public Sub DrawConnectors(ByVal graphics As Graphics)
        Dim designerTheme As CompositeDesignerTheme = _
            CType(DesignerTheme,CompositeDesignerTheme)
```

Get all the required outer container bounds to calculate the connectors.

```
        Dim bounds As Rectangle = Bounds
        Dim parallelConnectorTop As Integer = bounds.Top
            parallelConnectorTop = (parallelConnectorTop  _
            + (TitleHeight - 15))
```

Next, get the array of designers and retrieve their connection points.

```
        Dim activityDesigners As ReadOnlyCollection = ContainedDesigners
        Dim firstDesigner As ActivityDesigner = activityDesigners(0)
        Dim firstDesignerConnections() As Point = _
            firstDesigner.OuterConnectionPoints
```

```
Dim secondDesigner As ActivityDesigner = activityDesigners(1)
Dim secondDesignerConnections() As Point = _
    secondDesigner.OuterConnectionPoints
Dim thirdDesigner As ActivityDesigner = activityDesigners(2)
Dim thirdDesignerConnections() As Point = _
    thirdDesigner.OuterConnectionPoints
Dim parallelLinks(2) As Point
```

Here, you draw a small vertical line at the top of the designer between the first and second designers:

```
parallelLinks(0).X = (bounds.Left + (bounds.Width / 2))
parallelLinks(0).Y = (parallelConnectorTop + 10)
parallelLinks(1).X = (bounds.Left + (bounds.Width / 2))
parallelLinks(1).Y = (parallelConnectorTop + 15)
DrawConnectors(graphics, designerTheme.ForegroundPen, parallelLinks, _
    System.Workflow.ComponentModel.Design.LineAnchor. _
        None, LineAnchor.None)
```

Here, you draw the horizontal line above the designers:

```
parallelLinks(0).X = firstDesignerConnections(0).X
parallelLinks(0).Y = (parallelConnectorTop + 15)
parallelLinks(1).X = secondDesignerConnections(0).X
parallelLinks(1).Y = (parallelConnectorTop + 15)
DrawConnectors(graphics, designerTheme.ForegroundPen, parallelLinks, _
    System.Workflow.ComponentModel.Design.LineAnchor. _
        None, LineAnchor.None)
```

Here, you draw the top-left vertical line to the first designer:

```
parallelLinks(0).X = firstDesignerConnections(0).X
parallelLinks(0).Y = firstDesignerConnections(0).Y
parallelLinks(1).X = firstDesignerConnections(0).X
parallelLinks(1).Y = (parallelConnectorTop + 15)
DrawConnectors(graphics, designerTheme.ForegroundPen, parallelLinks, _
    System.Workflow.ComponentModel.Design.LineAnchor. _
        None, LineAnchor.None)
```

Here, you draw the top-right vertical line to the second designer:

```
parallelLinks(0).X = secondDesignerConnections(0).X
parallelLinks(0).Y = secondDesignerConnections(0).Y
parallelLinks(1).X = secondDesignerConnections(0).X
```

```
parallelLinks(1).Y = (parallelConnectorTop + 15)
DrawConnectors(graphics, designerTheme.ForegroundPen, parallelLinks, _
    System.Workflow.ComponentModel.Design.LineAnchor. _
    None, LineAnchor.None)
```

Here, you draw the bottom-right vertical line to half the distance to the bottom designer:

```
parallelLinks(0).X = secondDesignerConnections(1).X
parallelLinks(0).Y = secondDesignerConnections(1).Y
parallelLinks(1).X = secondDesignerConnections(1).X
parallelLinks(1).Y = (7 + secondDesignerConnections(1).Y)
DrawConnectors(graphics, designerTheme.ForegroundPen, parallelLinks, _
    System.Workflow.ComponentModel.Design.LineAnchor. _
    None, LineAnchor.None)
```

Here, you draw the bottom-left vertical line to half the distance to the bottom designer:

```
parallelLinks(0).X = firstDesignerConnections(1).X
parallelLinks(0).Y = firstDesignerConnections(1).Y
parallelLinks(1).X = firstDesignerConnections(1).X
parallelLinks(1).Y = (7 + firstDesignerConnections(1).Y)
DrawConnectors(graphics, designerTheme.ForegroundPen, parallelLinks, _
    System.Workflow.ComponentModel.Design.LineAnchor. _
    None, LineAnchor.None)
```

Here, you draw the horizontal bottom line:

```
parallelLinks(0).X = firstDesignerConnections(1).X
parallelLinks(0).Y = (firstDesignerConnections(1).Y + 7)
parallelLinks(1).X = secondDesignerConnections(1).X
parallelLinks(1).Y = (secondDesignerConnections(1).Y + 7)
DrawConnectors(graphics, designerTheme.ForegroundPen, parallelLinks, _
    System.Workflow.ComponentModel.Design.LineAnchor. _
    None, LineAnchor.None)
```

Here, you draw the bottom vertical line:

```
parallelLinks(0).X = (bounds.Left   _
            + (bounds.Width / 2))
parallelLinks(0).Y = (firstDesignerConnections(1).Y + 7)
parallelLinks(1).X = thirdDesignerConnections(0).X
parallelLinks(1).Y = thirdDesignerConnections(0).Y
DrawConnectors(graphics, designerTheme.ForegroundPen, parallelLinks, _
    System.Workflow.ComponentModel.Design.LineAnchor. _
    None, LineAnchor.None)
    End Sub
End Class
```

Activity Toolbox Item

The Toolbox item allows you to provide special "default configuration" logic that is executed when the activity is added to a workflow from the toolbox. As an example, the toolbox item for the activity defined previously would require three sequence activities added to its collection. The code for the toolbox item is as follows:

```
Public NotInheritable Class MyActivityToolBoxItem
    Inherits ActivityToolboxItem

    Public Sub New(ByVal type As Type)
        MyBase.New(type)
    End Sub

    Private Sub New(ByVal info As SerializationInfo, _
        ByVal context As StreamingContext)
        MyBase.New
        Deserialize(info, context)
    End Sub

    Protected Overrides Function CreateComponentsCore( _
        ByVal designerHost As IDesignerHost) As IComponent()
        Dim myActivity As CompositeActivity = New MyActivity
        myActivity.Activities.Add(New Sequence)
        myActivity.Activities.Add(New Sequence)
        myActivity.Activities.Add(New Sequence)
        Return CType(New IComponent() {myActivity},IComponent())
    End Function
End Class
```

Summary

In this chapter you learned about custom activities. You learned about creating basic and composite custom activities and how to create a custom activity in code. You learned about the many types of components that can be added to custom activities to implement different functionality.

CHAPTER 8

Advanced Activities and Activity Behaviors

T his chapter provides a more detailed discussion of the advanced activities provided with Windows Workflow Foundation, which include the following:

- Replicator

- Conditioned Activity Group (CAG)

- Policy

These activities help support more sophisticated, flexible, and powerful workflows. The first two activities are composite activities, designed to provide behavior to the child activities added to them. The third, Policy, is a basic activity that provides rule-based behavior. This chapter provides an overview of each activity followed by an example.

In addition, the second part of the chapter describes special types of behaviors that exist on a Sequential Workflow and can be added to custom activities to support, among other things, transactions and exception handling.

Replicator

The Replicator activity is designed to support scenarios where you need to execute an activity "n" number of times, but the value of "n" is only known at runtime. The Replicator operates over a collection of instances in much the same way that a For-Each statement in .NET does.

Replicator **Overview**

A Replicator can contain one and only one child activity, although that activity may be a Sequence or any other composite activity.

Other salient features of a Replicator are the ability to execute the child activities in sequential or parallel fashion and the ability to short-circuit execution of the activities using conditional logic.

The Replicator has four properties for which you can provide handlers:

- Initialized—Handler invoked when the Replicator is initialized; you must provide a value for this property

- ChildInitialized—Invoked each time an instance of the child activity is initialized

- ChildCompleted—Invoked each time an instance of the child activity completes

- Completed—Invoked after the Replicator completes

The Replicator also provides an UntilCondition that allows you to halt execution of the Replicator prior to all the child activity instances completing. As with other activities such as IfElse and While, the UntilCondition should point to a CodeCondition or a RuleConditionReference. The Replicator will exit as soon as the UntilCondition returns true, canceling any currently executing child instances.

The use of the various handlers and the UntilCondition is probably best explained with an example.

Replicator **Example**

A sample workflow with a Replicator is shown in Figure 8.1. The sample scenario is an application that queries a group of people for their dinner preference; they have the choice of Pizza or Hamburgers and a majority vote will determine what is ordered. The Replicator contains a custom, composite "VoteManager" activity that in turn contains a pair of activities that request an individual's vote and wait for the response. The VoteManager activity may represent a call on a local service that interacts with an application, sends an email, or any other mechanism that requests a user response. In the sample code this is done with a dialog box that prompts for a response, but the details of the VoteManager implementation are not important to understanding the Replicator's core behavior. Execution of the Replicator will result in a VoteManager instance being created for each assignee.

The minimal requirements for configuring a Replicator are adding a child activity and adding a handler for the Initialized method. Within the Initialized method, you specify a collection of instance data that will be used to create each instance of the child activity. One instance of the child activity will be created for each object in the collection. Additionally, within the Initialized handler you specify whether the Replicator should execute the activity instances in parallel or sequential fashion. The implementation of the Initialized handler for this example is as follows:

```
Dim voters As ArrayList
Private Sub ReplicatorInitialized( _
    ByVal sender As System.Object, _
    ByVal e As System.Workflow.Activities.ReplicatorEventArgs)
    voters = New ArrayList
    voters.Add("Samuel")
    voters.Add("Ava")
    voters.Add("Fred")
    e.Children = voters
    e.ExecutionType = ExecutionType.Sequence
End Sub
```

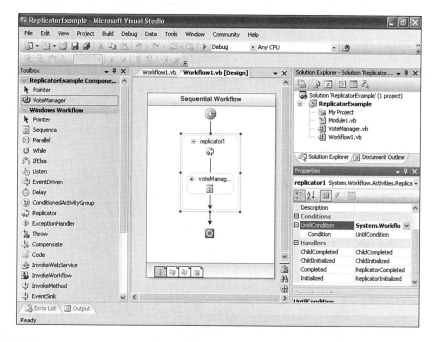

FIGURE 8.1   Replicator example.

In the example, an ArrayList is created with the names of individuals whose vote you are seeking; this is passed to the Children property on the ReplicatorEventArgs, which must contain an object collection implementing IEnumerable. The ExecutionType is set to Sequence, indicating that the votes should be gathered in sequence (in the order defined in the collection); the value can be changed to Parallel to execute all VoteManager instances concurrently.

The VoteManager activity has Voter and VoteResult properties, used to store the individual associated with a given VoteManager instance and his vote. You now must have a way to pass the Voter value to each VoteManager instance. You can do this in the ChildInitialized handler, which is called for each child activity instance prior to execution. The code should look as follows:

```
Private Sub ChildInitialized(ByVal sender As System.Object, ByVal e As _
    System.Workflow.Activities.ReplicatorChildEventArgs)
    Dim child As VoteManager = CType(e.Activity, VoteManager)
    child.Voter = CType(e.InstanceData, String)
End Sub
```

In the `ReplicatorChildEventArgs` event args, the `Activity` and `InstanceData` are passed. The `Activity` property, as the name implies, is the current `VoteManager` instance, whereas the `InstanceData` property contains the associated object for this activity from the `Children` collection that was provided in the `ReplicatorInitialized` handler. In `ChildInitialized`, the `InstanceData` will contain the string name from the `Children` collection (for example, "Samuel" the first time the handler is called). This value is assigned to the `Voter` property on the activity instance.

During `VoteManager` activity execution, the `VoteResult` field will be set to `Pizza` or `Hamburgers`, using a `Vote` enum. After a `VoteManager` instance completes, the `ChildCompleted` handler will be called, which can be used to pass the `VoteResult` information back to the `Replicator`. Assume that the `Replicator` defines two counters to tally the results, `pizzaCount` and `hamburgerCount`. These fields can be incremented in the `ChildCompleted` handler as shown in the following code:

```
Dim pizzaCount As Integer
Dim hamburgerCount As Integer

Private Sub ChildCompleted(ByVal sender As System.Object, ByVal e As _
    System.Workflow.Activities.ReplicatorChildEventArgs)
    If (CType(e.Activity, VoteManager).VoteResult = Vote.Pizza) Then
        pizzaCount = (pizzaCount + 1)
    Else
        hamburgerCount = (hamburgerCount + 1)
    End If
End Sub
```

After all `VoteManager` instances have completed, the `Replicator` will complete and the `ReplicatorCompleted` handler will be called, in which the vote totals are evaluated and the winner is chosen.

```
Private Sub ReplicatorCompleted(ByVal sender As System.Object, ByVal e As _
    System.EventArgs)
    If (pizzaCount >= hamburgerCount) Then
        Console.WriteLine("The winner is Pizza")
    Else
        Console.WriteLine("The winner is Hamburgers")
    End If
End Sub
```

As a final exercise, you can make your voting mechanism a little more sophisticated. Because you are doing a simple majority vote between two options, you do not have to wait for all voters to respond to know the result (and go ahead and order the food). You can implement this behavior with the `Replicator` using the `UntilCondition`. In this example the condition looks as follows:

```
Private Function UntilCondition(ByVal sender As System.Object, ByVal e As _
    System.EventArgs) As System.Boolean
      Return (pizzaCount > voters.Count * 0.5) Or (hamburgerCount > _
        voters.Count * 0.5) Or (pizzaCount + hamburgerCount = voters.Count)
End Function
```

This condition returns true as soon as the `pizzaCount` or `hamburgerCount` has reached a majority. This will cause the `Replicator` to stop creating new child instances (in the case of sequential execution), cancel any running child instances (in the case of parallel execution), and exit. The `UntilCondition` is evaluated after each of the `VoteManager` instances has completed.

Additional `Replicator` Topics

You can use APIs on the `Replicator` activity to update the information in the collection originally passed in the `Initialized` method. For example, you could use the following code to dynamically add a new person whose food preference you want to gather:

```
Me.replicator1.AddChild("Otto")
```

You could do this at any point while the `Replicator` is executing. You could also use the `RemoveChild` API to remove a person from our list.

Conditioned Activity Group (CAG)

The `Conditioned Activity Group` (CAG) activity provides condition-driven activity execution that allows you to define very flexible behavior within your workflow. The CAG contains a collection of child activities whose execution order is defined not by a strict sequencing as in a `Sequence`, but by conditions that are applied to the activities themselves.

The conditional logic can result in many different permutations of activity execution, including parallel (but optional) execution of activities, partially sequential execution, interleaving of activities with looping behavior, and so on.

CAG **Overview**

An empty CAG is shown in Figure 8.2.

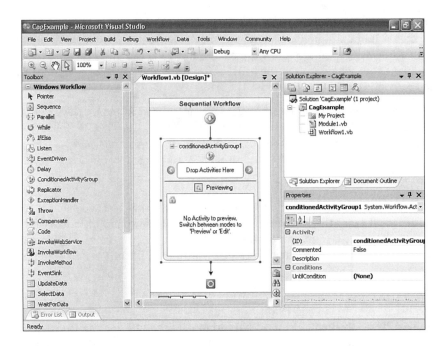

FIGURE 8.2   Empty Conditioned Activity Group.

The child activities are dragged from the toolbox into the filmstrip section at the top of the CAG that contains the text "Drop Activities Here."

Figure 8.3 shows two Code activities dropped into the CAG. If you select an activity in the filmstrip section, you will see its properties in the Properties window.

By clicking the icon next to Previewing [1/2], you can switch between preview and edit mode on the child activity. Edit mode would let you drag activities into the CAG child if it were a composite activity such as a Sequence. In addition to the standard properties of the activity, you will also see a WhenCondition property. You use this property to define the condition under which this activity will execute; the activity will continue to execute as long as its When condition evaluates to true. As with other activities, conditions can be defined either as CodeConditions or as RuleConditionReferences. The default value for the When condition specifies that the activity should execute one time.

In addition to the When conditions on the contained activities, the CAG itself has a condition, the Until condition. The UntilCondition property on the CAG determines when the CAG should exit. A value of true prevents new child activities from being executed and cancels activities that are currently being executed. The default value of the Until condition is to return true and exit when all activities have reached a quiescent state—that is, no activities are executing and none have a When condition that evaluates to true.

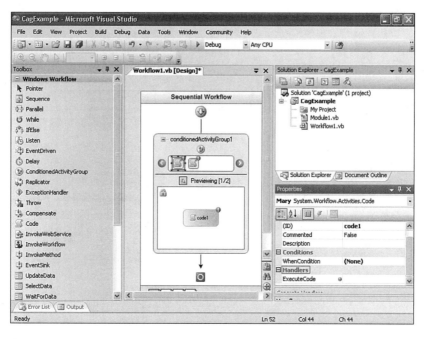

FIGURE 8.3 Conditioned Activity Group with two code activities.

When a CAG first begins execution, it will evaluate its Until condition. If it evaluates to false, the When condition of all the activities contained in the CAG will be evaluated. If an activity's When condition evaluates to true it will be scheduled for execution. The Until condition and the When conditions for all activities will then be reevaluated each time an activity completes, which may cause activities to be scheduled for execution (or the same activity to be rescheduled). Note that reevaluation occurs when an immediate child activity of the CAG completes, not when activities contained within the child activities of the CAG complete. For example, the CAG may contain a Sequence activity that in turn contains a number of activities; the CAG conditions will be reevaluated when the Sequence completes, not when child activities of the Sequence complete.

CAG Examples

The following sections provide examples of how the CAG conditions can be used to implement various kinds of activity execution behaviors.

Parallel Execution

Let's start by building a simple CAG that executes both activities and then exits. The CAG in Figure 8.4 has two code activities, titled "Phil" and "Mary," that represent approval steps by those two individuals.

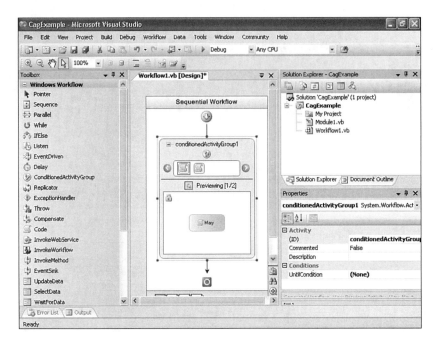

FIGURE 8.4   Simple CAG example-parallel execution.

After adding a reference to System.Windows.Forms to your project, add the PhilApproval method as the handler for the ExecuteCode property on the Phil activity and add the MaryApproval handler to the Mary activity:

```
Imports System.Windows.Forms
    Dim philCompleted As Boolean = False
    Dim maryCompleted As Boolean = False
    Dim philApproved As Boolean = False
    Dim maryApproved As Boolean = False

    Private Sub MaryApproval(ByVal sender As System.Object, ByVal e As _
        System.EventArgs)
        Dim result As DialogResult = MessageBox.Show("Mary, do you approve the _
            order?", "Order Review", MessageBoxButtons.YesNo)
        If (result = DialogResult.Yes) Then
            maryApproved = True
        End If
        maryCompleted = True
    End Sub
    Private Sub PhilApproval(ByVal sender As System.Object, ByVal e As _
        System.EventArgs)
        Dim result As DialogResult = MessageBox.Show("Phil, do you approve _
            the order?", "Order Review", MessageBoxButtons.YesNo)
```

```
        If (result = DialogResult.Yes) Then
            philApproved = True
        End If
        philCompleted = True
    End Sub
```

If you execute the workflow you will see the dialog box pop up for Phil and then for Mary; after you close both dialog boxes the Code activities will complete and the CAG will complete. In this simplest example, you have not defined any conditions, and the CAG has executed as if the Code activities were in a Parallel activity.

Parallel But Optional

Now assume that you still want to execute the same code, but that you do not always need both Phil and Mary to review the order. Use a variable to specify an ArrayList containing the individuals who need to review the order. To do this, add a When condition to the Phil and Mary condition. In the designer, click on the Phil activity at the top of the CAG. In the WhenCondition property in the Properties window, select System.Workflow.Activities.CodeCondition. Expand the WhenCondition property and type **PhilWhenCondition** into the Condition field under the WhenCondition property; this will create the corresponding method in the Workflow1.vb file. Do the same for the Mary activity (see Figure 8.5).

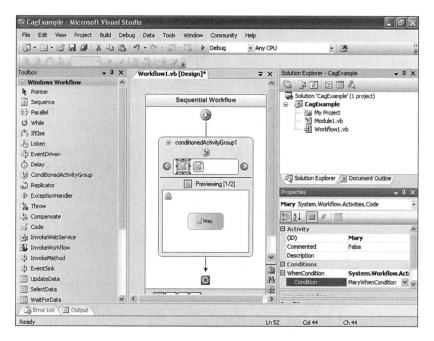

FIGURE 8.5 CAG example—parallel but optional execution.

In the Code view of the `Workflow1.vb` file, add the assignees variable and code in the workflow constructor to populate the `assignees` collection:

```
Dim assignees As ArrayList = New ArrayList
Public Sub New()
    MyBase.New()
    InitializeComponent()
    assignees.Add("Phil")
    assignees.Add("Mary")
End Sub
```

Then add the implementations for the `When` condition methods:

```
Private Function MaryWhenCondition(ByVal sender As System.Object, ByVal e _
    As System.EventArgs) As System.Boolean
    Return (assignees.Contains("Mary") AndAlso Not maryCompleted)
End Function

Private Function PhilWhenCondition(ByVal sender As System.Object, ByVal e _
    As System.EventArgs) As System.Boolean
    Return (assignees.Contains("Phil") AndAlso Not philCompleted)
End Function
```

By commenting out one or both of the `assignees.Add` lines in the constructor, you can control which of the activities executes.

Dependent Activities

To continue adding to this example, assume that you now want to make one activity dependent on another activity. In this case, you do not want Mary to get her pop-up until Phil has reviewed the order. You can do this with a modification to Mary's `When` condition that adds a check on whether the `Phil` activity has been executed, using a method on the `CAG` activity.

```
Private Function MaryWhenCondition(ByVal sender As System.Object, ByVal e _
    As System.EventArgs) As System.Boolean
    Return (assignees.Contains("Mary") AndAlso (Not maryCompleted AndAlso _
    (Me.conditionedActivityGroup1.GetChildActivityExecutedCount(Me.Phil) = 1)))
End Function
```

Looping Behavior and the `Until` Condition

Finally, assume that if Mary does not approve the order, it gets sent back to Phil to edit the order and then reapprove it. In such a scenario Mary should also not get the order unless Phil has approved it. This means that the Mary and Phil activities may need to execute multiple times until Mary finally approves the order.

First, modify the When condition to ensure that Mary only gets a request if Phil has approved it:

```
Private Function MaryWhenCondition(ByVal sender As System.Object, ByVal e _
    As System.EventArgs) As System.Boolean
        Return (assignees.Contains("Mary") AndAlso (philApproved = True))
End Function
```

Next, modify the When condition on the Phil activity so that Phil does not get a request unless his approval is marked as false. This ensures that Phil does not continue to get a request as soon as he approved it (in this scenario, it would not make sense for Phil to *not* approve it because he would be doing the modification of the order and should always approve it once he has made the correct edits). This also requires a change to Mary's code executor to reset philApproval to false if she rejects the order.

```
Private Function PhilWhenCondition(ByVal sender As System.Object, ByVal e _
    As System.EventArgs) As System.Boolean
        Return (assignees.Contains("Phil") AndAlso (philApproved = False))
End Function

Private Sub MaryApproval(ByVal sender As System.Object, ByVal e As _
    System.EventArgs)
        Dim result As DialogResult = MessageBox.Show("Mary, do you approve _
            the order?", "Order Review", MessageBoxButtons.YesNo)
        If (result = DialogResult.Yes) Then
            maryApproved = True
        Else
            philApproved = False
        End If
        maryCompleted = True
End Sub
```

Finally, you should add an Until condition on the CAG. In the UntilCondition property on the CAG, specify a CodeCondition with the name UntilCondition. Add the code to the function to evaluate whether Mary has approved the order:

```
Private Function UntilCondition(ByVal sender As System.Object, ByVal e As _
    System.EventArgs) As System.Boolean
        Return maryApproved
End Function
```

Policy

The Policy activity leverages an integrated, forward-chaining rules engine and allows you to use rules technology to model units of business and application logic.

Policy **Overview**

A `Policy`'s logic is defined as a collection of `If-Then-Else` rules organized into a `RuleSet` that is defined in and executed by the `Policy` activity. The rules are largely modeled using `CodeDom` types. Unlike other activities discussed in this book, the `Policy` activity is not used directly, though, and is not available in the toolbox. Instead you will use the `Policy` activity as a base class for custom activities that you create.

Let's start with a simple example.

Policy **Example**

This example uses a scenario where you must calculate the tax on a product based on the state to which it is being shipped.

You begin by defining a new activity. You can either add a Workflow Activity Library project to your solution or add a new Activity item to your existing workflow project. In the Designer view of the new activity you will first want to change the Base Class property of the activity to `System.Workflow.Activities.Policy`. For this example, you will also change the name of your activity to `TaxPolicy`. After this, the project and activity will look like Figure 8.6.

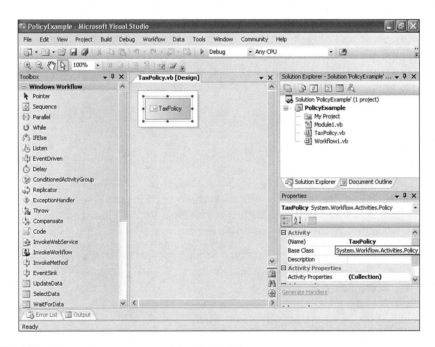

FIGURE 8.6   Custom `TaxPolicy` activity derived from `System.Workflow. Activities.Policy`.

Now add properties onto the activity. Select the ellipses in the `Activity Properties` property of the activity to launch the dialog shown in Figure 8.7.

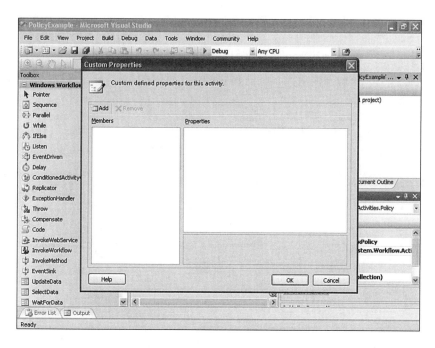

FIGURE 8.7   Custom activity property dialog.

Click on the Add button at the top left to add a new custom property, and give it a name of State and a type of System.String as shown in Figure 8.8.

By clicking Add again, you should also add a TaxRate property of type System.Double. Click OK and you are returned to the activity designer.

The next step is to create the rules that define the logic. Right-click on the activity in the Designer view or the .vb file in the Solution Explorer and select View Code. In the TaxPolicy class, override a method on the base Policy activity by adding the following:

```
Public Overrides Function CreateRuleSet() As _
    System.Workflow.Activities.Rules.RuleSet

End Function
```

Within this method is where you define the logic. Start by creating a RuleSet and adding a Rule object to it:

```
Dim ruleSet As RuleSet = New RuleSet("TaxPolicy")
Dim waTaxRule As Rule = New Rule("WashingtonTaxRule")
ruleSet.Rules.Add(waTaxRule)

Return ruleSet
```

Now define the rule itself, which is expressed as

```
IF State == "WA" THEN TaxRate = 10
```

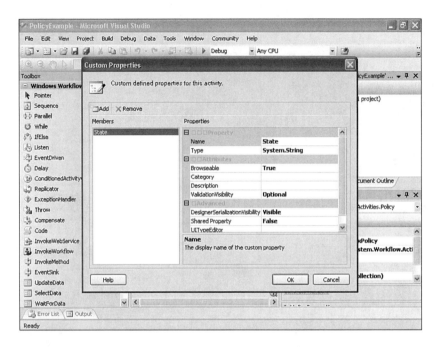

FIGURE 8.8   Adding a State property on the `TaxPolicy` activity.

Begin by adding the IF conditional test:

```
' "this" reference to the activity
      Dim thisRef As CodeThisReferenceExpression = _
        New CodeThisReferenceExpression
' reference to the State property on the activity
      Dim stateRef As CodePropertyReferenceExpression = _
        New CodePropertyReferenceExpression(thisRef, "State")

      Dim waCondition As CodeBinaryOperatorExpression = _
        New CodeBinaryOperatorExpression
      waCondition.Left = stateRef
      waCondition.Operator = CodeBinaryOperatorType.ValueEquality
      waCondition.Right = New CodePrimitiveExpression("WA")
      waTaxRule.Condition = New RuleExpressionCondition(waCondition)
```

Note that you may need to add an `Imports` statement:

```
Imports System.CodeDom
```

Next, define the THEN action:

```
      Dim taxRateRef As CodePropertyReferenceExpression = _
        New CodePropertyReferenceExpression(thisRef, "TaxRate")
```

```
        Dim waThen As CodeAssignStatement = New CodeAssignStatement
        waThen.Left = taxRateRef
        waThen.Right = New CodePrimitiveExpression(10)
        waTaxRule.ThenActions.Add(New RuleStatementAction(waThen))
```

You could add additional rules to the RuleSet, but we'll stop there for now. Your CreateRuleSet method should now look like this:

```
    Public Overrides Function CreateRuleSet() As _
        System.Workflow.Activities.Rules.RuleSet
        Dim ruleSet As RuleSet = New RuleSet("TaxPolicy")

        Dim thisRef As CodeThisReferenceExpression = _
            New CodeThisReferenceExpression
        Dim stateRef As CodePropertyReferenceExpression = _
            New CodePropertyReferenceExpression(thisRef, "State")
        Dim taxRateRef As CodePropertyReferenceExpression = _
            New CodePropertyReferenceExpression(thisRef, "TaxRate")

        Dim waTaxRule As Rule = New Rule("WashingtonTaxRule")
        ruleSet.Rules.Add(waTaxRule)
        Dim waCondition As CodeBinaryOperatorExpression = _
            New CodeBinaryOperatorExpression
        waCondition.Left = stateRef
        waCondition.Operator = CodeBinaryOperatorType.ValueEquality
        waCondition.Right = New CodePrimitiveExpression("WA")
        waTaxRule.Condition = New RuleExpressionCondition(waCondition)
        Dim waThen As CodeAssignStatement = New CodeAssignStatement
        waThen.Left = taxRateRef
        waThen.Right = New CodePrimitiveExpression(10)
        waTaxRule.ThenActions.Add(New RuleStatementAction(waThen))

        Return ruleSet
    End Function
```

You can now compile your project and the TaxPolicy activity will be added to the toolbox; it is available for use in any workflows in your project or any projects that reference this project. You can now use this activity in your workflow in the same way as any other activity. For this example, drag and drop the TaxPolicy into an empty workflow in the project, set the OrderValue and State properties, add some Console.Writeline statements to the workflow Completed handler to print all the property values, and execute the workflow.

```
    Private Sub WorkflowCompleted(ByVal sender As System.Object, ByVal e _
        As System.EventArgs)
        Console.WriteLine(("State = " + Me.taxPolicy1.State))
```

```
        Console.WriteLine(("OrderTotal = " + Me.taxPolicy1.OrderTotal.ToString))
        Console.WriteLine(("TaxRate = " + Me.taxPolicy1.TaxRate.ToString))
    End Sub
```

Additional `Policy` **Topics**

Now, you might be asking yourself why you would use a `Policy` activity. Couldn't you
just write the same logic in code? In very simple scenarios, the answer would be yes.
However, as the rules become more complex, the advantages of using a `RuleSet` become
increasingly clear. First, by providing an object model for authoring the rules, you can
develop custom tools for building, navigating, and analyzing your rules. Furthermore, the
rule properties and corresponding `RuleSet` execution semantics discussed in the following
sections would be increasingly difficult to mimic in a purely procedural, code-based
approach.

Priorities

If you add multiple rules to your `RuleSet`, you might want those rules to evaluate in a
specific order because the outcome of one rule affects the conditions of another.
Alternatively, if multiple rules update the same field, you might want to specify which
rule takes precedence. You can accomplish both of these scenarios with the Priority field
on the rule. Assume that you want to define a second rule that says if the state is equal to
Washington, but the value of the order is more than $10,000, then a higher, luxury goods
tax rate of 12% must be applied. First, add a new `OrderTotal` property of type
`System.Double` to the activity and define a corresponding reference:

```
        Dim orderTotalRef As CodePropertyReferenceExpression = _
            New CodePropertyReferenceExpression(thisRef, "OrderTotal")
```

Then you can define your new rule as follows:

```
        Dim waLuxuryTaxRule As Rule = New Rule("WashingtonLuxuryTaxRule")
        waLuxuryTaxRule.Priority = -5
        ruleSet.Rules.Add(waLuxuryTaxRule)

        Dim waLuxuryCondition As CodeBinaryOperatorExpression = _
            New CodeBinaryOperatorExpression
        waLuxuryCondition.Left = orderTotalRef
        waLuxuryCondition.Operator = CodeBinaryOperatorType.GreaterThan
        waLuxuryCondition.Right = New CodePrimitiveExpression(10000)

        ' combine two predicates into a single condition
        waLuxuryTaxRule.Condition = New RuleExpressionCondition( _
        New CodeBinaryOperatorExpression(waCondition, _
        CodeBinaryOperatorType.BooleanAnd, waLuxuryCondition))

        Dim waLuxuryThen As CodeAssignStatement = New CodeAssignStatement
```

```
waLuxuryThen.Left = taxRateRef
waLuxuryThen.Right = New CodePrimitiveExpression(12)
waLuxuryTaxRule.ThenActions.Add(New RuleStatementAction(waLuxuryThen))
```

Note that you set a priority value of –5 to this rule. Rules are executed in priority order from higher priorities to lower priorities; the default value is 0. Because you did not give a priority value to the first WashingtonTax rule, it has the default value. This means that your second rule, WashingtonLuxuryTax rule, will execute after the first rule. The first rule can be considered the default tax rate for Washington purchases, but its calculated tax rate will be overwritten by the second, luxury tax rule if it applies.

If you do not assign priorities to the rules they will all have the default value of 0 and their execution sequences will be established by the engine.

As a note, it may seem unusual in the previous example that the *lower* priority rule over-wrote the *higher* priority rule. Keep in mind that in other scenarios the action of a higher priority rule could change data that would actually prevent a lower priority rule from ever executing.

Chaining

The rules engine in Windows Workflow Foundation provides forward-chaining capabilities, which allows you to define sophisticated policies in a simple way. Briefly put, *forward chaining* means that the actions of one rule can cause another rule to be reevaluated. You can use priorities to order rule evaluation to achieve a similar effect in certain situations, but rule chaining provides two key advantages:

- Rule dependencies and sequencing do not have to be explicitly defined.

- Rules that have already been evaluated can be reevaluated.

The first item makes policy construction and maintenance easier, whereas the second item would not be achievable using priorities alone.

For example, assume that you wanted to add a "MinimumTax" rule that ensured that a minimum tax rate of 11% was always applied, irrespective of other rules. In other words:

```
IF TaxRate < 11 THEN TaxRate = 11
```

You could give this rule the lowest priority to ensure it gets fired or you could simply define the rule and let forward chaining take care of the rest. Any other rule that sets TaxRate will cause this rule to be reevaluated.

To a large degree, forward chaining in the RuleSet is implicit. The engine will evaluate the activity properties referenced in the actions of one rule against the property references in the conditions of other rules. If the first rule executes, the other rules will be reevaluated. For example, the WashingtonTax rule is defined as follows:

```
IF State == "WA" THEN TaxRate = 10
```

Because `TaxRate` is assigned in the actions and the `MinimumTax` rule uses `TaxRate` in its condition, the `MinimumTax` rule will be reevaluated when the `WashingtonTax` rule fires.

It should be noted that the implicit chaining evaluation is performed on immediate properties of the activity. If those properties are complex types, calls against the members of those complex types will be interpreted as calls on the property itself. For example, if the `TaxRate` property instead contained a `TaxAssessment` object with `State`, `Federal`, and `Local` properties, a change to the `State` property of the `TaxAssessment` instance would be interpreted—for chaining purposes—as a change to the `TaxRate` property itself.

Method Access

In addition to using activity properties in your rules, you might also want to define methods on the activity that you use in the rules. For example, define a `CalculateLuxuryTax` method as follows:

```
Public Sub CalculateLuxuryTax()
    Me.TaxRate = ((((Me.OrderTotal - 10000) / Me.OrderTotal) * 5) + 10)
End Sub
```

Note that this method must be public to be accessed by the rules engine.

Then change the action on the `WashingtonLuxuryTax` rule to reference this method:

```
waLuxuryTaxRule.ThenActions.Add(New RuleStatementAction( _
    New CodeMethodInvokeExpression(thisRef, "CalculateLuxuryTax")))
```

When using a method, you need to consider that its code might read or write against the activity properties. Therefore, you need a mechanism for defining chaining behavior associated with these indirect reads and writes; you can do this by attributing the methods. There are three attributes: `RuleRead`, `RuleWrite`, and `RuleInvoke`. The first two, as the name suggests, declare reads and writes on properties. The third declares that the method invokes another method, which might have its own attributes, so that even more indirect reads/writes can be identified. You would use the `RuleWrite` attribute on your method as follows:

```
<RuleWrite("TaxRate")> _
Public Sub CalculateLuxuryTax()
```

This indicates that your method writes to the `TaxRate` property. Based on this attributing, if the `WashingtonLuxuryTaxRule` is executed and its actions fired, your `MinimumTaxRule` would be reevaluated, and, depending on the calculated luxury tax, fired.

Halt **and** Update **Functions**

In addition to updating activity properties and calling activity methods, your rules can also use two built-in commands, `Halt` and `Update`. `Halt` stops execution of the `RuleSet` and the activity. `Update` is used to indicate that rule has updated a property. For example, in the `WashingtonLuxuryTaxRule`, instead of attributing the method, you could add an `Update` statement to the `ThenActions` that refers to the property name.

```
waLuxuryTaxRule.ThenActions.Add(New RuleUpdateAction("TaxRate"))
```

Maximum Execution Count

In some scenarios, forward chaining can cause unintended looping behavior, such as when a rule causes itself to be reevaluated. Excessive looping can be addressed by setting the `MaxExecutionCount` property on a rule. The default is 0, which represents unlimited looping. Any other positive value defines the maximum number of times that a rule can execute. Note that if you do not want the rule to execute (such as during testing) you should set the `Active` property on the rule to false.

Externalization and Programmatic Execution

A likely scenario is that you will want to externalize the `RuleSet` definition from the `Policy` activity itself. This would allow you to maintain and manage the `RuleSets` separately and have them retrieved and executed by the `Policy` activity at runtime. Instead of defining the tax `RuleSet` within the activity, you could replace the code in `CreateRuleSet` with the following:

```
Dim serializer As WorkflowMarkupSerializer = New WorkflowMarkupSerializer
Dim reader As StreamReader = New StreamReader("TaxPolicy.xml")
Dim ruleSet As RuleSet = CType(serializer.Deserialize(reader), RuleSet)
reader.Close()
Return ruleSet
```

This would retrieve the `RuleSet` definition from a `TaxPolicy.xml` file (in the application's directory). Similarly, you could replace this code with code that retrieves the `RuleSet` definition from a database. The point is that you can define any logic you would like in the `CreateRuleSet` method, as long as it returns a `RuleSet` object.

As you have probably figured out, you could serialize your `RuleSet` object using the following code:

```
Dim serializer As WorkflowMarkupSerializer = New WorkflowMarkupSerializer
Dim writer As StreamWriter = New StreamWriter("TaxPolicy.xml")
serializer.Serialize(ruleSet, writer)
writer.Flush()
writer.Close()
```

Advanced Activity Behaviors

The creation of custom activities was covered in Chapter 7, "Developing Activities." In this section you will take a look at additional behaviors that can be added to activities. These behaviors, which help support robust and long-running workflows, include the following:

- Transactions
- Compensation
- Exception handling
- Event handling
- Synchronization

In addition to being available to custom activities, these behaviors already exist on sequential workflows. In a sequential workflow, you can use the icons in the bottom left of the design canvas, which allows you to navigate to the design surfaces for exception handling, event handlers, and compensation behavior. Furthermore, a TransactionalContext activity is available in the toolbox, which supports transactions, compensation, and exception handling. The majority of this section, however, will focus on adding these behaviors to custom activities. After adding an activity with these behaviors to a workflow, you can right-click and use the context menu to navigate to the various design surfaces.

The behaviors are added to custom activities using a set of attributes applied to the activity class:

- SupportsTransaction
- SupportsExceptionHandlers
- SupportsEventHandlers
- SupportsSynchronization

Any activity with the SupportsTransaction attribute also gets support for compensation behavior.

The attributes can be added directly to the activity class definition as follows:

```
[SupportsExceptionHandlers]
[SupportsEventHandlers]
[SupportsTransaction]
[SupportsSynchronization]
public partial class TransactionalActivity : Sequence
```

Alternatively, the attributes can be added in the custom activity designer by changing the values of the SupportsEventHandlers, SupportsExceptionHandlers, and SupportsTransaction properties in the Advanced section of the Properties window when the activity is selected in the custom activity designer. SupportsSynchronization is not supported in the activity designer and must be directly added to the code. Note that all properties are available for composite activities, but only the SupportsTransaction property is available on basic activities derived from Activity.

Now that you know how to provide these behaviors to your workflow and activities, let's discuss the nature of the behaviors themselves.

Transactions

After the `SupportsTransaction` attribute is added to an activity, the activity will gain a `Transaction` property that allows you to specify the transactional characteristics applied to the execution of the activity (and its child activities). The three options are `None`, `Atomic`, and `LongRunning`. As the name implies, `None` provides no special transactional behavior.

Atomic Transactions

A value of `Atomic` provides ACID (Atomic, Consistent, Isolated, and Durable) semantics to the execution of the activity. If the atomic transaction fails because of an exception or timeout, all actions within the activity are rolled back. On an atomic transaction, a number of other properties are made available:

- `IsolationLevel`—Specifies the locking behavior associated with the transaction. The provided values and associated semantics match those found on the `IsolationLevel` enumeration in the `System.Transactions` namespace.

- `Retriable`—Indicates whether the transaction should be retried if it fails. The transaction will only be retried if specific exceptions are encountered: a `RetryTransactionException`, which can be explicitly thrown in the transaction, or a `PersistenceException`, which would be thrown from the host. The transaction will retry 20 times before the workflow is suspended. A delay of two seconds will be used between retries unless a specific delay is passed in the `RetryTransactionException`.

- `Timeout`—If the transaction is not successfully completed in this amount of time (specified in seconds), the transaction will be rolled back and a `TransactionAbortedException` will be thrown.

There are a few rules that govern the use of an atomic transaction in a workflow. An atomic transaction activity cannot contain another atomic transaction activity. Furthermore, an atomic transaction activity can only be contained within an activity designated as a long-running transaction because the outer activity must manage its state to support an inner atomic transaction. However, a sequential workflow can itself be an atomic transaction.

An atomic transaction activity may not have exception handlers because an exception in an atomic transaction will always roll back the transaction. In addition, an atomic transaction activity may not contain a `Suspend` or `InvokeWorkflow` activity.

It is also useful to note that rolling back an atomic transaction rolls back the state of the entire surrounding workflow.

Within an atomic transaction activity you might use transactional objects, and they will participate in the same transaction as the activity. For example, you can use an EnterpriseServices' `ServicedComponent` and the workflow will create a DTC transaction to

8

support it. Similarly, database calls that you make within an atomic transaction will automatically be transactional. For example, if you have a Code activity with the following ExecuteCode handler inside an atomic activity, the database update would only commit if and when the atomic activity commits:

```
Private Sub code1_ExecuteCode(ByVal sender As Object, ByVal e As EventArgs)
    Dim sqlConnection As SqlConnection = _
        "Initial Catalog=CustomerData;Data Source=(local);Integrated
Security=SSPI;"
    sqlConnection.Open
    Dim update As String = "UPDATE CustInfo SET CreditCardBalance = 505 _
        WHERE ID='1'"
    Dim cmd As SqlCommand = New SqlCommand(update, sqlConnection)
    cmd.ExecuteNonQuery
    sqlConnection.Close
End Sub
```

Similarly, the new TransactionScopes from the 2.0 version of the .NET Framework may also be used inside an atomic transaction.

The use of communications with workflows is covered in the next chapter, but I will mention them briefly here in this context. An outbound method call from within an atomic activity to a local service is not automatically transactional; however, the local service implementation may use the work batch information on the thread to participate in the same transaction as the workflow. An EventSink activity for an incoming event will be transactional, meaning that retrieval of the event from the queue will be part of the transaction. These two notions will become clearer after the hosting and communications discussions in Chapter 9, "Workflow Communications with .NET," and Chapter 11, "Hosting Workflows in Your Application."

Before you start using atomic transaction activities, you need to know that they require the host to provide a persistence service. The SqlStatePersistenceService provided with the Windows Workflow Foundation is one example of this; see Chapter 11 on hosting for more detail on the services and how to configure them.

Long-Running Transactions

The third value for Transaction is LongRunning, which is applied to activities that are expected to run over the course of hours, days, or months. This will typically involve communications activities that are waiting for events from external sources. Because the lifespan of the activity might be significant, it is not practical to hold locks in the same manner as atomic transactions. While activities within a long-running activity are waiting for these external events, the workflow may be "dehydrated," meaning that it is removed from memory and its state is maintained via the persistence service. Because a long-running workflow can be persisted, only serializable objects may be used as variables or parameters on a long-running activity, unless they are marked with the NonSerialized attribute.

A long-running transaction has an `LRTTimeout` property, where you specify a `DateTime` value. If the timeout is reached, a `System.TimeoutException` exception will be thrown to the surrounding activity.

The transaction containment rules can be summarized as follows:

- An atomic transaction must be contained in a long-running transaction, and can only contain a transaction marked as `None`.

- A long-running transaction must be contained in another long-running transaction, but may contain any other transaction type.

- A transaction marked as `None` can be contained in any other transaction type, but may only contain another `None` transaction.

Compensation

A compensation handler on an activity can be called after the activity has successfully completed. It is used to provide a business-level rollback of the actions in the activity. In other words, the activity cannot be rolled back in a true transactional sense because it has been committed, but compensation logic can be defined to help provide business consistency. Assume, for example, that the actions in an activity reserve inventory from a warehouse as part of an order processing workflow. If the activity completes but an exception occurs later in the workflow, the compensation handler of the activity can be called to release the inventory reservation.

The default compensation behavior of an activity is to call the compensation handlers of each of its completed child activities in the reverse order of their completion. If a complete child activity has executed multiple times (if it was contained in a `While`, `Replicator`, or `CAG`, for example), compensate will be called for each execution instance of that activity in reverse order of the executions.

The compensation handler is typically called by the default compensation handler of the surrounding activity, described previously. However, a compensation handler can also be explicitly called using the `Compensate` activity, either in the exception handler or compensation handler of the surrounding activity. The `Compensate` activity can be used to call the handler on any contained activity that supports transactions and compensation behavior (the activity must be an immediate child of the calling activity; calls on the compensation handler of nested activities are not allowed). The `Compensate` activity can also point to the surrounding activity's own compensation handler. If an activity calls its own compensation handler from within its compensation handler, it will invoke the default compensation behavior.

An activity's compensation handler can only be executed once; any subsequent calls to an activity's compensation handler will be ignored.

Exception Handling

The Exceptions view on an activity (see Figure 8.9) shows an ExceptionHandler's activity, which allows you to model multiple ExceptionHandler activities in the same way that you might add multiple catch statements to a try-catch statement in your code. The Exceptions view can be accessed by right-clicking on the workflow or activity (the activity must support exception handlers). From the toolbox, drag and drop the ExceptionHandler activity into the filmstrip at the top of the exception handler's block. Each exception handler must have its Type property populated, specifying the exception type that it will process. In addition, the handler has an optional Variable property where the exception will be stored.

Selecting an individual ExceptionHandler in the filmstrip displays the child activities of that handler; this is where you model the logic for how a particular type of exception will be processed.

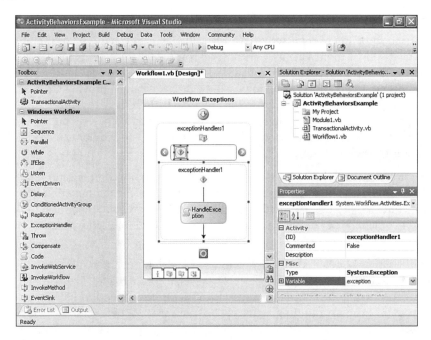

FIGURE 8.9   Exception handler defined on a workflow.

If an exception is thrown within the course of an activity's execution, the runtime will look for a corresponding exception handler in the left-to-right order that the exception handlers are shown in the filmstrip; this allows you to process exceptions in an exception hierarchy from more to less specific types in exactly the same way that catch blocks in code are given the opportunity to handle an exception in the order that they are defined. For example, assume that you access a file within the main body of the activity. To account for possible exceptions accessing and opening the file, you might first add an ExceptionHandler that handles a System.IO.FileNotFoundException. Then you might add a second ExceptionHandler activity to the right of the first ExceptionHandler that handles the next exception in the hierarchy, `System.IO.IOException`, in order to handle, for example, a network access failure exception.

Within a handler, you can use any other activity that you might use in the main body of the activity, including blocking activities such as a `Delay` or communications activities. In addition, you may use a `Throw` activity to throw (or rethrow) an exception. The `Exception` property on `Throw` should point to an `Exception` instance. A typical scenario would be that a `Throw` activity would be placed at the end of the `ExceptionHandler` and its `Exception` property would point to the same variable specified in the `Variable` property of its parent `ExceptionHandler`. This would cause the `Throw` statement to rethrow the original exception. Note that if the exception handler completes normally and does not throw an exception, the outer activity will continue execution. The inner activity—the activity that caught the exception—will not be reexecuted and will be marked with a status of completed and an outcome of cancelled.

A `Compensate` activity may also be placed in an exception handler in order to call previously defined compensation logic. In fact, if an activity does not have an exception handler for a given exception, the default exception-handling behavior is to call the compensation handler of each completed activity within the current activity and then rethrow the exception. The compensation handlers would be called in reverse order of how the associated activities executed prior to the exception being thrown, as with default compensation behavior.

Event Handling

Event handlers are used to process events that might be received at any point during execution of the activity. These typically involve events that are possible in some scenarios but do not occur in the course of "normal" activity execution. One example might be an activity that participates in order processing. An event handler might be modeled on the activity to receive a `CancelOrder` event.

After switching to the Events view, you will see the `EventHandlers` activity, which has a filmstrip window as with the exception handlers. In this case, you will drag an `EventDriven` activity from the toolbox into the filmstrip to model the receipt of a single event type.

Within an `EventDriven` activity, the first activity must be an `EventSink` or a `Delay` activity (more precisely it must be an activity that implements `IEventActivity`). After this first activity you model the behavior to be triggered by the event. The event can be delivered at any point during the activity's execution and it will be processed.

Synchronization

Synchronization is used in scenarios where multiple activities may access a shared variable in concurrent fashion; it is analogous to a lock statement used in code. For example, you might have a parallel activity where activities in multiple branches have reads of and writes to a variable on the workflow. An activity can be marked synchronized to ensure that it completes before any activity that it is synchronized with begins. Synchronization requirements are specified by populating the `SynchronizationHandles` property of the activity with a comma-delimited set of string values (quotes are not required when entering the values). Two activities are considered synchronized if they have a matching synchronization handle, analogous to a named Mutex instance used for thread synchronization. In other words, if one of the comma-delimited values matches, the activities' execution will be synchronized. In the following example, the Synch1 and Synch2 activities have a SynchronizationHandles value of "a". This ensures that only one of the two activities will execute at a time, so that the actions of their child activities will not interfere with each other. Without synchronization, the read activities will both see the value of the second update to the shared variable, from the RightWriteA activity. With synchronization, the LeftReadA activity will see the value as written by the LeftWriteA activity, and the RightReadA activity will see the value as written by the RightWriteA activity (see Figure 8.10).

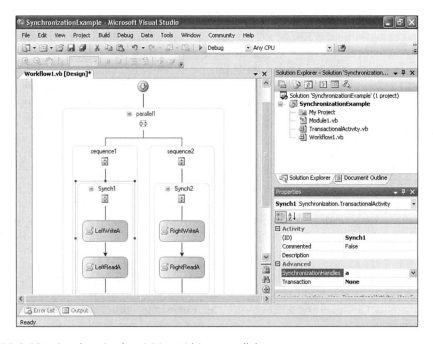

FIGURE 8.10   Synchronized activities within a parallel.

The values do not have to match a workflow variable name; they do not have any significance other than to provide a match across activities. For example, if you have three activities with the following values for SynchronizationHandles, Activity1 would be synchronized with Activity2, and Activity2 would be synchronized with Activity3:

- Activity1 – a,b
- Activity2 – b,c
- Activity3 – c,d

Note that atomic transaction activities are, by their nature, always synchronized because no other part of a workflow can execute while an atomic transaction is executing.

Behavior Relationships

Table 8.1 summarizes the behaviors that different transaction types can have.

TABLE 8.1 Activity Behavior and Transaction Relationships

Behaviors	None	Atomic	Long Running
Exception handlers	Yes (if not in atomic activity)	No	Yes
Compensation handler	No	Yes	Yes
Event handlers	Yes	Yes	Yes
Synchronization handlers	Yes	Yes	Yes

Activity Behaviors Example

Figure 8.11 shows a workflow that incorporates several of the behaviors described previously.

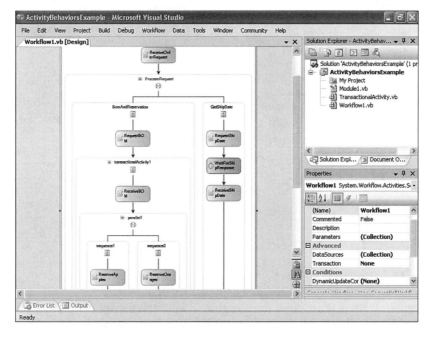

FIGURE 8.11 Activity behaviors example.

This example uses an order confirmation process. In this process, an order request is received by the first activity. The workflow then enters the ProcessRequest parallel activity, which reserves the required inventory and gets a ship date. The BomAndReservation sequence activity has a RequestBOM activity that sends a message to an external application to get the bill of materials associated with the product ordered. In this example, the bill of materials represents the number of apples and oranges in a type of fruit basket. The `ReceiveBOM` activity receives the response event and then two parallel `ReserveInventory` activities reserve the required number of apples and oranges based on the BOM breakdown. The `ReceiveBOM` and `ReserveInventory` activities are nested inside an atomic activity, so that the event received is transactional with the inventory reservation.

The `GetShipDate` activity sends a message to an external system to request a ship date and receives the response. Between the request and response activities there is a `Delay` activity to simulate a delayed response. The use of inbound and outbound events is simulated in the sample, but could be replaced by communications events, as described in Chapters 9 and 11.

On the activity titled `transactionalActivity1`, there is a compensation handler that reverts the inventory reservation if the activity is compensated as shown in Figure 8.12.

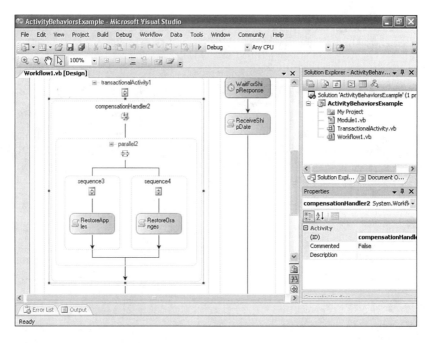

FIGURE 8.12   `transactionalActivity1` compensation handler.

On the workflow there is an event handler that mimics the receipt of an order cancellation event. Because there isn't an actual inbound event, a `Delay` activity is used to simulate it (see Figure 8.13). After the delay timeout is met, the event handler will throw an exception.

The exception will then be caught by an exception handler defined on the workflow, as shown in Figure 8.14.

The exception handler will then call the compensation handler on the `transactionalActivity1` activity.

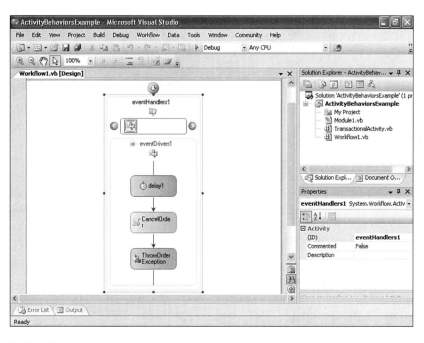

FIGURE 8.13   Workflow event handler.

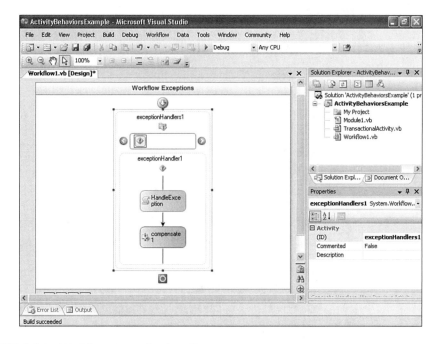

FIGURE 8.14   Workflow exception handler.

When the sample is run, the BomAndReservation activity will execute and complete. Meanwhile, the delay in the GetShipDate will prevent the workflow from completing. This will allow the CancelOrder event handler to execute, which will throw the exception. This will in turn cause the exception handler to compensate the transactionalActivity1 activity. See the code associated with this chapter to execute this sample and follow these interactions.

Summary

In this chapter you've taken a brief tour of some of the more advanced activities provided with Windows Workflow Foundation. You've seen how the Replicator allows you to dynamically spawn new activity instances from collection data, and how the Conditioned Activity Group provides flexible, condition-driven activity execution. You've also seen how the Policy activity serves as a base type to allow you to build powerful and flexible business logic that leverages a forward-chaining rules engine.

In addition, you have seen the more advanced activity behaviors that can easily be added to your custom activities to enable robust workflows in support of business processes. These behaviors include exception handling, transactional support, event handling, business-level compensation semantics, and execution synchronization.

CHAPTER 9

Workflow Communications with .NET

This chapter describes how workflows communicate with local objects contained by host applications. It describes how workflows call methods on local objects and handle events raised by local objects. The key to understanding this communication mechanism lies in the local services registered with the host application and the asynchronous queuing layer used by the Local Communication Service (LCS).

What You Need

The required software, hardware, and knowledge required and in some cases recommended to set and work with Windows Workflow Foundation are:

- Required software—.NET Framework 2.0 SDK and Windows Workflow Foundation Beta1

- Recommended software—Visual Studio .NET 2005 (any edition)

- Recommended hardware—Any PC that meets .NET Framework 2.0 SDK minimum requirements

- Recommended skills—C# 1.1 familiarity

Workflow Communications at a Glance

This chapter describes the low-level mechanisms used by workflows to communicate with host applications. The information that will be covered includes the following:

- Local Services and their purpose and advantage

- Data activities versus Local Services

- Local Service Interface—its purpose and usage

- What is correlation?

- `WorkflowMessageEventArgs` and its purpose and usage

- `InvokeMethodActivity` and its relationship to Local Service Interface

- `EventSinkActivity` and its relationship to Local Service Interface

- Service Request Form Application and WinForm Application with Local Service Actiivities in Workflow

Local Communication Services Overview

The workflow and the .NET application executing it need to be able to communicate with each other. To support this interaction a contract in the form of a .NET interface is defined. The implementation of this interface is registered with the workflow runtime and used to mediate the communications between the workflow and the application hosting or executing the workflow. Mediating the exchange of events between the application hosting the workflow and a specific workflow instance is the responsibility of the workflow runtime. Not all workflows are loaded in memory; some long-running workflows keep their state in disk. It is the responsibility of the workflow instance to load workflow instances whose state has been unloaded to disk and deliver raise events. In summary, local services are the implementation of that communication interface that is registered with the workflow runtime to handle events raised by the application hosting the workflow.

Why Local Services?

As we discussed briefly in Chapter 5, "Workflow Integration with Data Activities," the mechanisms for exchanging information between the host application and the workflow are *queues*. These queues provide a separation between the actual workflow instance and the host application. This separation, or proxy layer, allows workflow instances to hydrate and dehydrate as required without using any in-memory references that may be held by the host application. Queues are used to implement any asynchronous inbound data passing to the workflow. Workflows register for insert events on queues and when information is written to the queues from the host applications, these events are fired. The reason for this asynchronous model when sending information to the workflow is that the workflow instance state is not required to be in-memory; it could be unloaded. Queues provide a mechanism for ensuring the message will be delivered when the workflow instance state is reloaded.

Communications from the workflow to the host application are performed synchronously using the object registered with the workflow runtime service. These objects are accessed directly by the workflow to invoke methods on them. When method execution on this object returns, the workflow's thread is allowed to continue execution. Thus, method invocation is used to implement the synchronous outbound data passing from the workflow to the host.

The abstraction layer that sits on top of the queues, making this possible, is the Local Communication Service. The Local Communication Service provides a mechanism to access the workflow runtime, help manage local services, and manage events raised for specific workflow instances (see Figure 9.1). This abstraction allows workflows and host applications to exchange information by implicitly defining event handlers to receive queue messages and methods on local services that are called by the workflow.

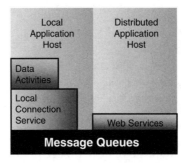

FIGURE 9.1   Windows Workflow Foundation communication stack.

All local services need to be registered with the workflow runtime in order for them to be available to the host application to receive messages from the workflow. Also, they are registered with the runtime so they can be available to the workflow instance to send messages to the host application. On the workflow side, the local service is accessed from the activity execution environment using the `ActivityExecutionContext`. Once registered with the workflow runtime, the local service follows a single pattern, where all communications of a specific type are done using the registered object.

Data Activities Versus Local Services

Data activities leverage the Local Communication Service to exchange data between the workflow and the host application. They implement an interface that defines a fixed contract between the host application and the workflow. This minimizes the exposure to the messaging layer and allows developers to focus on defining the payload that the message needs to consume and deliver. They provide an out-of-the-box mechanism for sending and querying data from the workflow to the host and vice versa.

Data sources used by data activities require the payload of the information being transmitted to be of the same `Type` or `Object` class. Local services, on the other hand, are more flexible. They provide a mechanism for exchanging data where the inbound payload doesn't have to match the outbound payload. In addition, data activities provide only two types of built-in events: data queries and data saves. Local services are able to support an unlimited number of events.

Data activities provide a subset of the functionality delivered by local services but simplify the development by allowing developers to focus on the data being exchanged. The main difference between the two is that local services require an interface, the implementation of that interface, and the definition of local service activities whereas data activities don't.

The guidelines to differentiate when to use local services or data activities are shown in Table 9.1.

TABLE 9.1   Local Services or Data Activities Guidelines

Guidelines	Technology
Same data inbound and outbound	Data activities
Query and save data events only	Data activities
Different data inbound and outbound	Local services
Additional events (such as cancel, resubmit, submit)	Local services
Out-of-the-box activities; no interface or activity development	Data activities
Fine-grain activity separation, requires interface development	Local services

Data exchanges between host applications and workflows require knowledge of data sources, Data Handlers, and unique keys, not message protocols (see Figure 9.2). Data sources describe the makeup of the data that will be exchanged between the workflow and the host application. Data Handlers provide a mechanism for managing data that was sent by the workflow to the host. Unique keys specify the tokens in the information that make the data exchange between the workflow and host application self-contained. The host application service that enables the communications to take place without exposing the protocol semantics is the *Data Source Service*. The Data Source Service is responsible for allowing the host application to send and query data from the workflow and managing the incoming requests that come from the workflow to the host application. This service lives as part of the workflow runtime services.

Local Service Interface

Local services require an interface that defines the methods that the workflow will invoke (outbound communications) and the events the workflow will receive (inbound communications). This interface will be implemented by a local object inside the host application and used by a workflow activity to call methods in it or register event listeners. The interface needs to contain a `DataExchangeService` attribute. When the local service is registered with the workflow runtime, it uses this attribute to discover the interface for which it needs to mediate communications. The mediation provided by the workflow instance is responsible for intercepting events raised by the local object, load unloaded workflows instances, and deliver events to the right workflow instance. This is the only required attribute in the interface.

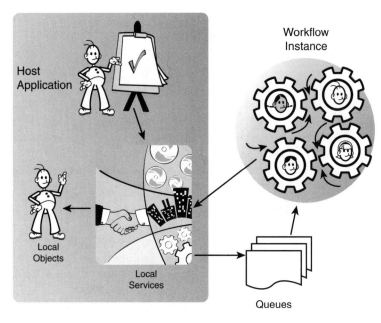

FIGURE 9.2   Data activities communications.

Imagine a company that wants to implement a Service Request Management System to create and track trouble tickets or customer problems. Trouble tickets are going to be created in the server using a customer ID and customers will be allowed to close or cancel their request. Requests are closed when customers feel they have received adequate resolution to their problems and are canceled when customers feel they don't need help anymore.

This problem requires an interface that facilitates the creation of a trouble ticket by the workflow system and the sending of status information to the workflow.

```
<DataExchangeService()> _
Public Interface IServiceRequest

    Private Event CloseService As EventHandler
    Private Event CancelService As EventHandler
    Sub CreateServiceRequest(ByVal requestId As String, _
        ByVal customerId As String, ByVal description As String)


End Interface
```

The `CreateServiceRequest` method is used by the workflow to create a service request and communicate its creation to the host application. The two `EventHandler` delegates are used by the host application to send status updates to the workflow on the Service Requests.

Defining Correlation Values

By default, the workflow instance is serving as a unique key to map inbound events coming from a single local object. This behavior is known as default correlation. Default correlation doesn't require any knowledge about the payload of the message. It assumes that events being sent to the workflow are related to the same object. Although this approach is simple and useful, it doesn't suffice in many situations.

Imagine you are reviewing a proposal and you submit the proposal for approval to five managers. The approvals will come back to the workflow using the implementation of the local service you registered with the workflow runtime. All the approvals share the same data definition or type. In order to be able to distinguish between these approvals inside the workflow, you need a unique key or correlation parameter value that distinguishes the various payloads. The correlation parameter (that is, a correlation token) will be used to differentiate between the various object instances contained by the workflow. The correlation parameter will define the payload property or parameter used to uniquely identify the payload or the message (that is, the unique key).

Correlation could also be viewed as a channel between the host application and the workflow that is used to exchange messages with a unique ID.

There are several correlation attributes that could be used to decorate the interface, shown in Table 9.2.

TABLE 9.2   Several Correlation Attributes that Can Be Used to Decorate the Interface

Attributes	Description
`[CorrelationInitializer]`	Used to decorate an interface method or event. It signals the workflow that the invocation of this method from the workflow or the receiving of this event by the workflow will start or opens a communication channel between the workflow and the host application.
`[CorrelationParameter]`	Used to decorate the interface, methods, and events. It defines the parameter inside the interface methods and events that will be used as the unique identifier. The value inside this parameter will be treated as the unique key for the communication channel.
`[CorrelationAlias]`	Used to override the `CorrelationParameter` setting for a specific method or event. Maps the `CorrelationParameter` value to a different parameter that is being used to hold the correlation value.

In the previous scenario, in order to allow customers to submit multiple Service Requests in one case or trouble ticket, the interface would have to define a `CorrelationParameter`:

```
DataExchangeService(), _
 CorrelationParameter("requestId")> _
Public Interface IServiceRequest

    <CorrelationAlias("requestId", "e.RequestId")> _
    Private Event CloseService As EventHandler

    <CorrelationAlias("requestId", "e.RequestId")> _
    Private Event CancelService As EventHandler

    <CorrelationInitializer()> _
    Sub CreateServiceRequest(ByVal requestId As String, _
        ByVal customerId As String, ByVal description As String)

End Interface
```

This interface defines the request ID to be used as the `CorrelationParameter`. This means each request object will be identified using a unique request ID. The `CorrelationInitializer` is the `CreateServiceRequest` method, which means that every time the workflow invokes this method in the host application, a new communication channel will be created between the workflow and the host. The `CorrelationAlias` tells the system where to find the `CorrelationParameter`, requestId, in the `ServiceEventArgs` parameter. The variable e comes from the delegate defined by the `System.EventHandler<T>` signature. For event handlers e will always be used as the prefix to the parameter.

WorkflowMessageEventArgs

The `WorkflowMessageEventArgs` type provides a mechanism for sending messages from the host application to the workflow via the local service. It requires the passing of the workflow instance ID together with the value for the correlation parameter. This information provides the required context to the workflow to be able to route the incoming message via the correct communication channel.

All the event arguments defined in the local service interface need to inherit from the `WorkflowMessageEventArgs` class and invoke a base method in the constructor. This sets the correct context to deliver the message to the correct workflow instance and provides the information required to rehydrate the workflow when it has been dehydrated.

`WorkflowMessageEventArgs` subclasses need to implement the [Serializable] property. This allows the message to be stored into the queues for delivery to the workflow.

For the scenario described earlier, a `ServiceEventArgs` class was defined to store the Service Request ID of the trouble ticket on the event being sent to the workflow.

```
<Serializable()> _
Public Class ServiceEventArgs
    Inherits WorkflowMessageEventArgs
```

```
    Private _id As String

    Public Sub New(ByVal instanceId As Guid, ByVal serviceId As String)
        MyBase.New(instanceId)
        _id = serviceId
    End Sub

    Public ReadOnly Property RequestId As String
        Get
            Return _id
        End Get
    End Property
End Class
```

The solution invokes the base (instanceId) constructor of the WorkflowMessageEventArgs class and provides a public property that could be accessed by the workflow code-beside to determine the correlation property of the object that triggered the event.

InvokeMethodActivity

After the interface has been defined, a custom activity is created for each method and event that exists in the interface. Each activity represents the invocation of a method on a local service from the workflow. This custom activity inherits from InvokeMethodActivity. The InvokeMethodActivity is responsible for accessing the workflow runtime, retrieving a local service of the specified interface type, and invoking a specific method in it. After the method finishes executing on the local service, the thread of execution is returned to the workflow and it continues to process its other activities.

Custom activities for invoking local service methods are implemented by creating two classes that derived from InvokeMethodActivity and ActivityExecutor<T>. The InvokeMethodActivity subclass defines the InterfaceType, MethodName, properties, and attributes required to manipulate a design-time activity definition. The ActivityExecutor<T> subclass defines the execute behavior of the activity at runtime. This executor is responsible for retrieving the registered runtime information of the local service and invoking the method on the local object.

Invoked method activities could also be used to explicitly initiate the correlation between the workflow and the host application. This opens a communication channel to exchange data between the host and workflow using a predefined unique key (that is, CorrelationParameter) when a message is sent by the workflow. This is accomplished by adding the [CorrelationInitializer] attribute to the method definition in the local service interface.

For the Service Request Management scenario, there is only one method in the interface CreateServiceRequest, thus there is only going to be one InvokeMethodActivity. This activity will be used to hold the design-time information and properties of the CreateServiceRequest activity. Once defined, a visual design representation of the CreateServiceRequest activity will be available inside Visual Studio (see Figure 9.3).

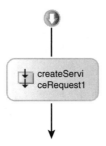

FIGURE 9.3   Design view of newly defined `CreateServiceRequest InvokeMethodActivity`.

```
ToolboxItemAttribute(GetType(ActivityToolboxItem)), _
 ExecutorAttribute(GetType(CreateServiceRequestExecutor))> _
Public Class CreateServiceRequest
    Inherits InvokeMethodActivity

    Public Shared RequestIdProperty As DependencyProperty = _
            System.Workflow.ComponentModel.DependencyProperty.Register( _
            "RequestId", GetType(String), GetType(CreateServiceRequest))

    Public Shared CustomerIdProperty As DependencyProperty = _
            System.Workflow.ComponentModel.DependencyProperty.Register( _
            "CustomerId", GetType(String), GetType(CreateServiceRequest))

    Public Shared RequestDescriptionProperty As DependencyProperty = _
            System.Workflow.ComponentModel.DependencyProperty.Register( _
            "RequestDescription", GetType(String), GetType(CreateServiceRequest))

    <DesignerSerializationVisibility(DesignerSerializationVisibility.Hidden)> _
    Public Overrides ReadOnly Property InterfaceType As System.Type
        Get
            Return GetType(IServiceRequest)
        End Get
    End Property

    <DesignerSerializationVisibility(DesignerSerializationVisibility.Hidden)> _
    Public Overrides ReadOnly Property MethodName As String
        Get
            Return "CreateServiceRequest"
        End Get
    End Property

    <ValidationVisibilityAttribute(ValidationVisibility.Required)> _
    Public Property RequestId As String
```

```
        Get
            Return CType(MyBase.GetValue( _
                         CreateServiceRequest.RequestIdProperty),String)
        End Get
        Set
            MyBase.SetValue(CreateServiceRequest.RequestIdProperty, value)
        End Set
    End Property

    <ValidationVisibilityAttribute(ValidationVisibility.Required)>  _
    Public Property CustomerId As String
        Get
            Return CType(MyBase.GetValue( _
                         CreateServiceRequest.CustomerIdProperty),String)
        End Get
        Set
            MyBase.SetValue(CreateServiceRequest.CustomerIdProperty, value)
        End Set
    End Property

    Public Property RequestDescription As String
        Get
            Return CType(MyBase.GetValue( _
                   CreateServiceRequest.RequestDescriptionProperty),String)
        End Get
        Set
            MyBase.SetValue(CreateServiceRequest.RequestDescriptionProperty, value)
        End Set
    End Property
End Class
```

In this scenario, you define the `InterfaceType` property to return an `IServiceRequest` interface, which is the type of the Local Service Interface you created earlier. In addition, define the name of the `MethodName` to be the name of the method in the `IServiceRequest` interface `CreateServiceRequest`. Next, three properties are defined on the activity—`RequestId`, `CustomerId`, and `Description`. `RequestId` holds the unique identifier for the new Service Request. `CustomerId` holds the unique identifier for the customer, and `Description` holds the reason for the Service Request. After the activity is created, it is available to workflow developers as part of the toolbar components (see Figure 9.4).

The runtime behavior of this activity is implemented using an `ActivityExecutor<T>;implementing>;implementing>` class. This class is defined as the execution attribute, `[ExecutorAttribute(typeof(CreateServiceRequestExecutor))]`, of the `CreateServiceRequest` activity.

FIGURE 9.4   Workflow component toolbar with `CreateServiceRequest` `InvokeMethodActivity`.

```
Public NotInheritable Class CreateServiceRequestExecutor
    Inherits ActivityExecutor

    Protected Overrides Function Execute(ByVal activity As _
        CreateServiceRequest, ByVal provider As System.Workflow. _
        ComponentModel.ActivityExecutionContext) As System.Workflow. _
        ComponentModel.Status
        Dim hostInterface As IServiceRequest = CType(provider.GetService( _
            GetType(IServiceRequest)),IServiceRequest)
        If (hostInterface = Nothing) Then
            Throw New System.InvalidOperationException
        End If
        hostInterface.CreateServiceRequest(activity.RequestId, _
            activity.CustomerId, activity.RequestDescription)
        Return System.Workflow.ComponentModel.Status.Closed
    End Function
End Class
```

This class is responsible for accessing the `IServiceRequest` interface implementation registered with the `WorkflowRuntime`, `CType(provider.GetService(typeof (IServiceRequest)), IServiceRequest)` and invoking the `CreateServiceRequest` method on it, `hostInterface.CreateServiceRequest(activity.RequestId, activity.CustomerId, activity.RequestDescription)`. After the method is executed, it marks the activity status as closed.

EventSinkActivity

A custom activity is created for each event handler that exists in the interface. Each activity represents an event sink that is being listened to by the workflow. This custom activity inherits from `EventSinkActivity`. The `EventSinkActivity` is responsible for registering an event handler during the activity's initialization. Registered handlers are called with a copy of the message when an event is received by a workflow queue. It is the responsibility of the registered event handler delegate to surface the event and the sender of the message via its `Activity` properties.

Custom activities for processing local service events are implemented using two classes, EventSinkActivity and EventSinkActivityExecutor<T>. The EventSinkActivity subclass defines the InterfaceType, MethodName, properties, and attributes required to manipulate a design-time activity definition. The EventSinkActivityExecutor <T> subclass defines the execute behavior of the activity at runtime. This executor is responsible for registering the event handler and processing the event when a message is received by the queue.

Event sink activities could also be used to explicitly initiate the correlation between the workflow and the host application. This behavior opens a communication channel to exchange data between the host and workflow using a predefined unique key (such as CorrelationParameter) when a message is received by the queue. This is accomplished by adding the [CorrelationInitializer] attribute to the event handler definition in the local service interface.

For the service request management scenario, there are two event handler delegates in the interface CreateServiceRequest, thus there are going to be two EventSinkActivities. These activities will be used to hold the design-time information and properties of the activity. The names of the activities are going to be CloseServiceRequest and CancelServiceRequest. Once defined, a visual design representation of the CloseServiceRequest (see Figure 9.5) and CancelServiceRequest (see Figure 9.6) activities will be available inside Visual Studio.

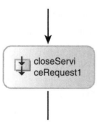

FIGURE 9.5   Design view of newly defined CloseServiceRequest EventSinkActivity.

```
<ToolboxItemAttribute(GetType(ActivityToolboxItem)), _
 Executor(GetType(CloseServiceRequestExecutor))> _
Public Class CloseServiceRequest
    Inherits EventSinkActivity

    Public Shared SenderProperty As DependencyProperty =
System.Workflow.ComponentModel.DependencyProperty.Register( _
    "Sender", GetType(Object), GetType(CloseServiceRequest))

    Public Shared EProperty As DependencyProperty =
System.Workflow.ComponentModel.DependencyProperty.Register("E",
GetType(ServiceEventArgs), GetType(CloseServiceRequest))
```

```
<DesignerSerializationVisibility(DesignerSerializationVisibility.Hidden)>  _
Public Overrides ReadOnly Property InterfaceType As System.Type
    Get
        Return GetType(IServiceRequest)
    End Get
End Property

<DesignerSerializationVisibility(DesignerSerializationVisibility.Hidden)>  _
Public Overrides ReadOnly Property EventName As String
    Get
        Return "CloseService"
    End Get
End Property

<ValidationVisibilityAttribute(ValidationVisibility.Required)>  _
Public Property Sender As Object
    Get
        Return CType(MyBase.GetValue( _
            CloseServiceRequest.SenderProperty),Object)
    End Get
    Set
        MyBase.SetValue(CloseServiceRequest.SenderProperty, value)
    End Set
End Property

<ValidationVisibilityAttribute(ValidationVisibility.Required)>  _
Public Property E As ServiceEventArgs
    Get
        Return CType (MyBase.GetValue( _
            CloseServiceRequest.EProperty),ServiceEventArgs)
    End Get
    Set
        MyBase.SetValue(CloseServiceRequest.EProperty, value)
    End Set
End Property
End Class
```

The InterfaceType property for this activity continues to return an IServiceRequest type, which is the type of the Local Service Interface you created earlier. In addition, you define the EventName property to be the name of the event handler delegate in the IServiceRequest interface CloseService. Next, two properties are defined for Activity— Sender and E. Sender holds the object responsible for submitting the message to the queue and E holds the message that was stored in the queue. These two properties surface the queue message to the workflow code-beside. After the activity is created, it is available to workflow developers as part of the toolbar components (refer to Figure 9.4). The same steps are performed for the CancelServiceRequest EventSinkActivity (see Figure 9.6).

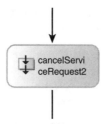

FIGURE 9.6   Design view of newly defined `CancelServiceRequest` `EventSinkActivity`.

The runtime behavior of this activity will be implemented using an
`EventSinkActivityExecutor<T>` class. This class is defined as the execution attribute,
`[Executor(typeof(CloseServiceRequestExecutor))]`, of the `CloseServiceRequest`
activity.

```
Public Class CloseServiceRequestExecutor
    Inherits EventSinkActivityExecutor

    Protected Overrides Sub Initialize(ByVal activity As CloseServiceRequest, _
            ByVal context As ActivityExecutionContext)
        Dim service As IServiceRequest = CType(context.GetService(GetType( _
            IServiceRequest)),IServiceRequest)
        AddHandler service.CloseService, AddressOf Me.OnCloseService
    End Sub

    Private Sub OnCloseService( _
        ByVal sender As Object, ByVal args As ServiceEventArgs)
        Dim context As ActivityExecutionContext = _
            WorkflowServiceContext.ActivityExecutionContext
        Dim activity As CloseServiceRequest = _
            CType(context.Activity,CloseServiceRequest)
        activity.Sender = sender
        activity.E = args
    End Sub
End Class
```

This class is responsible for initializing the event handler delegate to a local handler on
the class, `AddHandler service.CloseService, AddressOf Me.OnCloseService`. The
handler is invoked when the application executing the workflow places a close service
message on the workflow queue. At that point, the local service implementation of
the `CloseService` activity is executed by invoking the `OnCloseService` method. After
the event handler is executed, the activity is marked as completed. The same steps
are performed for the `CancelServiceRequest` `EventSinkActivityExecutor`,
`EventSinkActivityExecutor <CancelServiceRequest>`.

Due to the abstraction layer provided by the workflow runtime and local communication
service over the queues, the event handler being defined is registered against a proxy

provided by the workflow runtime. This abstraction layer supports the loading of work-flow instance state when events are sent to the workflow.

A Workflow Communications Activity (wca.exe) generator will be provided in the future to allow the autogeneration of EventSink and MethodInvoke activities from an interface definition. This tool is expected to ship as part of the SDK/tools. This will save developers the time to develop EventSink and MethodInvoke activities by hand. In addition, two new generic local service activities for sending and receiving uncorrelated data should be provided as out-of-the-box activities.

Service Request Form Application

To put it all together, implement the Service Request Management scenario using a WinForm application, a workflow definition, and your newly created local service activi-ties. The WinForm application will be used to allow customers to manage their own Service Requests, trouble tickets, or cases.

Workflow Development

Implement this scenario by creating a Sequential Workflow Library. The workflow applica-tion will be used to define the Service Request management process and your local service activities will define the data exchange protocol between the WinForm and the workflow. From the workflow toolbar, start by dragging and dropping the CreateServiceRequest activity into the workflow designer (see Figure 9.7). These activities show up in the toolbar when the project containing the activities representing the EventSink and MethodInvoke are built.

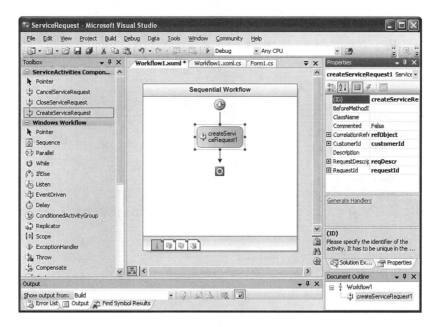

FIGURE 9.7 Workflow designer with CreateServiceRequest activity.

Configure the activity by defining a `CorrelationReference`, `CustomerId`, `RequestId`, and `RequestDescription` (see Figure 9.8). The `CorrelationReference` property holds the correlation information used to establish the communication channel. Each communication channel will use a different variable of this type. Whenever activities want to exchange messages on the same channel, they need to reuse the same `CorrelationReference` object.

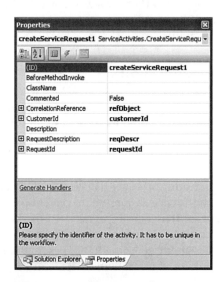

FIGURE 9.8 `CreateServiceRequest` activity properties.

The `CustomerId`, `RequestId`, and `RequestDescription` properties are passed into the workflow as variables. They are used to create a `ServiceTicket` object that is available to the host application via the local service object implementation.

```
Public Class ServiceTicket

    Public Id As String
    Public Description As String
    Public Status As String
    Public AssignedTo As String
    Public CustomerId As String

    Public Sub New(ByVal requestId As String, ByVal customerId As String, _
        ByVal description As String)
      MyBase.New
      CustomerId = customerId
      Id = requestId
      Status = "Opened"
```

```
            Description = description
            AssignedTo = "HongTao"
        End Sub
End Class
```

The implementation of the `IServiceRequest` interface, `ServiceRequestImpl`, contains additional methods that allow the host application to retrieve information set by the workflow instance, `RetrieveServiceRequest`. It provides a `Dictionary` that is used to store multiple `ServiceRequest` objects into a caseList `Dictionary` variable.

```
Public Class ServiceRequestImpl
    Inherits IServiceRequest

    Private caseList As Dictionary

    Public Sub New()
        MyBase.New
        caseList = New Dictionary
    End Sub

    Public Event CloseService As EventHandler

    Public Event CancelService As EventHandler

    Public Sub CreateServiceRequest(ByVal requestId As String, _
            ByVal customerId As String, ByVal description As String)
        'Create Service Request in Workflow and Send it to Host Application.
        Dim ticket As ServiceTicket = New ServiceTicket( _
            requestId, customerId, description)
        caseList.Add(requestId, ticket)
    End Sub

    Public Sub CloseServiceRequest(ByVal args As ServiceEventArgs)
        'Send Activate Order message to Workflow.
        If (Not (Me.CloseService) Is Nothing) Then
            Me.CloseService(Nothing, args)
        End If
    End Sub

    Public Sub CancelServiceRequest(ByVal args As ServiceEventArgs)
        'Send Cancel Order message to Workflow.
        If (Not (Me.CancelService) Is Nothing) Then
            Me.CancelService(Nothing, args)
        End If
    End Sub
```

```
    Public Function RetrieveServiceRequest(ByVal requestId As String) _
        As ServiceTicket
        Return CType(caseList(requestId),ServiceTicket)
    End Function
End Class
```

ServiceRequestImpl also provides two helper methods, CloseServiceRequest and
CancelServiceRequest, that allow the host to submit events to the workflow instance.
These two methods invoke their respective event handlers. The implementation class can
be located in the host application or the assembly with the interface definition.

Back in the workflow, a Conditioned Activity Group (CAG) is used to host the two
EventSink activities, CloseServiceRequest and CancelServiceRequest (see Figure 9.9).
The CAG allows you to listen for both events but terminate the listen when one of the
two events is received. After one event is received, the Until condition on the CAG is set
to true; this will mark all the activities inside of it as completed.

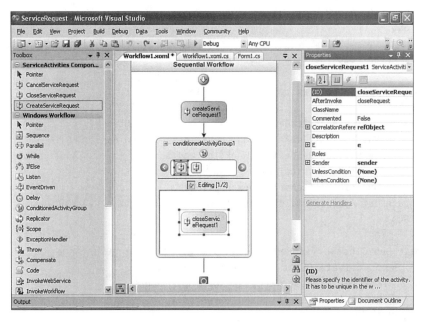

FIGURE 9.9   Workflow Designer with CloseServiceRequest and CancelServiceRequest
inside ConditionedActivityGroup.

The Correlation Reference property for the CloseServiceRequest and
CancelServiceRequest activities point to the same variable used in the
CreateServiceRequest activity. This implies that all local service activities will be
exchanging messages on the same communication channel. Similarly, the E and Sender
properties on the CloseServiceRequest and CancelServiceRequest activities are configured to point to the same variables. The E variable defined on the code-beside will be of
type ServiceEventArgs, which is a subclass of WorkflowMessageEventArgs.

An `AfterInvoke` property was defined on the `CloseServiceRequest` and `CancelServiceRequest`. These method handlers will be used to confirm the receiving of the event by the workflow instance and will set the CAG `Until` expression to true:

```
Public Sub closeRequest(ByVal sender As Object, ByVal e As EventArgs)
       MessageBox.Show("Service Request has been closed")
       eventReceived = true
End Sub

Public Sub cancelRequest(ByVal sender As Object, ByVal e As EventArgs)
       MessageBox.Show("Service Request has been cancelled")
       eventReceived = true
End Sub
```

Setting the `eventReceived` variable to true causes the CAG `Until` expression to evaluate to true and completes the execution of the CAG. Completing the CAG marks all pending child activities as completed. This allows only one `EventSink` activity to receive a message, either Cancel or Close. The following code shows the CAG's condition handler:

```
Public Function ServiceRequestEventReceived(ByVal sender As Object, _
       ByVal e As EventArgs) As Boolean
        'eventReceived was initialized to false.
        Return eventReceived
End Function
```

The scenario modeled in this workflow, unfortunately, doesn't justify the added correlation complexity. However, in real-world scenarios most requests like approvals, help desk request, authorizations, and others come in groups and not a single reply. Imagine this scenario being modified to allow the user to submit multiple help desk requests simultaneously. This change would require the introduction of correlation values.

WinForm Development
The WinForm application used to submit Service Requests starts the workflow by passing a description and a customer identification name as variables to the workflow. The constructor of the WinForm application is responsible for registering the `Local` object with the workflow runtime.

```
Public Class Form1
    Inherits Form

    Private workflowRuntime As WorkflowRuntime

    Private sRequest As ServiceRequestImpl

    Private workflowInstanceId As Guid

    Private requestId As String
```

```
    Private workflowType As Type

    Public Sub New()
        MyBase.New
        InitializeComponent
        'Initialize Workflow Environment
        workflowRuntime = New WorkflowRuntime
        workflowType = GetType(Workflow1)
        sRequest = New ServiceRequestImpl
        workflowRuntime.AddService(sRequest)
        workflowRuntime.StartRuntime
    End Sub
End Class
```

The application starts the workflow when the customer enters the his or her customer ID and problem description into the application and clicks the Submit Request button. The button handler associated with this object is responsible for packaging the customer ID and problem description as parameters to the workflow and starting the workflow:

```
Private Sub button1_Click(ByVal sender As Object, ByVal e As EventArgs)
        Try
            'Retrieve Workflow Parameters
            Dim customerId As String = textBox1.Text
            Dim description As String = textBox2.Text
            requestId = Guid.NewGuid.ToString
            Dim parameters As Dictionary = New Dictionary
            parameters.Add("CustomerAccountNumber", customerId)
            parameters.Add("ProblemDescription", description)
            parameters.Add("ServiceRequestId", requestId)
            'Start workflow and pass parameters
            workflowInstanceId = Guid.NewGuid
            workflowRuntime.StartWorkflow(workflowType, workflowInstanceId, _
                parameters)
        Catch exception As Exception
            Console.WriteLine(exception.Message)
        End Try
End Sub
```

The workflow receives the customer identification and problem description as variables, creates a ServiceTicket, and stores it in the caseList Dictionary. After the ServiceTicket is created, the WinForm application is able to retrieve the status of the ServiceRequest (see Figure 9.10).

Retrieving the status allows the WinForm application to Close or Cancel the ServiceRequest using the Request ID as its correlation value. The following code shows the code-beside used to process the Close and Cancel workflow events:

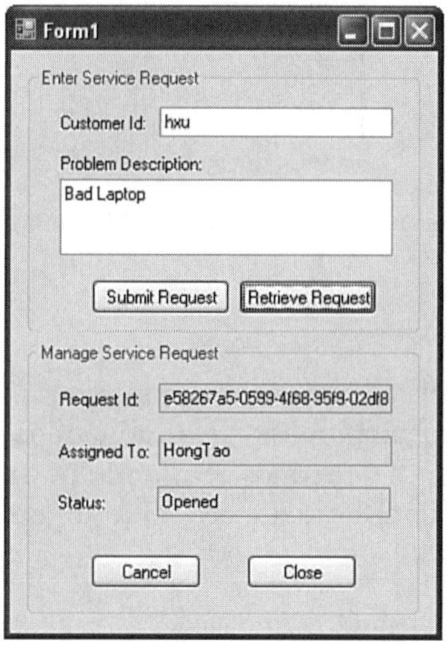

FIGURE 9.10   Service Request WinForm application described in scenario.

```vb
Private Sub Cancel_Click(ByVal sender As Object, ByVal e As EventArgs)
    sRequest.CancelServiceRequest(New ServiceEventArgs( _
    workflowInstanceId, requestId))
End Sub

Private Sub Close_Click(ByVal sender As Object, ByVal e As EventArgs)
    sRequest.CloseServiceRequest(New ServiceEventArgs( _
    workflowInstanceId, requestId))
End Sub
```

After the workflow processes the `Close` or `Cancel` event, it will go to its code-beside to set the `Until` condition on the CAG and display the `MessageBox` acknowledging the event (see Figure 9.11 and Figure 9.12). Only one of these two events will be executed per workflow instance.

FIGURE 9.11   Workflow message confirming `ServiceRequest` closing.

FIGURE 9.12   Workflow message confirming `ServiceRequest` cancellation.

Summary

Local services provide a flexible communication mechanism that allows data to be exchanged without payload restrictions or event limitations. They require an interface definition, implementation of the interface, and workflow runtime registration. They should be viewed as a more sophisticated mechanism for exchanging data that require knowledge of message protocols.

CHAPTER **10**

State Machine Workflow

The Business Process Landscape

The business process landscape has undergone a remarkable change in the last decade. In the 1990s business process reengineering was merely a buzzword used for automation of repeatable tasks. Any efficiency that was to be gained by automating repeatable tasks was gained. Today business users demand much more than automation for a business task; they demand visibility into the process and effective controls such that they can direct the process depending on their changing needs.

Today's business processes contain complex interactions between human beings and automated programs. Human participants need to control the automated components and be able to observe what is happening with them. With increasing interconnections between businesses, the business process spans across organizational and geographical boundaries. The participants in these processes need to know the context in which they are operating. The participants in the process need to understand what has happened so far and what will be the effect of their actions.

Another important aspect of today's business process is that the processes need to be very agile in responding to the changing demands of the customers. The business process needs to be flexible enough to accommodate situations that might be out of the ordinary. Thus a defined business process merely becomes a template of one set of possible actions. There may be other actions that come up when the business process is running. The business process must be amenable to change so that these situations can be handled, tracked, and reported on.

State Machine Workflows: A New Way of Creating Business Applications

In most cases, business processes today are embedded in business applications. Currently such business applications are large monolithic blocks and are difficult to change. In contrast, the demands of the business require the creation of applications that can react to the changing needs of the business, competition, and other forces. What businesses need is for the business applications to be flexible to keep up with the changing demands of the business. Today the application comes in the way of change and the businesses have to adapt to the application rather than the application adapting to the business needs.

The varying demands of the business mean that different parts of the business application evolve at different speeds. The core entities that take part in the business application might evolve slowly but the business process that is embedded in the business application might evolve much more rapidly. Every time a change is needed there are too many resources spent on versioning and deploying the application as a whole.

For example, you might have a CRM application that services requests from existing customers. You can store information about the customer as well as the service requests in the customer and service request entities. The way to service the request is the process that is embedded within the business application. Now you can start a new Gold Customer service program to service your most valued customers. With the way business applications are written, you would need to version the entire CRM application to provide this new service. Ideally, you should be able to provide this service by just adding new features to the process embedded within the application. The customer and service request entities by and large remain the same but the process needs to change to support the gold customers.

Another important factor to consider while creating a model for flexible business processes is that the number of exceptions can be very large. At almost every step of the process there can be exceptions.

These requirements quickly turn a process with only a handful of actions into a complex set of possible flows. Coding these flows as simple branching sequences becomes tedious because from any given process state there are many things that can happen next. In many cases the same action can occur at any point in the process (such as resend, handle exception, cancel) so checks for each one of these actions would need to be done at every step. A flowchart that coded all possible paths would be very complex even if the "main path" contained only a few steps. The number of possible paths is much greater than the number of unique actions. This leads one to want to describe the process not in terms of the paths through the process but in terms of the actions themselves.

The concept of business events and the actions in response to them provides a rich metaphor for describing business processes. Business analysts are familiar with this concept and tend to describe their processes in this manner. If a design environment is provided to them with this metaphor then they can be much more effective. They would need to describe the business events and the actions they would take in response to those events. The actions themselves can be prepackaged activities or code or can even be the hook for the developer to plug in the required functionality.

State machines provide a very suitable design pattern for the creation processes using business events and actions. State machines are familiar design patterns that have been in use for long time. It is a very well understood design pattern. The states in a state machine correspond to the states in a business process. If you consider the transitions in a state machine, they have two components to it: the event that causes the state machine to respond and the action that is performed as a result to change the state from the current state to the next.

The way the state machine is described can help to solve a lot of interesting problems. For instance, static analysis can be done on the state machines, which can help predict the possible next states that can be transitioned to. Using the state machine design pattern, a lot of interesting patterns can be implemented. For example, the skip and rework patterns can be implemented using a state machine. In case of the skip pattern the idea is to skip a state and move on to the next one. This can be achieved by finding out the definition of the target state and then making the appropriate changes to the shared context. The rework pattern is a variation on the skip pattern.

State machines are also a useful design pattern because they provide a very natural way to observe a business process. The current state of the state machine is the current state of the process. One can also get a quick understanding of the process by simply looking at the state machine of the process. This is in contrast to a sequential design of a business process. It is very hard to figure out what is happening in the business process by simply looking at a visual representation of the sequential process. Also, while a sequential process is running, the only information one can get is the step at which the process is. The user then has to extrapolate the state of the process from that information.

In many cases it becomes simply too hard to create a sequential design of a process. This is most notable in entity lifecycle kinds of processes like document lifecycle processes or purchase order lifecycles. These entity lifecycles can contain arbitrary transitions from one state to another. Modeling these transitions in a sequential workflow can get to be a challenging task. The only control flow constructs available in the sequential design for making transitions are the `while` loop and the `If` statements. Trying to construct the arbitrary jumps from one state to another using these two constructs can make the business process completely unreadable and unmanageable.

Consider the example of a document lifecycle and compare the implementations in a sequential workflow design and state machine design. As shown in Figure 10.1, a simple purchase order process can be mapped as a state machine.

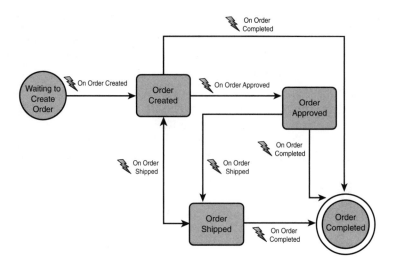

FIGURE 10.1 Document lifecycle implemented as a state machine.

In contrast, Figure 10.2 shows the equivalent purchase order process when implemented as a sequential flow.

You can see the ease with which one can create the state machine implementation of the process. The sequential design of the PO process is possible but is hard to follow. First the concept of state is completely lost. It has to be managed by the workflow author. The model is hard to query and the current state of the process has to be deciphered based on user variables. Also, if you examine closely the model also caters to any event in any state and whether an event is valid for a state has to be determined by the workflow author by putting conditional logic inside the workflow. Of course, it should be recognized that there may be multiple other ways of modeling the PO process using a sequential workflow, which may alleviate some of the problems, but the fact remains that it is inherently hard to model event-driven processes in a sequential workflow.

Having said this, it must be noted that not all workflow problems can be solved better by state machines rather than sequential workflows. There is a class of problems for which state machine workflows are better suited and a class of problems for which the sequential workflows are better suited. Towards the end of this chapter we will discuss in detail when to use state machine workflows and when to use sequential workflows.

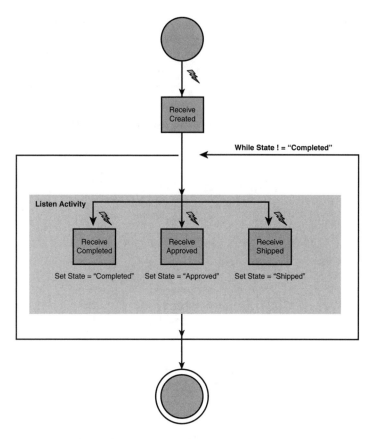

FIGURE 10.2   Document lifecycle implemented as a sequential process.

Structure of the State Machine Workflows

State machine as a construct is nothing new. It has been in use since the advent of computing. What you need to look at is how the state machine has been implemented using the metaphor of activities in Windows Workflow Foundation.

As mentioned in previous chapters, the state machine workflow is a root activity just like the sequential workflow root activity. The state machine workflow root activity is made up of a set of state activities. Each state activity represents a state in the state machine. Each state activity can contain an optional state initialization activity and one or more event-driven activities. Each event-driven activity can handle one event. In response to the event handled in the event-driven activity, some processing can be done and a transition can be made to another state. We will shortly take a look at how transitions are made using the Set State activity.

10

Later on in this chapter you will look at the concept of reusable event-driven activities. To reuse event-driven activities across states, the states can be grouped together and be contained within another state activity. That state activity can also contain the event handlers that are common to all the states that are contained within it. We will go over this concept in more detail later. Suffice it to say at this point that recursive composition of states is allowed.

Figure 10.3 illustrates the hierarchy of activities that can be contained within the state machine workflow.

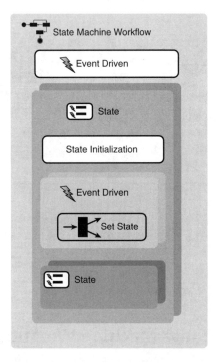

FIGURE 10.3   Hierarchy of activities in a state machine workflow.

A Simple State Machine Workflow

At this point you are probably eager to start creating your own state machine workflows. There are a lot of concepts that we need to cover before you can start implementing your business processes as a state machine. But just to get ourselves acquainted with state machine, let's create a very simple state machine.

Create a state machine with three states in it, State 1, State 2, and State 3. State 3 will be a completed state and hence will not contain any other activity. The state machine will transition from State 1 to State 2 and then from State 2 to State 3.

Put one event handler each in State 1 and State 2 (see Figure 10.4). As you have seen in earlier chapters, the event-driven activity must contain an input activity as its first activity or it can contain a delay activity as its first activity. The significance of using delays is to provide temporal signals to a state machine. In this case, use delays with a time span of five seconds. Thus after you create an instance of this state machine, the delay in State 1 will get a signal after five seconds. It will transition to State 2. After five seconds the delay activity in State 2 will get a signal. A transition will be made to State 3. State 3 is a completed state for the state machine and at this point the state machine will stop executing.

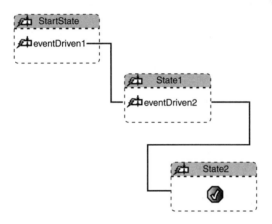

FIGURE 10.4   A simple state machine sample.

Listing 10.1 shows how this state machine can be created in code. The code listing also contains a simple console application that acts as a host for the workflow.

LISTING 10.1   StateMachineSample.cs

```
Namespace StateMachineSampleNameSpace
    Imports System
    Imports System.ComponentModel
    Imports System.ComponentModel.Design
    Imports System.Collections
    Imports System.Drawing
    Imports System.Workflow.ComponentModel
    Imports System.Workflow.ComponentModel.Design
    Imports System.Workflow.Runtime
    Imports System.Workflow.Activities
    Imports System.Workflow.Activities.Rules


    Public NotInheritable Class StateMachineSample
        Inherits StateMachineWorkflow
```

LISTING 10.1 Continued

```vbnet
    Private StartState As State

    Private eventDriven1 As EventDriven

    Private delay1 As Delay

    Private setState1 As SetState

    Private state1 As State

    Private eventDriven2 As EventDriven

    Private delay2 As Delay

    Private setState2 As SetState

    Private code1 As Code

    Private code2 As Code

    Private state2 As State

    Public delay1Value As TimeSpan = TimeSpan.Parse("0.00:00:02")

    Public delay2Value As TimeSpan = TimeSpan.Parse("0.00:00:02")

    Public Sub New()
        MyBase.New
        InitializeComponent
    End Sub

    Private Sub InitializeComponent()
        Dim activitybind1 As System.Workflow.ComponentModel.ActivityBind = _
            New System.Workflow.ComponentModel.ActivityBind
        Dim activitybind2 As System.Workflow.ComponentModel.ActivityBind = _
            New System.Workflow.ComponentModel.ActivityBind
        Dim activitybind3 As System.Workflow.ComponentModel.ActivityBind = _
            New System.Workflow.ComponentModel.ActivityBind
        Dim activitybind4 As System.Workflow.ComponentModel.ActivityBind = _
            New System.Workflow.ComponentModel.ActivityBind
        Me.StartState = New System.Workflow.Activities.State
        Me.state1 = New System.Workflow.Activities.State
        Me.state2 = New System.Workflow.Activities.State
        Me.eventDriven1 = New System.Workflow.Activities.EventDriven
```

LISTING 10.1 Continued

```
Me.eventDriven2 = New System.Workflow.Activities.EventDriven
Me.delay1 = New System.Workflow.Activities.Delay
Me.code1 = New System.Workflow.Activities.Code
Me.setState1 = New System.Workflow.Activities.SetState
Me.delay2 = New System.Workflow.Activities.Delay
Me.code2 = New System.Workflow.Activities.Code
Me.setState2 = New System.Workflow.Activities.SetState
'
' StartState
'
Me.StartState.Activities.Add(Me.eventDriven1)
Me.StartState.ID = "StartState"
'
' state1
'
Me.state1.Activities.Add(Me.eventDriven2)
Me.state1.ID = "state1"
'
' state2
'
Me.state2.ID = "state2"
'
' eventDriven1
'
Me.eventDriven1.Activities.Add(Me.delay1)
Me.eventDriven1.Activities.Add(Me.code1)
Me.eventDriven1.Activities.Add(Me.setState1)
Me.eventDriven1.ID = "eventDriven1"
'
' eventDriven2
'
Me.eventDriven2.Activities.Add(Me.delay2)
Me.eventDriven2.Activities.Add(Me.code2)
Me.eventDriven2.Activities.Add(Me.setState2)
Me.eventDriven2.ID = "eventDriven2"
'
' delay1
'
Me.delay1.ID = "delay1"
activitybind1.ID = "/Workflow"
activitybind1.Path = "delay1Value"
Me.delay1.SetValue(System.Workflow.Activities.Delay. _
    TimeoutDurationProperty, activitybind1)
```

10

LISTING 10.1   Continued

```
        activitybind2.ID = "/Workflow"
        activitybind2.Path = "TestCodeHandler"
        '
        ' code1
        '
        Me.code1.ID = "code1"
        Me.code1.AddHandler( _
          System.Workflow.Activities.Code.ExecuteCodeEvent, activitybind2)
        '
        ' setState1
        '
        Me.setState1.ID = "setState1"
        Me.setState1.TargetState = "state1"
        '
        ' delay2
        '
        Me.delay2.ID = "delay2"
        activitybind3.ID = "/Workflow"
        activitybind3.Path = "delay2Value"
        Me.delay2.SetValue( _
          System.Workflow.Activities.Delay.TimeoutDurationProperty, _
          activitybind3)
        activitybind4.ID = "/Workflow"
        activitybind4.Path = "Code2Handler"
        '
        ' code2
        '
        Me.code2.ID = "code2"
        Me.code2.AddHandler( _
          System.Workflow.Activities.Code.ExecuteCodeEvent,activitybind4)
        '
        ' setState2
        '
        Me.setState2.ID = "setState2"
        Me.setState2.TargetState = "state2"
        '
        ' StateMachineSample
        '
        Me.Activities.Add(Me.StartState)
        Me.Activities.Add(Me.state1)
        Me.Activities.Add(Me.state2)
        Me.CompletedState = "state2"
        Me.DynamicUpdateCondition = Nothing
        Me.InitialState = "StartState"
    End Sub
```

LISTING 10.1   Continued

```
        Public Sub TestCodeHandler(ByVal sender As Object, ByVal e As EventArgs)
            Console.WriteLine("In Start State. Transitioning to State 1")
        End Sub

        Public Sub Code2Handler(ByVal sender As Object, ByVal e As EventArgs)
            Console.WriteLine("In State 1. Transitioning to State 2")
        End Sub
    End Class
End Namespace
```

The class in Listing 10.2 is a console application that will initiate the simple state machine sample workflow.

LISTING 10.2   Program.cs

```
Namespace StateMachineSampleNameSpace
    Imports System
    Imports System.Threading
    Imports System.ComponentModel
    Imports System.Workflow.ComponentModel
    Imports System.Workflow.Runtime
    Imports System.Workflow.Activities


    Class Host

        Private Shared waitHandle As AutoResetEvent = New AutoResetEvent(false)

        Private Shared Sub Main(ByVal args() As String)
            Dim wr As WorkflowRuntime = New WorkflowRuntime
            wr.StartRuntime
            Try
                wr.WorkflowCompleted = (wr.WorkflowCompleted _
                    + OnWorkflowCompletion)
                wr.StartWorkflow(GetType(StateMachineSample))
                waitHandle.WaitOne
                Console.WriteLine("Done Running The workflow. Press Any _
                    Key To Exit...")
                Console.ReadLine
            Finally
                wr.StopRuntime
            End Try
        End Sub
```

10

LISTING 10.2   Continued

```
        Private Shared Sub OnWorkflowCompletion(ByVal sender As Object, _
            ByVal instance As WorkflowCompletedEventArgs)
                waitHandle.Set
        End Sub
    End Class
End Namespace
```

The state machine that you created is very simplistic. The idea was to show how state machines can be built using Windows Workflow Foundation.

As you can see from the code, the state machine workflows can be created in the same way as the sequential workflows. The authoring model is exactly the same. What differs is the set of activities that make up the state machine workflow.

The state machine example shown previously is a code-based workflow sample. You can try to visualize this state machine in the designer in Visual Studio. Simply open a state machine console application project and delete the workflow that is added in it. Now add a code-only state machine workflow. Copy all the code from the previous workflow listing in it. You can now see the workflow in the designer.

The State Machine Workflow Root Activity

Now that you have created your first state machine workflow, let's look at the different activities that make up the state machine workflow in detail. Start with the state machine workflow root activity. The state machine workflow root activity is one of the two root activities that are available out of the box; the other is the sequential workflow root activity.

The state machine root activity has all the same characteristics as that of a root activity. In addition, it has properties that are required for the execution of the state machine. Most notably, the state machine workflow root activity has two properties that are important:

- The initialstate
- The completedstate

The initialstate of the state machine, as the name suggests, is the state in which the state machine will be when an instance of the state machine is created. The initialstate property is mandatory and must be provided when a state machine workflow is created. The initialstate of the state machine is like any other state activity that is contained within the state machine. The initialstate activity can be a direct child of the state machine workflow root activity, or it can be contained within another state activity. A state machine workflow can have only one initialstate.

The `completedstate` of the state machine is a state activity that is designated as the end state of the state machine. When a transition is made to the `completedstate`, the workflow execution is completed. The `completedstate` is not mandatory. This means that you can have a state machine workflow that does not complete. This does not mean that the state machine workflow is always active in memory. It may get dehydrated as it waits for an event.

In the majority of cases you would create a state machine process that has a `completedstate` because most business processes have a definite end. But in some cases there may be a need to create processes that live as long as the application in which they live is active. If the application shuts down, the process also shuts down. For example, consider a purchase order application. There may be a shipping process that is created as a state machine and it gets activated once the purchase order application is started. The shipping process takes requests from purchase order processes and as purchase orders are fulfilled they are queued up for shipping. The shipping subprocess here does not have a definite end. It is alive as long as the purchase order application is alive. It keeps waiting for shipping requests from other purchase order processes. It processes the shipping request and then waits. It may get shut down when the purchase order application is shut down.

Not having a `completedstate` is a definite exception and not the norm. While creating a state machine workflow, care must be taken to ensure that there is a `completedstate` if the process you are modeling has a logical end. If not, the workflow compiler will not point out a validation error and the process may never complete and it would be hard to figure out what has gone wrong.

The state machine workflow root activity is a composite activity. It can contain other activities in it. The activities that can be contained are

- The state activity
- The event-driven activity

The fact that state activities can be contained may be obvious. I have also mentioned that the state activities can be recursively composed, thus a state could contain other states. What may be a little puzzling is the fact that the root state machine activity can contain event-driven activities also. The reason is that the root activity itself acts like a state. When the root state machine activity contains an event handler the set of allowable events in any state would be the set of events handled within the state and the containing state up to and including the root activity itself.

The State Activity

The state activity is the most important activity within the state machine. It represents a state in the state machine. To be in a state in the state machine means to be executing a particular state activity. Transitions in the state machine are made from one state activity to another state activity. A state activity can contain event-driven activities. Each event-driven activity can handle one event, which can be received by virtue of being in that state. Figure 10.5 shows the structure of a state activity and the activities that can be contained within it.

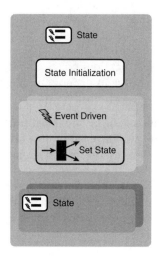

FIGURE 10.5   Structure of the state activity.

A state in the state machine represents a logical state of the process. When creating a state machine for your business process, you must first think of the different logical states the process might be in. Then create a state activity for each logical state. A good rule of thumb to use is to first find out the different milestones in the process and then create one state per milestone. You must also keep in mind that a user or participant in the business process will want to know where the process is currently. The state represents a natural answer to this query. For example, in a document life cycle process, the different states of the process are document created, document approved, document published, and so on. Each one of them is also a logical milestone for the process and something a business user would expect to get back for the query "Where is the process currently?" While designing your state machine, you must keep the user query requirements also in mind. It will make the job of building a query model for your process simpler.

As explained in the section on state machine root activities, there are two activities in the state machine; one is designated as the `initialstate` and other is designated as the `completedstate`.

The `initialstate` activity is like any other state activity and can contain event-driven activities.

When a transition is made to the `completedstate`, the state machine workflow instance execution is completed. The state machine workflow instance is shut down. So as you can guess, there is no need to have any activities within the `completedstate`. Due to this if a state activity is designated as a `completedstate`, it must be empty.

In some cases, as soon as a state transition is made certain initialization logic must be run. As an example, create a state machine workflow for implementing page navigation in a UI system for buying a phone. Create a very simple navigation as shown in Figure 10.6. Assume that there is a UI program that simply does the job of displaying the page that the state machine workflow tells it to display. Figure 10.6 shows the state machine work-flow for the page navigation for a UI system to buy a phone.

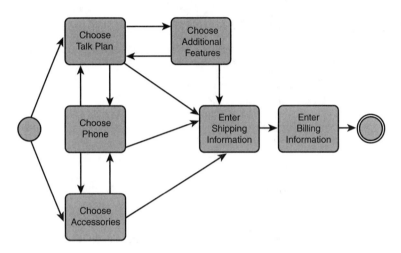

FIGURE 10.6   An example of a very simple navigation.

Each page can correspond to a state in the state machine. Every button on the page will correspond to an event that will be handled by an event-driven activity within that state. Now consider the navigation from the Choose Talk Plan to the Choose Phone form. Say that based on different payment plans the price of the phones varies. So when the user clicks on the Payment Plan Chosen button the event corresponding to that action will be handled in the Choose Talk Plan state of the state machine. A transition will be made to the Choose Phone state and the Choose Phone state is now executing. Now the State machine has to tell the UI program about the next page and also provide the data (the prices of the phones based on the payment plan) to the UI program. In order to pass this information a state initialization activity can be placed inside the Choose Phone state. The State initialization activity is executed by default as soon as the state activity starts executing. You can also see that in the absence of the state initialization activity you would not have a nice way of sending the information to the UI program. Agreed, you could have used the event handler in the Choose Talk Plan to send the information, but then you would not have been able to create encapsulation of one state to one page. Moreover, within the event handler you would have to have complex condition logic to send different data based on different transitions to be made. With the state initialization activity you can create a very clean design.

Figure 10.7 shows the implementation of the page navigation workflow.

The state initialization activity can be contained within any state except the state marked as `completedstate`.

As mentioned earlier the state activity can be recursively composed. Thus a state activity can contain other state activities. This topic is covered in more detail in the section "Recursive Composition of State Activities" later in this chapter.

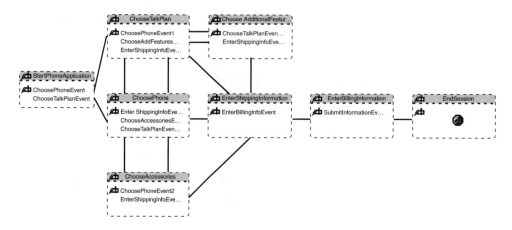

FIGURE 10.7   Page navigation workflow.

The Event-Driven Activity in a State Machine Workflow

The event-driven activity is used in the state machine workflow to handle an event. The event-driven activity can be contained within a state activity or can be contained directly within the root state machine workflow activity.

The structure of the event-driven activity is the same as how the event-driven activity would be used in the sequential workflow. There are some additional restrictions put when the event-driven activity is used in the state machine.

Let us start by summarizing how the event-driven activity is used. The event-driven activity is a composite activity in which the first activity must be an activity of type IEventActivity. The IEventActivity interface is implemented by those activities that are going to handle events. The Object connection service activities are a set of activities that handle incoming events. The Delay activity is also any activity that handles the timeout event. Let us refer to the activity that implements the IEventActivity interface as *event handling activity*. Figure 10.8 shows the typical structure of an event-driven activity when used inside a state activity.

When the event-driven activity is used in the state machine the first event handling activity is the only event-handling activity allowed within the event-driven activity. Note that this is a little different than how the event-driven activity is used in the sequential workflow. In a sequential workflow any subsequent activity can also be an event-handling activity. The reason why the state machine does not allow any subsequent activity to be an event handling activity is that the state machine workflow expects the execution of the event-driven activity to be non-blocking in nature. It is desirable that the execution of the event-driven activities is in a nonblocking manner. The ideal behavior of the state machine is to handle an event, execute the event handler, perform some state transition if required, and then wait for the next event. This modeling pattern provides ease of execution and implementation of the state machine. If events are allowed to be received while the event-driven activity is being processed then the event handler would have to block and wait for the event to arrive. This wait may not be good because the conditions that are valid for the state machine to be in that particular state may become invalid while waiting.

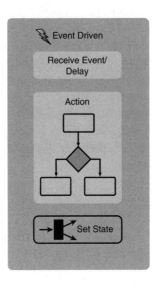

FIGURE 10.8   Event-driven activity used inside a state machine.

For example, if you design an event-driven activity that sends the PO for approval and then blocks till the approval is not received, the whole state machine will be blocked till the approval is received. Now say that in the meanwhile the PO is changed. Because the state machine is blocked the change cannot be handled. This is not desirable because the change may potentially invalidate the approval and you would want the approver to know it before he goes through the process of approving a PO that is no longer valid.

If any non-blocking activity needs to be performed rather than performing it inline within the event-driven activity, a better design pattern is to invoke an instance of another state machine workflow that can handle the blocking event. After the event is received the invoked instance can finish and send a message back to the workflow that invoked it. The workflow that invoked another instance is free to receive any other events while the invoked workflow is waiting for the blocking event. This, of course, requires asynchronous communication between instances, which is a little harder. Another pattern would be to split the work into two different event handlers.

As such, not all blocking behaviors can be detected. For example, if the author has a Code activity that blocks by making calls to some external entity, it cannot be detected. By not allowing certain activities, you are minimizing the chances of blocking behavior. But if the workflow author does want to block and that is the desired behavior then she is free to do so.

Apart form the restriction of not being able to have multiple event-handling activities in the event handler, the event-driven activity within the state machine cannot contain the

`Listen` activity. The reason again is simple. The `Listen` activity contains multiple event-handling activities within it and hence violates the rule for having only one event-handling activity.

There are situations where it is useful to have a `Delay` activity as the first activity in the event handler. For example, when a document is sent for review by the author the workflow might change its state to `Waiting for Review` state. In this state there may be two event handlers, one that receives the approval message from the reviewer and the other event handler that contains a delay that will fire after a set time interval. This way the author can handle a case where the reviewer has not sent a reply in a fixed amount of time.

Transitions from One State to Another— The `Set State` Activity

Transitions are a very important aspect of a state machine. *Transitions* provide the ability to change the state of the state machine based on an external stimulus. The state machine workflow provides a `Set State` activity that can be used to make the transition from one state to another. The `Set State` activity can be placed inside the event handlers that are used to handle an event, as is illustrated in Figure 10.3.

The `Set State` activity provides a property called `Target State`. In order to make a transition whenever the `Set State` activity executes, the execution of the state activity in which the `Set State` activity is contained is stopped. The state activity that is provided in the `Target State` property starts executing.

The `Set State` activity is contained within an event handler, the idea being that in a given state an event is handled by an event handler. In response to the event, some work is done and then a transition is made to the target state. For example, in a document life cycle workflow, the workflow might be in `Document Waiting for Review` state. When the manager completes the review, an event called `ReviewComplete` is received by an event handler, which is contained within the `Document Waiting for Review` state. Now at this point there may be some work to be done, like copying the review comments to variables. After that work is done, the state of the process can now move to `Document Review Complete`. In order to make this transition happen, a `Set State` activity is put inside the event handler. Figure 10.9 illustrates the event handler and the `Set State` activity.

As such, the transition to a target state is the last work that needs to be done as part of handling an event in a state. For this reason the `Set State` activity has to be the last executing activity within the event handler. There can be more than one `Set State` activity within an event-driven activity, but then all of them have to be the last ones to execute in the event-driven activity. For example, in a document lifecycle workflow you might have an event-driven activity that handles the event `Document Reviewed`. As part of the event payload, the reviewer might include a decision whether the document is approved for publishing or rejected and wants some changes. This means that the transition can be either to the document published state or to the document edited state. To do this, you would need to put two `Set State` activities in the event driven, each in one branch of the If activity. Figure 10.9 illustrates how two Set State activities can be put in the same event-driven activity.

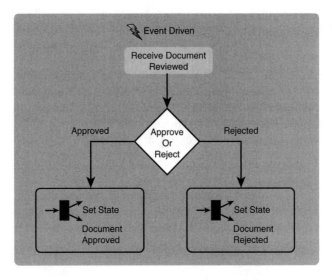

FIGURE 10.9   The Event Handler activity and the Set State activity.

The execution of the Set State activity causes a chain of events to happen. First, the execution of the event-driven activity in which the Set State activity is contained is completed. Next, the execution of the state activity in which the event-driven activity is contained is completed. The root activity then will schedule the execution of the state activity, which is the target of the transition. After the execution of the target state starts, the transition is completed. At this point the state machine is ready to receive events that are contained within the target state that is now executing.

Recursive Composition of State Activities

In certain situations, the same event has to be handled in multiple states. The choice is to repeat the same event handler in multiple states or to somehow define the event handler only once and then reuse it in all the states where the same event occurs.

Recursive composition of states allows the reuse of event handlers. You can think of it as a way of grouping the states for the purpose of sharing an event.

As an example, consider a purchase order process that includes the following states:

- Waiting to create order
- Order Created
- Order Changed
- Order Approved

10

- Order Shipped

- Order Completed

As shown in Figure 10.10, a set of events can be handled in each of the states. The Purchase Order Changed event can be handled in the Order Created state and Order Approved state. In each case, the state machine needs to be put in the Order Changed state. You have two choices. You can put the same event handler in both the states where the Purchase Order Changed event can happen. Alternatively, you can create a state called PO Processing and then add all the concerned states in it. You can now place the event handler in that state. Figure 10.10 shows the PO Processing state and the event-driven activity for the Purchase Order Changed event, which is handled in the PO Processing state.

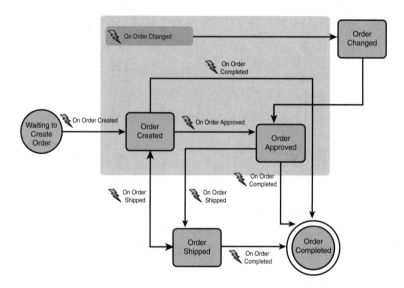

FIGURE 10.10   Recursive composition of states.

The effect is that at runtime the state that is active can handle all the events handled by event handlers within it and in addition, all the events handled by the enclosing state up to and including the root activity itself can be handled.

You might think that just to reuse an event-driven activity, the recursive composition of states seems to be overkill. Actually, the recursive composition of states allows some very powerful patterns for business exception handling. As such, when you create a state machine you can think of the events that can be handled when the state machine is in a particular state. But in most human workflow situations, out-of-band events happen all the time. For example, in the PO process illustrated before, there can be many more out-of-band events like PO Canceled or PO Re-Opened that can happen. The recursive composition pattern allows a nice way to handle such out-of-sync events. Another way to think about the recursive composition and exception handling is that when a state machine is in a particular state it can handle a certain set of events. If an event happens that cannot be handled in that state, it is a business exception. The way then to handle the business exception is to handle the event in the enclosing state or at the root state machine workflow level. Remember that the state machine workflow root activity also behaves like a state.

States can be nested to any levels. At each level of nesting you can add states or event-driven activities or other states. The one thing, though, that is not possible with state composition is that a single state activity cannot be in two states at the same time. For example, if a state activity State 1 in your state machine shares an event E1 with state State 2 and another event E2 with another state State 3, there is no way to create two states, State 11, in which you have State 1 and State 2, and another state, State 22 in which you have State 1 and State 3. Figure 10.11 shows the composition of states that is not possible.

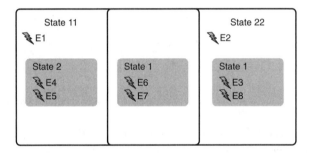

FIGURE 10.11   A state cannot be recursively contained within two states at the same time.

Transitions in the state machine can only be made to a state that does not contain other states. There is no transition possible to a state that contains other states. Of course, the event handler contained within such a state can transition to another state.

Dynamic Update in State Machine Workflows

You will learn about dynamic update in much more detail in Chapter 12, "Dynamic Update of Workflow." This chapter covers the need for dynamic update and the patterns for dynamic update in state machine workflows.

Dynamic update is the ability to change the workflow logic while the workflow is running. There are several types of dynamic updates that can be made to a workflow and particularly to a state machine workflow. A new state can be added to the state machine or a new event handler can be added to an existing state to handle a new event. In some cases, the way the transitions are done in the state machine can be changed by changing the Target State property of the Set State activities.

Consider the purchase order process that you saw in the last section. Now consider a case where a particular PO has very high cost items in it and the creator of the PO thinks that in addition to the normal approval from the manager, he needs to get an approval from the vice president of the group. To do that, the PO author must be able to add a new state to the workflow called VP Approved. This would involve doing a dynamic update to the PO process. Figure 10.12 shows the addition of a new state in the state machine.

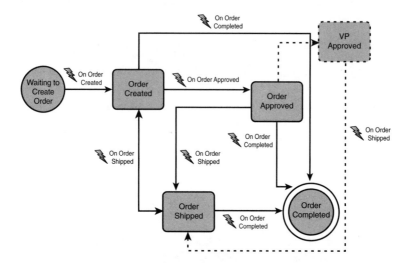

FIGURE 10.12   Dynamically adding a new state to the state machine workflow.

Of course, there are a lot of factors that go into doing the dynamic update. There is the issue of the exact mechanics of doing the dynamic update. Those aspects will be covered in Chapter 12. The other issue is that of how an end user who is interacting with the process gets to trigger the dynamic update. The workflow visualization that is created for the business process must support the end-user actions of starting the dynamic update. One way could be that based on some action on the user interface, an event is generated that is sent to the state machine. The state machine can have an event handler to handle this event (usually such a handler will be attached at the root level because the dynamic update may happen any time and hence is available in all the states). In the event handler the logic for adding a new state to the state machine can be done.

Skip and Rework Patterns in State Machine Workflows

Human workflows have a lot of ad hoc processing in them. A process may be defined in a particular way but then while running the process there may be situations where the works need to diverge from the manifest of the process. Sure, dynamic update is a way to add the extra steps that are required, but then in some situations you may want to simply repeat a step or skip over a step. In the PO example we discussed in the section "Dynamic Update in State Machine Workflows," consider the case where there is a PO for which the PO owner thinks that there is no need for approval because he already has verbal approval for it. He may want to skip the approval step.

The state machine workflow allows for skipping and repeating steps. The state machine workflow handles a special type of event called the `Set State` event. This event can be raised from the host program. The payload of the event includes the ID of the target state. Figure 10.13 shows moving the state machine from one state to another using the `Set State` event.

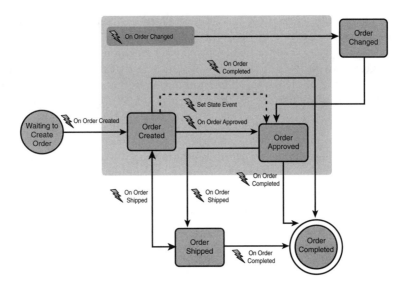

FIGURE 10.13   Skipping a step in a state machine workflow.

Both the skip and rework patterns can be implemented using the `Set State` event. In both cases all you need to do is simply set the state of the state machine to the appropriate state.

Let us look at a function that illustrates how to send the `Set State` event to the workflow instance. In order to raise the `Set State` event an instance of `SetStateEventArgs` is needed. The `SetStateEventArgs` constructor requires the instance ID of the state machine workflow that will receive the event and the ID of the state activity that will be the state that will be set as the current state after handling the event. In order to raise the event, the `EnqueueItem` method on the workflow instance class is called. The `EnqueueItem` method requires the queue name in which the event will be enqueued and the `SetStateEventArgs`. The queue in which the `SetState` event is enqueued is provided as a static property on the `StateMachineWorkflow` class.

```
Public Sub SetState(ByVal stateId As String)
        Dim eventArgs As SetStateEventArgs = New
SetStateEventArgs(Me.WorkflowInstance.InstanceId, stateId)
        wi.EnqueueItem(StateMachineWorkflow.SetStateQueueName, eventArgs, _
            Nothing, Nothing)
    End Sub
```

10

Summary

State machine workflows provide a very powerful paradigm for implementing business processes. State machines are a very useful pattern in modeling processes where there is a lot of ad hoc steps involved in the workflow and where it may not be possible to model all the paths using a sequential flow.

State machines have been represented in Windows Workflow Foundation through a set of activities. The root state machine workflow activity represents a single state machine. One or more state activities can be contained within a state machine workflow. Each state represents a logical state in the state machine. A state activity can contain event handlers. Each event handler can handle a unique event and then optionally transition to another state. The transition is made possible by the use of the `Set State` activity.

State machine workflows offer a natural query model where the state of the process is the state activity that is currently executing. In contrast to a sequential workflow, in order to answer the same question, some amount of translation has to be done to figure out the state of the process from the activity that is currently executing.

The state machine workflow also provides a way to intercept the execution of the workflow and skip or repeat the execution of states. Such patterns are very useful in human-centric workflow.

CHAPTER **11**

Hosting Workflows in Your Application

One of the major benefits of Windows Workflow Foundation is that any type of application that can execute managed code on the .NET Framework 2.0 can also execute workflows. An application that executes workflows and manages their lifetime is referred to as a *workflow host*.

In earlier chapters, you saw some simple examples showing how the WorkflowRuntime class can be used to start and execute new instances of workflows. You were essentially building a workflow host. In Chapter 6 "Using Web Services," you also learned how workflows can execute within ASP.NET applications and ASP.NET web services by using IIS as the workflow host. In this chapter, you're going to drill into the workflow runtime and hosting APIs in much more detail. Let's start by looking at the Windows Workflow Foundation runtime architecture.

Runtime Architecture

Windows Workflow Foundation provides a flexible and extensible runtime architecture. Rather than imposing specific requirements on a hosting application, it allows developers to plug in various runtime services depending on the application's requirements. For example, if you need to track the runtime execution of workflows, you can configure an optional tracking service. If you need to execute long-running workflows, you can use a persistence service to save the state of workflows to a data store.

The Windows Workflow Foundation runtime architecture is illustrated by the diagram in Figure 11.1. As you can see in this diagram, workflow instances are created and managed by the WorkflowRuntime. Based on the configuration of the hosting application, additional runtime services can be plugged into the runtime to provide support for behavior such as transactions, persistence, tracking, and timers.

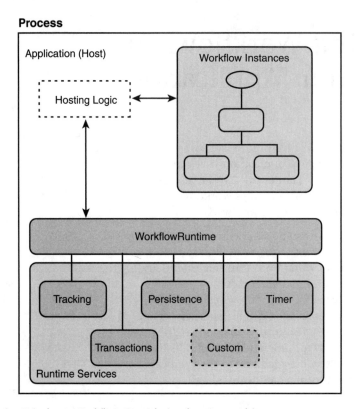

FIGURE 11.1   Windows Workflow Foundation hosting architecture.

Notice in Figure 11.1 that the WorkflowRuntime executes in the same process and application domain as the hosting application. It is not a separate process or background service. Consequently, the hosting application must be running in order for workflows to be executed. The functionality available to the hosts and workflow instances depends on the services registered with the workflow runtime.

As you learned earlier, a Windows Workflow Foundation host can be any application that can execute managed code on the .NET Framework 2.0. For example, you could build a Workflow host that is a Windows Forms application, a Windows Service, an ASP.NET application, or even a console application. When deciding what type of host to build, you should consider factors such as the following:

- How will communication occur with the host and other tiers of the application?

- Should the host execute on the client or server or both?

- Will the host be responsible for executing workflows on behalf of multiple users?

- Should the workflow execution and data be isolated from other workflow instances?

- How should workflows be versioned, deployed, and managed?

Workflow Runtime APIs

The Workflow Runtime APIs are contained in the `System.Workflow.Runtime` assembly. The .NET types defined in the `System.Workflow.Runtime` assembly are organized in the following four namespaces:

- `System.Workflow.Runtime`—Contains the .NET types that define the core runtime.

- `System.Workflow.Runtime.Hosting`—Contains the .NET types used to build a workflow host. Most of the runtime services are defined in this namespace.

- `System.Workflow.Runtime.Messaging`—Contains the .NET types that are used for workflow communications.

- `System.Workflow.Runtime.Configuration`—Contains the classes that are used to define the configuration sections for a host's configuration file.

The `WorkflowRuntime` class is the core component of the runtime APIs. The `WorkflowRuntime` class manages the collection of runtime services, provides methods to start and stop the runtime, and provides the ability to create new workflow instances. It also provides a set of events that can be used to monitor and change the behavior of the workflow runtime. The `WorkflowRuntime` class is illustrated in Figure 11.2. A host can start multiple instances of the WorkflowRuntime and each instance can have a different configuration or collection of runtime services.

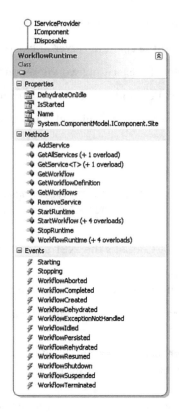

FIGURE 11.2   WorkflowRuntime class.

Building a Workflow Host

From a high level, there are four basic steps involved with building a workflow host. These steps include the following:

1. Create an instance of the WorkflowRuntime class.

2. Add runtime services to the workflow runtime (optional).

3. Start the WorkflowRuntime.

4. Start a new instance of the workflow.

Getting Started with the WorkflowRuntime Class

To understand how the WorkflowRuntime APIs can be used, let's create a simple Windows Forms application that will host a Windows Workflow Foundation workflow. A Windows Forms (WinForm) application works well for these examples because you can visually see information about the WorkflowRuntime or workflow instances. Initially your WinForm will just contain two toolbar buttons; one for starting the workflow runtime and another for stopping the workflow runtime. You'll also display the current status of the runtime in a status bar on the bottom of the form.

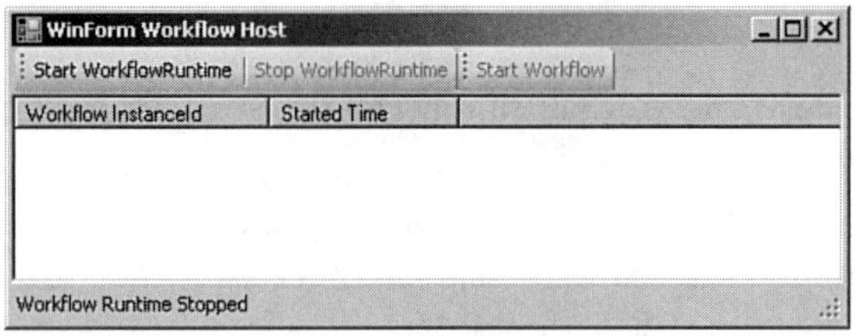

FIGURE 11.3 WinForm workflow host.

> **NOTE**
>
> The complete code for the WinForm workflow host is included in the code download for this book in both VB.NET and C#.

First, you need to include a using statement for the `System.Workflow.Runtime` namespace:

```
Imports System.Workflow.Runtime
```

Then you need to declare a member-level variable in the form to hold a reference to an instance of the `WorkflowRuntime` class. You need to maintain the workflow runtime in a member-level variable rather than a method-level variable so it doesn't go out of scope. If the variable holding a reference to an instance of the `WorkflowRuntime` goes out of scope, the `WorkflowRuntime` would be stopped and consequently, all the workflow instances executing on the runtime would be terminated.

```
Public Class Form1
    Private workflowRuntime As WorkflowRuntime
End Class
```

To start the workflow runtime, you'll simple create a new instance of the `WorkflowRuntime` class and call the `StartRuntime` method on the new object. There are several overloaded versions of the constructor for the `WorkflowRuntime` class. In this case you're creating a new workflow runtime with the default configuration, so the `WorkflowRuntime` will only use a minimal set of services. You can check the started status on the `WorkflowRuntime` by its `IsStarted` property.

```
Private Sub btnStartWorkflowRuntime_Click(ByVal sender As System.Object, ByVal e _
   As System.EventArgs) Handles btnStartWorkflowRuntime.Click

    If workflowRuntime Is Nothing Then
        workflowRuntime = new WorkflowRuntime();
    End If
```

```
        If workflowRuntime.IsStarted = False Then
            workflowRuntime.StartRuntime()
        End If
    End Sub
```

To stop the `WorkflowRuntime`, you can simply call the `StopRuntime` method on the `WorkflowRuntime` object.

```
Private Sub btnStopWorkflowRuntime_Click(ByVal sender As Object, ByVal e As _
    EventArgs) Handles btnStopWorkflowRuntime.Click
    If Not (workflowRuntime Is Nothing) Then
        ' If the WorkflowRuntime is started, then stop it now.
        workflowRuntime.StopRuntime()
    End If

    ' Release the WorkflowRuntime, and recreate it when we need it again.
    workflowRuntime = Nothing
End Sub
```

Starting Workflows

The `WorkflowRuntime` class provides a `StartWorkflow` method that can be used to create and start new instances of workflows. There are several overloads of the `StartWorkflow` method. The simplest `StartWorkflow` method takes just a single parameter of the type `System.Type`, which represents the type of workflow to start. For example, with one line of code you can start a new instance of our workflow named `SimpleWorkflow1`:

```
Dim workflowInstance As WorkflowInstance = _
    workflowRuntime.StartWorkflow( _
        GetType(HostingExampleWorkflows.SimpleWorkflow1))
```

The second overloaded version of the `StartWorkflow` method also takes a GUID as a parameter. The GUID is used as the `InstanceId` for the new workflow instance. This can be helpful for situations where you have a GUID value from another application or system and you want the workflow instance to share the same value so you can associate data outside the workflow with a workflow instance. In this example you'll create a new GUID for the workflow `InstanceId` and pass it in as a parameter to the `StartWorkflow` method:

```
Dim workflowInstanceId As Guid = Guid.NewGuid()
Dim workflowInstance As WorkflowInstance

workflowInstance = workflowRuntime.StartWorkflow( _
    GetType(HostingExampleWorkflows.SimpleWorkflow1), workflowInstanceId)
```

The third overloaded version of the `StartWorkflow` method that you will look at takes a generic dictionary containing the parameter values for the workflow. In this example, the workflow named `HostingExampleWorkflow.SimpleWorkflowWithParams` has defined two parameters: `FirstName` and `LastName`.

```
Dim workflowInstanceId As Guid = Guid.NewGuid()
Dim parameters As New Dictionary(Of String, Object)
parameters.Add("FirstName", "James")
parameters.Add("LastName", "Conard")

Dim workflowInstance As WorkflowInstance

' Create a new instance of the SimpleWorkflowWithParams
workflowInstance = workflowRuntime.StartWorkflow( _
    GetType(HostingExampleWorkflows.SimpleWorkflowWithParams), _
                workflowInstanceId, parameters)
```

Notice that each of these methods returns a class called `WorkflowInstance`. The `WorkflowInstance` class represents a specific instance of a workflow model. It can be used to control the execution of a workflow instance from the hosting application. You will learn how to use these methods of the `WorkflowInstance` class later in this chapter.

Starting Workflows Using Reflection

The previous examples assume that the workflow host has a reference to the assembly containing the `HostingExampleWorkflows.SimpleWorkflow1` workflow when the host is compiled. However, in many cases you will need to build a host that can support a variety of workflows that cannot be referenced at compile time, perhaps because the workflows haven't been created yet or because they are being developed by someone else. In these situations, you can use reflection to load the assembly and workflow type using the `System.Reflection.Assembly` class.

In the following code example you can see how to start the `SimpleWorkflow1` using reflection. First, you will load the `HostingExampleWorkflows.dll` assembly by calling the static `Load` method on the `Assembly` class. The `Load` method returns an instance of the `Assembly` class that represents your `HostingExampleWorkflows` assembly. Next, you can use the `Assembly` object to get a reference to a `System.Type` representing the `HostingExamplesWorkflows.SimpleWorkflow1` contained in the assembly. Finally, you can start the `SimpleWorkflow1` by providing the `Type` as a parameter.

```
Dim asm As System.Reflection.Assembly

' Load the HostingExampleWorkflows.dll.  For this example, assume
' ...that executing assemblies path.
asm = System.Reflection.Assembly.Load("HostingExampleWorkflows")
```

```
' Get the type for the SimpleWorkflow1, so we can start a new instance of it
Dim workflowType As System.Type = _
  asm.GetType("HostingExampleWorkflows.SimpleWorkflow1")

Dim workflowInstance As WorkflowInstance

' Create a new instance of the workflow type
workflowInstance = workflowRuntime.StartWorkflow(workflowType, workflowInstanceId)
```

This example assumes that the `HostingExampleWorkflows.dll` is in the same directory as the host. To load an assembly from a different location, you could use the `LoadFromFile` static method on the `Assembly` class. An in-depth discussion on the `System.Reflection` APIs is beyond the scope of this book. For more information about reflection in .NET, please refer to .NET Framework documentation on the `System.Reflection` namespace located at http://msdn.microsoft.com/library/en-us/cpref/html/frlrfSystemReflection.asp.

Workflow Lifecycle and Events

The `WorkflowRuntime` class exposes several events so the host can perform processing at different stages in the life cycle of the workflow (see Table 11.1).

TABLE 11.1 WorkflowRuntime Events

Event Name	Description
ExceptionNotHandled	An unhandled exception has occurred in a workflow.
Started	The workflow runtime has started.
Stopped	The workflow runtime has stopped.
WorkflowAborted	A workflow has been aborted.
WorkflowCompleted	A workflow has completed.
WorkflowCreated	A workflow has been created.
WorkflowIdled	A workflow is idle.
WorkflowLoaded	A workflow has been loaded from the persistence store.
WorkflowPersisted	A workflow has been persisted to the persistence store.
WorkflowResumed	A workflow has been resumed.
WorkflowShutdown	A workflow has been shut down. This typically occurs if the WorkflowRuntime is stopped while a workflow is still executing.
WorkflowSuspended	A workflow has been suspended. Workflows that are suspended can be resumed.
WorkflowTerminated	A workflow has been terminated.
WorkflowUnloaded	A workflow has been unloaded to the persistence store.

You can attach event handlers for these events on the `WorkflowRuntime` class. For example, you can customize your previous code sample to attach to the `WorkflowRuntime` events:

```
If workflowRuntime Is Nothing Then
    workflowRuntime = new WorkflowRuntime();
End If

If workflowRuntime Is Nothing Then
    workflowRuntime = new WorkflowRuntime();

    AddHandler workflowRuntime.Started, AddressOf Me.WorkflowRuntime_Started
    AddHandler workflowRuntime.Stopped, AddressOf Me.WorkflowRuntime_Stopped
    AddHandler workflowRuntime.WorkflowCompleted, _
                        AddressOf Me.WorkflowRuntime_WorkflowCompleted
    AddHandler workflowRuntime.WorkflowCreated, _
                        AddressOf Me.WorkflowRuntime_WorkflowCreated
End If

If workflowRuntime.IsStarted = False Then
    workflowRuntime.StartRuntime()
End If
```

When the `Started` and `Stopped` events occur on the `WorkflowRuntime`, simply update the text on the status bar using the `UpdateStatusText` helper method:

```
Sub WorkflowRuntime_Started(ByVal sender As Object, ByVal e As _
    WorkflowRuntimeEventArgs)
    Me.UpdateStatusText("Workflow Runtime has started...")
End Sub

Sub WorkflowRuntime_Stopped(ByVal sender As Object, ByVal e As _
    WorkflowRuntimeEventArgs)
    Me.UpdateStatusText("Workflow Runtime has stopped...")
End Sub
```

The `WorkflowRuntime` events execute on a different thread than the controls on the Windows Form. Consequently, you cannot update the status bar control directly from these event handlers. Rather, the `UpdateStatusText` private method must use a delegate and call the WinForm's `Invoke` method to update the status bar on the WinForm's thread. First, you need to define the delegate and then the `UpdateStatusText` method:

```
Delegate Sub UpdateStatusTextDelegate(ByVal status As String)

Private Sub UpdateStatusText(ByVal status As String)
    If Me.lstvwWFInstances.InvokeRequired Then
        ' This code is running on a different thread than the UI.  We need to
        ' ...use a delegate to update the status bar text
        Dim dlgtUpdateStatusText As _
                New UpdateStatusTextDelegate(AddressOf Me.UpdateStatusText)
```

```
        Dim args() As Object = {status}

        ' Update the status bar text through the delegate on the UI's thread
        Me.Invoke(dlgtUpdateStatusText, args)

    Else
        Me.lblWorkflowRuntimeStatus.Text = status
    End If
End Sub 'UpdateStatusText
```

When an event related to a workflow instance occurs, such as WorkflowCreated and WorkflowCompleted, we'll update the status of the workflow in the list on the WinForm. The UpdateListViewItem private method included in this code example is used to update the workflow status displayed in our ListView control.

```
Sub WorkflowRuntime_WorkflowCreated(ByVal sender As Object, _
                                    ByVal e As WorkflowEventArgs)
    UpdateListViewItem(e.WorkflowInstance, "Created")
End Sub

Sub WorkflowRuntime_WorkflowCompleted(ByVal sender As Object, _
                                    ByVal e As WorkflowCompletedEventArgs)
    UpdateListViewItem(e.WorkflowInstance, "Completed")
End Sub
```

The UpdateListViewItem private method must also use a delegate to update the user interface from the WorkflowRuntime event handler:

```
Delegate Sub UpdateListviewItemDelegate( _
        ByVal workflowInstance As WorkflowInstance, ByVal status As String)

Private Sub UpdateListViewItem(ByVal workflowInstance As WorkflowInstance, _
                        ByVal status As String)

    If Me.lstvwWFInstances.InvokeRequired Then
        ' This code is running on a different thread than the UI.  We need to
        ' ...use a delegate to update the ListViewItem
        Dim dlgtUpdateListViewItem As New UpdateListviewItemDelegate( _
                                    AddressOf Me.UpdateListViewItem)

        Dim args() As Object = {workflowInstance, status}

        ' Update the listviewitem through the delegate on the UI's thread
        Me.lstvwWFInstances.Invoke(dlgtUpdateListViewItem, args)
```

```
    Else
        ' Get the WorkflowInstanceId
        Dim instanceId As String = workflowInstance.InstanceId.ToString()

        ' Get a reference to the corresponding ListViewItem
        Dim lvitemWFInstance As ListViewItem = lstvwWFInstances.Items(instanceId)

        If Not (lvitemWFInstance Is Nothing) Then
            lvitemWFInstance.SubItems(3).Text = status
        End If
    End If
End Sub
```

The WinForm workflow host, shown in Figure 11.4, can now display the status for the `WorkflowRuntime` in the status bar and the status for each individual workflow in the `ListView` control.

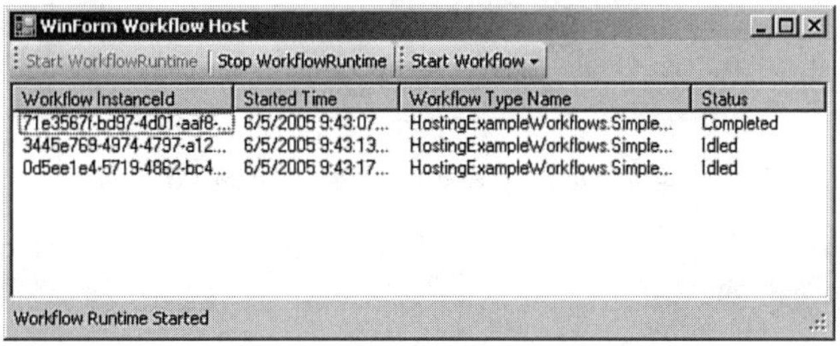

FIGURE 11.4   WinForm workflow host with workflow status information.

Controlling Workflow Instances

As mentioned previously, the `WorkflowInstance` class represents an instance of a workflow executing within the `WorkflowRuntime`. The `WorkflowInstance` class provides several methods for controlling the lifecycle for an instance of a workflow from the host application. The members of the `WorkflowInstance` class are listed in the diagram shown in Figure 11.5.

To demonstrate how you can use the `WorkflowInstance` class to control an instance of a specific workflow, you're going to enhance the WinForm Workflow Host to include toolbar buttons for each control method. The modified form is shown in Figure 11.6.

The following code handles a click event for each of the new toolbar buttons. When a button such as Abort or Suspend is clicked, you'll get a reference to the `WorkflowInstance` from the `WorkflowRuntime` for the item in the `ListView` control that is selected. Then you'll call the appropriate method on the `WorkflowInstance`. For example, if the Abort method is clicked, you'll simply call the `Abort()` method on the `WorkflowInstance`:

FIGURE 11.5   WorkflowInstance class.

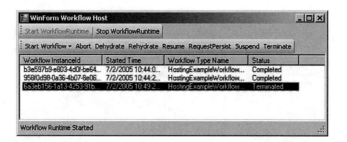

FIGURE 11.6   WinForm workflow host with control toolbar buttons.

```
Private Sub btnControlWorkflowInstance_Click(ByVal sender As Object, _
                                             ByVal e As EventArgs) _
    Handles btnUnloadWorkflow.Click, btnTerminateWorkflow.Click, _
      btnSuspendWorkflow.Click, btnResumeWorkflow.Click, btnRequestpersist.Click, _
      btnLoadWorkflow.Click, btnAbortWorkflow.Click

    ' Get the WorkflowInstanceId for the workflow selected in the listview
    Dim workflowInstanceId As Guid = GetSelectWorkflowInstanceId()

    ' Get a reference to the WorkflowInstance object from the runtime
    Dim workflowInstance As WorkflowInstance
    workflowInstance = workflowRuntime.GetWorkflow(workflowInstanceId)

    ' Get the name of the Menuitem that was clicked
    Dim menuItemName As String = CType(sender, ToolStripItem).Name
```

```
Select Case menuItemName
    Case "btnAbortWorkflow"
        workflowInstance.Abort()

    Case "btnUnloadWorkflow"
        workflowInstance.Unload()

    Case "btnLoadWorkflow"
        workflowInstance.Load()

    Case "btnResumeWorkflow"
        workflowInstance.Resume()

    Case "btnRequestpersist"
        workflowInstance.RequestPersist()

    Case "btnSuspendWorkflow"
        ' Suspend the selected WorkflowInstance
        workflowInstance.Suspend("Suspending workflow...")

    Case "btnTerminateWorkflow"
        ' Terminate the selected WorkflowInstance
        workflowInstance.Terminate("Terminated from the host machine")
    End Select
End Sub
```

> **NOTE**
>
> If you attempt to call the `Dehydrate` method on a workflow instance without a Persistence Runtime Service, you will receive a `System.InvalidOperationException`. You will learn how to configure runtime services and use the `SqlStatePersistenceService` later in this chapter.

Runtime Services

Windows Workflow Foundation includes several runtime services that can be plugged into the `WorkflowRuntime`. These services are divided into five categories:

- Threading Services

  - `DefaultThreadingService`—Uses the default .NET thread pool to allocate threads for the workflow runtime.

  - `ASPNETThreadingService`—Uses the ASP.NET thread servicing an HTTP request to execute the workflow. This service is designed to be used with the ASP.NET workflow host.

- Timer Services

  - `InMemoryTimerService`—Manages timers for delay activities in memory. Because the timers are maintained in memory, they are not durable across Workflow runtime restarts.

  - `ASPNETTimerService`—Manages timers for delay activities in the web server's process. This timer service behaves differently than the `InMemoryTimerService` because it calls into a workflow through an HTTP request. The `ASPNETTimerService` is designed for use with the ASP.NET Workflow Host.

  - `SqlTimerService`—Manages timers for delay activities in a SQL Server database.

- Tracking Services

  - `SqlTrackingService`—Stores tracking data in a SQL Server database using a predefined SQL database schema.

  - `TerminationTrackingService`—Logs events to the system event log on the local machine when a workflow instance is terminated for any reason.

- State Persistence Services

  - `SqlStatePersistenceService`—Stores the state for workflow instances in a SQL Server database.

- Transaction Services

  - `DefaultWorkflowTransactionService`—Provides a transactional context for performing transactional operations.

  - `SharedConnectionWorkflowTransactionService`—Used to share database connections and transactions across multiple services.

NOTE

The `WorkflowRuntime` can only use one Threading, Timer, Transaction, or State Persistence service at a time. However, multiple tracking services can be added to the workflow runtime and used at the same time.

Keep in mind that you are not limited to the runtime services provided with Windows Workflow Foundation. Later in this chapter you will see how you can build a custom tracking service.

The `SqlTimerService`, `SqlTrackingService`, and `SqlStatePersistenceService` are referred to as durable services because the data they manage is durable across a shutdown of the `WorkflowRuntime` or hosting process. These durable services support single SQL Server databases running on SQL Server 2000 or SQL Server 2005. The services rely on a predefined database schema. The SQL scripts for creating the databases are included with Windows Workflow Foundation, but the databases are not created automatically during setup. You will learn how to configure and use these durable services later in this chapter.

Using Runtime Services

When an instance of the WorkflowRuntime is started, by default it will use the following four services:

- DefaultWorkflowTransactionService

- InMemoryTimerService

- DefaultThreadingService

Runtime services can be added to the WorkflowRuntime by simply calling the AddService method. For example, in the following code sample you create and initialize a new instance of the TerminationTrackingService and add it to the WorkflowRuntime collection of services by calling the AddService method:

```
workflowRuntime = New WorkflowRuntime()


' Create an instance of the TerminationTracking service
Dim terminationTracking As New TerminationTrackingService()


' If the WWF event source doesn't exist, then create it.
If Not System.Diagnostics.EventLog.SourceExists("WWF") Then
    System.Diagnostics.EventLog.CreateEventSource("WWF", "Application")
End If


' Assign the EventSource for the TerminationTracking Service
terminationTracking.EventSource = "WWF"
workflowRuntime.AddService(terminationTracking)
```

Notice that the TerminationTrackingService will use the EventLog Event Source name of "WWF" for logging events. If the Event Source specified doesn't already exist then you will receive an exception when you call the StartWorkflow method to start a new workflow instance.

Runtime services can also be specified in the configuration file for the host application. The configuration file must include a <section> element defining the name of the configuration section for the WorkflowRuntime. The section's name should refer to an element in the configuration file that contains the list of runtime services that should be started with the WorkflowRuntime. For example, the following App.Config file for your WinForm Workflow Host includes a section named WorkflowRuntimeConfig. With the WorkflowRuntimeConfig configuration, you will start the TerminationTrackingService. Notice that the EventSource property for the TerminationService is specified as an attribute for the <add> element.

```
<?xml version="1.0" encoding="utf-8" ?>
<configuration xmlns="http://schemas.microsoft.com/.NetConfiguration/v2.0">
  <configSections>
    ' Reader Note: Define a ConfigSection named WorkflowRuntimeConfig
    <section name="WorkflowRuntimeConfig"
```

```
type="System.Workflow.Runtime.Configuration.WorkflowRuntimeSection,
System.Workflow.Runtime, _
   Version=3.0.0.0, Culture=neutral, PublicKeyToken=31bf3856ad364e35>
  </configSections>
  <WorkflowRuntimeConfig UnloadOnIdle"true">
    ' Reader note: List the services that should be included in _
       WorkflowRuntimeConfig
    <Services>
      <add type="System.Workflow.Runtime.Hosting.TerminationTrackingService,
System.Workflow.Runtime, Version=3.0.0.0, Culture=neutral, _
   PublicKeyToken=31bf3856ad364e35 EventSource="WWF" />
    </Services>
  </WorkflowRuntimeConfig>
</configuration>
```

A configuration file can contain multiple WorkflowRuntime configuration sections with each section containing a different list of services. To use the configuration file with the WorkflowRuntime, you need to simply specify the name of the configuration section when instantiating the WorkflowRuntime. For example, the following code sample provides the name WorkflowRuntimeConfig as a parameter to the WorkflowRuntime constructor:

```
workflowRuntime = New WorkflowRuntime("WorkflowRuntimeConfig")
```

> **NOTE**
>
> If you specify a configuration section name in the constructor for the WorkflowRuntime, you will need to add a reference to System.Configuration assembly.

Now that you've learned how to add runtime services to the WorkflowRuntime, let's learn how to use some of the more advanced runtime services starting with the SqlStatePersistenceService.

Using Persistence with the SqlStatePersistanceService

By default, workflow instances execute entirely in memory within the process space of the hosting application. Consequently, workflow instances are not durable across restarts of the WorkflowRuntime or the host application. If the WorkflowRuntime is stopped for any reason or the host application is shutdown, then all running workflow instances running will be aborted. This default behavior might be fine for simple, short-running workflows when there are only a few workflow instances. However, it is not ideal when using workflows that might be long running or when executing numerous workflow instances because workflow instances are always consuming resources, such as threads and memory, from the host application.

A persistence service provides the ability to persist and restore the entire state of a work-flow instance to a durable data store, such as a database or a file. This behavior, illustrated in Figure 11.7, allows workflow instances to be completely removed from memory, saved to a durable data store, and restored back in memory at a later point in time.

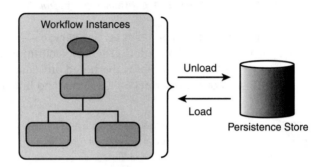

FIGURE 11.7   Workflow dehydration and rehydration.

Using the SqlStatePersistenceService

There are three steps that are necessary for using the SqlStatePersistenceService runtime service:

1. Create a SQL Server database for persisting workflow state.

2. Create the table structures and database objects required for the SqlStatePersistenceProvider.

3. Register and configure the SqlStatePersistenceService with the WorkflowRuntime.

Let's walk through these steps in more detail.

Create the SQL Server Database

There are a number of ways to create a SQL Server database. For example, you could use Visual Studio 2005's Server Explorer tool window to create a new database. In this case, simply use the command-line utility OSQL, which is included with SQL Server and SQL Server 2005 Express. The following command creates a new SQL Server database named PersistenceStore. In this case you're using the instance of SQL Express on the local machine that is installed by Visual Studio 2005:

```
osql -S .\SQLExpress -E -Q "CREATE DATABASE PersistenceStore"
```

> **NOTE**
>
> The code sample for this chapter includes batch files for executing OSQL to create the SQL Server database.

Create the Tables and Database Objects

Windows Workflow Foundation provides SQL scripts for creating the tables and database objects required by the SQL durable services. These SQL scripts are installed in the following directory:

```
C:\WINDOWS\Microsoft.NET\Framework\v2.0.50215\Windows Workflow Foundation\SQL
```

There are two scripts that are specific to the SqlPersistenceService—SqlPersistenceService_Schema.sql, which contains the table definitions, and SqlPersistenceService_Logic.sql, which contains the stored procedures for the SQL Persistence database. Execute both of these scripts on the command line using the OSQL utility:

```
Osql -S localhost\SQLExpress -E  -n -d PersistenceStore -i
"C:\WINDOWS\Microsoft.NET\Framework\v2.0.50215\Windows Workflow _
    Foundation\SQL\SqlPersistenceService_Schema.sql"
Osql -S localhost\SQLExpress -E  -n -d PersistenceStore -i
"C:\WINDOWS\Microsoft.NET\Framework\v2.0.50215\Windows Workflow _
    Foundation\SQL\SqlPersistenceService_Logic.sql"
```

> **NOTE**
>
> This example uses the SQL Server 2005 Express instance that was installed with Visual Studio 2005. Consequently, the value for the server name parameter includes the SQL Server instance name of "SQLExpress".

Add the SqlStatePersistenceService to the WorkflowRuntime

To use the SqlStatePersistenceService with the WorkflowRuntime, you simply need to create an instance of the service and add the new instance to the WorkflowRuntime by calling the AddService method. The constructor for the SqlStatePersistenceService takes both a reference to the WorkflowRuntime and a connection string for the Persistence database as parameters. Notice that you still need to call the AddService method on the WorkflowRuntime to register the new SqlStatePersistenceService object with the runtime.

```
workflowRuntime = New WorkflowRuntime()

Dim sqlStatePersistence As New SqlStatePersistenceService( _
    "Initial Catalog=PersistenceStore;Data Source=.\SQLEXPRESS; _
    Integrated Security=SSPI;")

workflowRuntime.AddService(sqlStatePersistence)
```

Alternatively, you can add the SqlStatePersistenceService to the list of runtime services in your host's configuration file. Notice that when adding the

SqlStatePersistenceService to the configuration file, you must also provide the full SQL connection string for the PersistenceStore database in the ConnectionString attribute:

```xml
<?xml version="1.0" encoding="utf-8" ?>
<configuration xmlns="http://schemas.microsoft.com/.NetConfiguration/v2.0">
  <configSections>
    <section name="WorkflowRuntimeConfig"
type="System.Workflow.Runtime.Configuration.WorkflowRuntimeSection,
System.Workflow.Runtime, Version=3.0.0.0, Culture=neutral,
PublicKeyToken=31bf3856ad364e35>
  </configSections>
  <WorkflowRuntimeConfig>
    <Services>
      <add type="System.Workflow.Runtime.Hosting.TerminationTrackingService,
System.Workflow.Runtime, Version=3.0.0.0, Culture=neutral,
PublicKeyToken=31bf3856ad364e35>
      <add type="System.Workflow.Runtime.Hosting.SqlStatePersistenceService,
System.Workflow.Runtime, Version=3.0.0.0, Culture=neutral,
PublicKeyToken=31bf3856ad364e35 ConnectionString="Initial Catalog= _
    PersistenceStore;Data
Source=.\SQLEXPRESS;Integrated Security=SSPI;"/>
    </Services>
  </WorkflowRuntimeConfig>
</configuration>
```

Load and Unload Workflow Instances

Now that you have configured the SqlStatePersistenceService, you can dehydrate and rehydrate a WorkflowInstance to and from the PersistenceStore database. This is accomplished by simply calling the Unload and Load methods on the WorkflowInstance, as you saw in the earlier example:

```
workflowInstance.Unload()
workflowInstance.Load()
```

You can also instruct the WorkflowRuntime to dehydrate workflows automatically when they are in an idle state. This is accomplished by setting the UnloadOnIdle property on the WorkflowRuntime class. By default this property is set to false. The following code sample shows how you can set the UnloadOnIdle property after creating an instance of the WorkflowRuntime:

```
workflowRuntime = New WorkflowRuntime()
workflowRuntime.UnloadOnIdle = True
```

```
Dim sqlStatePersistence As New SqlStatePersistenceService( _
    "Initial Catalog=PersistenceStore;Data Source=.\SQLEXPRESS;Integrated _
    Security=SSPI;")
```

```
workflowRuntime.AddService(sqlStatePersistence)
```

The `UnloadOnIdle` option can also be specified in the host's configuration file for the `WorkflowRuntime` by setting the `UnloadOnIdle` attribute of the `WorkflowRuntime` configuration section. For example, in the following sample, you can see how we've added the `UnloadOnIdle` attribute for the `WorkflowRuntimeConfig` section:

```
...
  <WorkflowRuntimeConfig UnloadOnIdle="true">
     <Services>
        <add type="System.Workflow.Runtime.Hosting.TerminationTrackingService,
System.Workflow.Runtime, Version=3.0.0.0, Culture=neutral,
PublicKeyToken=31bf3856ad364e35>
        <add type="System.Workflow.Runtime.Hosting.SqlStatePersistenceService,
System.Workflow.Runtime, Version=3.0.0.0, Culture=neutral,
PublicKeyToken=31bf3856ad364e35 ConnectionString="Initial Catalog= _
   PersistenceStore;Data
Source=.\SQLEXPRESS;Integrated Security=SSPI;"/>
     </Services>
  </WorkflowRuntimeConfig>
</configuration>
```

Using Tracking with the `SqlTrackingService`

Tracking provides the ability to capture data and events that occur during the execution of a workflow. These workflow data and events can be used for a variety of scenarios, such as real-time monitoring, calculating Key Performance Indicators (KPIs) that indicate the performance of a business process, or historical reporting. There are three types of events that you can track:

- Workflow Events—Events that indicate the status or state of the workflow. For example, the workflow tracking events include: `Created`, `Idle`, `Resumed`, `Persisted`, `Unloaded`, `Loaded`, `Exception`, `Terminated`, `Aborted`, `Changed`, `Completed`, and `Shutdown`. Except for the `Changed` event, the workflow events exposed through the tracking system are the same as the events that are raised on the `WorkflowRuntime` class.

- Activity Events—Activity events indicate the state of a specific activity within a workflow. For example, the activity events include: `Initialized`, `Executing`, `Faulting`, `Compensating`, `Canceling`, and `Closed`.

- User Events—User events allow you to extend the `WorkflowRuntime`'s behavior to track custom data during the execution of a workflow. For example, you might want to track the results from calling a web service or data that was received from an event into the workflow.

As you learned earlier in this chapter, tracking is supported by adding a tracking service into the `WorkflowRuntime`. The Tracking Service is responsible for receiving and processing tracking data from the `WorkflowRuntime`. In addition to the `TerminationTrackingService` that you used earlier, Windows Workflow Foundation also provides the `SqlTrackingService` that stores tracking data into a SQL Server database. Let's learn how to take advantage of tracking by configuring and using the `SqlTrackingService`.

Using the `SqlTrackingService`

There are three steps that are required to configure and use the `SqlTrackingService` runtime service. These steps are very similar to the steps you reviewed earlier for the `SqlStatePersistenceService`.

1. Create a SQL Server database for storing tracking data. For the examples later in this chapter, use the name "`TrackingStore`".

2. Create the table structures and database objects required for the `SqlTrackingService`. The `Tracking_Schema.sql` script contains the table definitions and `Tracking_Logic.sql` contains the definitions for the stored procedures that are used by the `SqlTrackingService`.

3. Register and configure the `SqlTrackingService` with the `WorkflowRuntime`.

> **NOTE**
>
> The code sample for this chapter includes batch files creating the SQL Server Tracking database.

Just like the `SqlStatePersistenceService`, the `SqlTrackingService` also requires a reference to the `WorkflowRuntime` and a connection string to be specified as parameters when it is instantiated. The following code example shows how we can create a new instance of the `SqlTrackingService` and add it to the `WorkflowRuntime`. You can also configure it in the host's configuration file.

```
workflowRuntime = New WorkflowRuntime()

Dim sqlTracking As New SqlTrackingService( _
  "Initial Catalog=TrackingStore;Data Source=.\SQLEXPRESS;Integrated _
  Security=SSPI;")

workflowRuntime.AddService(sqlTracking)

' Create an instance of the TerminationTracking service
Dim terminationTracking As New TerminationTrackingService()
```

```
If Not System.Diagnostics.EventLog.SourceExists("WWF") Then
    System.Diagnostics.EventLog.CreateEventSource("WWF", "Application")
End If

terminationTracking.EventSource = "WWF"
workflowRuntime.AddService(terminationTracking)
```

Notice that in addition to the `SqlTrackingService`, the previous code example also adds the `TerminationTrackingService` to the `WorkflowRuntime`. You can actually have multiple tracking services registered with the `WorkflowRuntime`. This behavior is unlike other types of runtime services, such as `Threading`, `Transactions`, or `Persistence` where only one instance can be registered with the `WorkflowRuntime`.

Viewing Workflow Tracking Data

To view the tracking data capturing by the `SqlTrackingService` you must execute queries against the tables in the tracking database. For example, the following code returns a DataSet with `WorkflowInstance` data from the Tracking database by executing a SQL statement against the `WorkflowInstance` table. The SQL statement also joins the data in the `WorkflowInstance` table to the data in the `Types` table so the results will also include the full type name of the workflow.

```
Public Shared Function GetWorkflowInstances( _
                 ByVal trackingDBConnectionString As String) As DataSet

    Dim commandText As String = "SELECT Type.TypeFullName, Type.AssemblyFullName, " _
        + " WorkflowInstance.WorkflowInstanceId " _
        + " FROM  WorkflowInstance INNER JOIN " _
        + " Type ON WorkflowInstance.WorkflowTypeId = Type.TypeId " _
        + " ORDER BY WorkflowInstance.CreatedDateTime DESC"

    Dim sqlconTrackingStore As New SqlConnection()
    Try
        sqlconTrackingStore.ConnectionString = trackingDBConnectionString
        sqlconTrackingStore.Open()

        Dim sqlcmdGetWorkflowInstances As SqlCommand = _
                    sqlconTrackingStore.CreateCommand()

        sqlcmdGetWorkflowInstances.CommandText = commandText
        sqlcmdGetWorkflowInstances.CommandType = CommandType.Text

        Dim ds As New DataSet()
        Dim sqlDataAdapter As New SqlDataAdapter()
```

```
        sqlDataAdapter.SelectCommand = sqlcmdGetWorkflowInstances
        sqlDataAdapter.Fill(ds)

        Return ds
    Finally
        sqlconTrackingStore.Dispose()
    End Try
End Function
```

To illustrate how you could use the tracking data captured by the SqlTrackingService, we can add a simple Windows Form to the workflow host application. This Tracking Viewer WinForm, illustrated in Figure 11.8, queries several tables in the Tracking database to display the WorkflowInstances and the Workflow, Activity, and User events associated with each WorkflowInstance. Notice that there are several events that were tracked during the lifetime of the HostingExampleWorkflows.SimpleWorkflow1 workflow, including two Persisted events and an Unloaded and Loaded event.

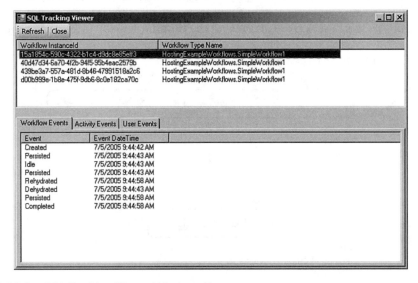

FIGURE 11.8   SQL Tracking Viewer Windows Form.

> **NOTE**
>
> For the sake of space, we will not cover all of the code for the SQL Tracking Viewer WinForm in this chapter. Rather, the Windows Form is included in the code download for this chapter.

Viewing Tracking Data with WorkflowMonitor

There are several potential ways you could use the rich tracking data stored by the SqlTrackingService. The SQL Tracking Viewer WinForm is just one very simple example.

The Windows Workflow Foundation SDK also includes a tool called Workflow Monitor that can be used to view the tracking data stored by the `SqlTrackingService`. Workflow Monitor is a helpful utility because in addition to displaying the tracking events, it can also display a graphical view of the workflow definition in the Windows Workflow Foundation workflow designer control.

The XML markup representing the workflow definition is serialized by the `SqlTrackingService` and stored in the `Workflow` table when the `TrackWorkflowDefinition` property for the `SqlTrackingService` is set to true. This property can be set on an instance of the `SqlTrackingService` or in the configuration file for the host. The `TrackWorkflowDefinition` property must be set to true in order for the `WorkflowMonitor` to behave correctly.

Tracking Profiles

By default, all events will be tracked with the `SqlTrackingService`. However, the data that is tracked can be customized by creating a custom tracking profile. A tracking profile is essentially a filter that specifies the types of events that will be sent to a tracking service. Rather than a tracking service filtering the events, the tracking service provides a tracking profile to the `WorkflowRuntime` and the runtime actually filters the events that are sent to the tracking service. Figure 11.9 illustrates the communication between the `WorkflowRuntime` and a Tracking Service.

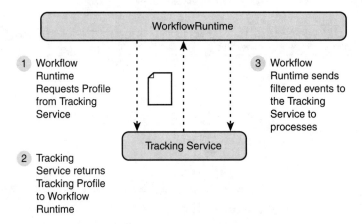

FIGURE 11.9   `WorkflowRuntime` and Tracking Service interaction.

Tracking profiles can be constructed programmatically using the tracking profile object model or they can be represented as XML. The .NET types that provide this programming model are defined in the `System.Workflow.Runtime.Hosting` namespace. The `TrackingProfile` class is the root of the object model. It exposes properties for managing a collection of `Activity`, `Workflow`, and `User` tracking points. The definition of the `TrackingProfile` class is illustrated in Figure 11.10.

FIGURE 11.10   TrackingProfile class.

The diagrams in Figure 11.11 show the definition for the WorkflowTrackPoint, ActivityTrackPoint, and UserTrackPoint classes. A TrackingProfile manages collections for each of these types of tracking points.

FIGURE 11.11   WorkflowTrackPoint, ActivityTrackPoint, and UserTrackPoint classes.

Learn how to use custom tracking profiles by looking at an example. There are two steps required to create a custom tracking profile for use the SqlTrackingService:

1. Create a TrackingProfile either by using the TrackingProfile object model or by creating a TrackingProfile XML file by hand.

2. Save the XML-formatted TrackingProfile to the tracking database.

For this example, you will see how to create a TrackingProfile through the object model and then serialize to XML. First, you need to define the custom TrackingProfile to track a subset of the workflow and activity events. In the following code sample, create a new TrackingProfile object and configure it to track only the Created, Completed, Aborted, and Terminated events of a workflow and the Initialized and Closed events of an activity.

```
Private Function CreateTrackingProfile() As TrackingProfile
    Dim profile As New TrackingProfile()

    profile.Version = New Version("1.0.0.0")

    Dim workflowTrackPoint As New WorkflowTrackPoint()
    Dim workflowLocation As New WorkflowLocation()
```

```
workflowLocation.Events.Add(WorkflowEvent.Created)
workflowLocation.Events.Add(WorkflowEvent.Completed)
workflowLocation.Events.Add(WorkflowEvent.Aborted)
workflowLocation.Events.Add(WorkflowEvent.Terminated)

workflowTrackPoint.MatchingLocation = workflowLocation
profile.WorkflowTrackPoints.Add(workflowTrackPoint)

Dim activityTrackPoint As New ActivityTrackPoint()

Dim activityLocation As New ActivityLocation(GetType(Activity))
activityLocation.MatchDerivedTypes = True
activityLocation.Events.Add(Status.Initialized)
activityLocation.Events.Add(Status.Closed)

activityTrackPoint.MatchingLocations.Add(activityLocation)

profile.ActivityTrackPoints.Add(activityTrackPoint)

    Return profile
End Function
```

Notice that when you create a new `ActivityLocation` object you pass the type for the base `Activity` class as a parameter to the constructor. An `ActivityLocation` can be used to filter the types of activities that are tracked by the tracking service. In this case you will track just the `Initialized` and `Closed` events for all activities because you specified the base `Activity` class and the `MatchDerivedTypes` property is set to true. The `MatchDerivedTypes` property controls whether activities that derive from the base `Activity` class are also tracked.

Before custom tracking profiles can be used with the `SqlTrackingService`, they must be serialized to XML and stored in the `TrackingProfiles` table in the SQL Server tracking database. The `TrackingProfileSerializer` class provides the ability to serialize and deserialize a `TrackingProfile` to and from XML. Define a method that uses the `TrackingProfileSerializer` to convert a `TrackingProfile` into an XML-formatted string:

```
Public Shared Function SerializeTrackingProfileToString( _
                    ByVal trackingProfile As TrackingProfile) As String
    Dim writer As New System.IO.StringWriter()

    Dim serializer As New TrackingProfileSerializer()
    serializer.Serialize(trackingProfile, writer)

    Return writer.ToString()
End Function
```

Here's the XML-formatted version of the new `TrackingProfile`:

```
<?xml version="1.0" encoding="utf-16" standalone="yes"?>
<TrackingProfile xmlns="http://www.microsoft.com/WWFTrackingProfile" _
    version="1.0.0.0">
    <TrackPoints>
        <WorkflowTrackPoint>
            <MatchingLocation>
                <WorkflowLocation>
                    <WorkflowEvents>
                        <WorkflowEvent>Created</WorkflowEvent>
                        <WorkflowEvent>Completed</WorkflowEvent>
                        <WorkflowEvent>Aborted</WorkflowEvent>
                        <WorkflowEvent>Terminated</WorkflowEvent>
                    </WorkflowEvents>
                </WorkflowLocation>
            </MatchingLocation>
        </WorkflowTrackPoint>
        <ActivityTrackPoint>
            <MatchingLocations>
                <ActivityLocation>
                    <Activity>
                        <Type>System.Workflow.ComponentModel.Activity, _
                        System.Workflow.ComponentModel, Version=3.0.0.0, _
                        Culture=neutral, PublicKeyToken=31bf3856ad364e35</Type>
                        <MatchDerivedTypes>true</MatchDerivedTypes>
                    </Activity>
                    <StatusEvents>
                        <Status>Initialized</Status>
                        <Status>Closed</Status>
                    </StatusEvents>
                </ActivityLocation>
            </MatchingLocations>
        </ActivityTrackPoint>
    </TrackPoints>
</TrackingProfile>
```

The SQL Server tracking database includes a stored procedure named `UpdateTrackingProfile` that can be used to insert or update a tracking profile for use by the `SqlTrackingService`.

```
Public Shared Sub SaveTrackingProfile(ByVal trackingDBConnectionString As String, _
            ByVal workflowTypeFullName As String, ByVal assemblyFullName As String, _
            ByVal versionId As String, ByVal trackingProfileXml As String)
```

```vb
    Dim sqlconTrackingStore As New SqlConnection()

    Try
        sqlconTrackingStore.ConnectionString = trackingDBConnectionString
        sqlconTrackingStore.Open()

        Dim sqlcmdUpdateTrackingProfile As SqlCommand = _
                                sqlconTrackingStore.CreateCommand()

        sqlcmdUpdateTrackingProfile.CommandText = "UpdateTrackingProfile"
        sqlcmdUpdateTrackingProfile.CommandType = CommandType.StoredProcedure

        Dim sqlParameters As SqlParameterCollection = _
                            sqlcmdUpdateTrackingProfile.Parameters
        sqlParameters.AddWithValue("@TypeFullName", workflowTypeFullName)
        sqlParameters.AddWithValue("@AssemblyFullName", assemblyFullName)
        sqlParameters.AddWithValue("@VersionId", versionId)
        sqlParameters.AddWithValue("@TrackingProfile", trackingProfileXml)

        sqlcmdUpdateTrackingProfile.ExecuteNonQuery()
    Finally
        sqlconTrackingStore.Dispose()
    End Try
End Sub 'SaveTrackingProfile
```

> **NOTE**
>
> The TrackingProfile version must increment before it is saved to the SQL Tracking database. If the TrackingProfile version number has not been incremented, the call to the UpdateTrackingProfile stored procedure will fail and an exception will be thrown.

The following code sample shows how the helper functions you just defined are used to create the TrackingProfile, serialize it to XML, and save it to the Tracking database:

```vb
Dim workflowType As Type = GetType(HostingExampleWorkflows.SimpleWorkflow1)

Dim trackingProfile As TrackingProfile = Me.CreateTrackingProfile()

Dim trackingProfileXml As String = _
        SerializeTrackingProfileToString(trackingProfile)

SaveTrackingProfile( _
    "Initial Catalog=TrackingStore;Data Source=.\SQLEXPRESS;Integrated _
    Security=SSPI;", workflowType.FullName, workflowType.Assembly.FullName,
    trackingProfile.Version.ToString(), trackingProfileXml)
```

Now that your custom tracking profile has been created, you can use your WinForm
Workflow Host to start a workflow and view the tracking data. As you can see in Figure
11.12, after the new `TrackingProfile` has been applied only the `Created` and `Completed`
workflow events are captured in the SQL Tracking database.

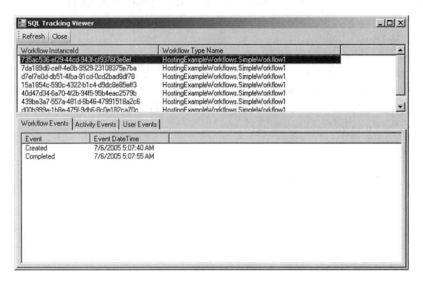

FIGURE 11.12   SQL Tracking Viewer with filtered events.

Creating a Custom Runtime Service

One of the most powerful features of Windows Workflow Foundation is that developers
can extend the `WorkflowRuntime` by building custom runtime services. Windows
Workflow Foundation defines an abstract base class for the common types of services.
These base classes include the following:

- `ThreadingService`

- `TimerService`

- `TrackingService`

- `StatePersistenceService`

- `WorkflowTransactionService`

The runtime services included with Windows Workflow Foundation ultimately derive
from these base classes. Consequently, custom services are treated as first class citizens
within the `WorkflowRuntime`. There are no special APIs for hidden functionality that the
included runtime services leverage that is not available to developers who want to build
custom services.

The work required to develop each type of custom service will vary significantly because of the different functionality and complexity of the service. For example, building a threading service or a transaction service can be much more complex than building a tracking service. For the purposes of this chapter, we'll keep the example simple by building a custom tracking service that writes out tracking data to the console.

The TrackingService class is an abstract base class for creating a custom tracking service. A custom tracking service must ultimately derive from TrackingService. The TrackingService class defines methods for managing the TrackingProfile that is used by the runtime. A custom workflow tracking service must also include a class that derives from the TrackingChannel base class. The TrackingChannel base class defines a single method, named Send, which is called when tracking data should be processed. These classes are illustrated in Figure 11.13.

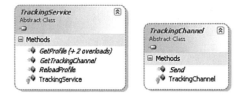

FIGURE 11.13   TrackingService and TrackingChannel classes.

There are three basic steps involved in building a custom tracking service. These steps include the following:

1. Create a new class that inherits from TrackingService.

2. Create a new class that inherits from TrackingChannel.

3. Add the new tracking service to the WorkflowRuntime.

Developing the Console Tracking Service

Start creating the custom tracking service by including using statements in your code file for the Windows Workflow Foundation namespaces:

```
Imports System
Imports System.Collections.Generic
Imports System.Text
Imports System.Workflow
Imports System.Workflow.ComponentModel
Imports System.Workflow.Runtime
Imports System.Workflow.Runtime.Hosting
```

Now define a new class named ConsoleTrackingService that derives from the TrackingService base class:

```
Public Class ConsoleTrackingService
    Inherits TrackingService
End Class
```

Then you can create a new class named `ConsoleTrackingChannel` that derives from the `TrackingChannel` base class:

```
Public Class ConsoleTrackingChannel
    Inherits TrackingChannel
End Class
```

In the `ConsoleTrackingService` you'll declare a member variable named `trackingChannel` to hold a reference to an instance of the `ConsoleTrackingChannel`. In the constructor for the `ConsoleTrackingService`, create the new instance of the `ConsoleTrackingChannel`:

```
Public Class ConsoleTrackingService
    Inherits TrackingService
    Private trackingChannel As ConsoleTrackingChannel = Nothing

    Public Sub New()
        trackingChannel = New ConsoleTrackingChannel()
    End Sub
End Class
```

The `GetProfile` methods are responsible for returning an instance of the `TrackingProfile` class that represents the tracking profile the `WorkflowRuntime` should use with the tracking service. There are three overloaded versions of the `GetProfile` method. The first overload takes a `WorkflowInstanceId` as a parameter. This `GetProfile` method is expected to return a tracking profile that applies to a specific instance of a workflow. The `ConsoleTrackingService` will not support instance-specific tracking profiles, so this overload of the `GetProfile` method should simply return null.

```
Overloads Public Overrides Function GetProfile(workflowInstanceId As Guid) _
        As TrackingProfile
    Return Nothing
End Function
```

The second overloaded version of the `GetProfile` method takes a `WorkflowType` and a version for the tracking profile. This method is responsible for returning a reference to a `TrackingProfile` object that represents a specific version of the tracking profile for the specified type of workflow. Again, the `ConsoleTrackingService` will not support version-specific tracking profiles, so this version of the `GetProfile` method should just return null.

```
Overloads Public Overrides Function GetProfile(workflowType As Type, _
                        profileVersionId As Version) As TrackingProfile
    Return Nothing
End Function
```

The third overloaded version of the `GetProfile` method simply takes a type representing the workflow that should be tracked. In this case, construct a default tracking profile by calling the private method `GetDefaultProfile`:

```
Overloads Public Overrides Function GetProfile(workflowType As Type) As _
    TrackingProfile
    Return GetDefaultProfile()
End Function
```

The `GetTrackingChannel` method is responsible for returning a reference to the object that derives from the `TrackingChannel` base class. In this case, return a reference to the `ConsoleTrackingChannel` that you instantiated in the constructor:

```
Public Overrides Function GetTrackingChannel(parameters As TrackingParameters) _
        As TrackingChannel
    Return trackingChannel
End Function
```

The `ReloadProfile` method is used by the workflow runtime to determine whether the `TrackingProfile` that was previously retrieved from the tracking service should be refreshed for a specific workflow instance. The tracking profile can be refreshed by the host by calling the `ReloadTrackingProfiles` method on the `WorkflowInstance` class.

```
Public Overrides Function ReloadProfile(workflowType As Type, workflowInstanceId _
    As Guid, ByRef profile As TrackingProfile) As Boolean
    profile = Nothing
    Return True
End Function
```

In the private method named `GetDefaultProfile` you'll create a new `TrackingProfile` to track all events. This is very similar to the `TrackingProfile` you created earlier in this chapter for use with the `SqlTrackingService`. However, in this case you are creating a profile to track all events:

```
Private Function GetDefaultProfile() As TrackingProfile
    Dim profile As New TrackingProfile()

    profile.Version = New Version("1.0.0.0")


    Dim activityTrackPoint As New ActivityTrackPoint()
    Dim activityLocation As New ActivityLocation(GetType(Activity))
    activityLocation.MatchDerivedTypes = True
```

```
    Dim status As Status
    For Each status In [Enum].GetValues( _
    GetType(System.Workflow.ComponentModel.Status))
        activityLocation.Events.Add(status)
    Next status

    activityTrackPoint.MatchingLocations.Add(activityLocation)
    profile.ActivityTrackPoints.Add(activityTrackPoint)

    Dim workflowTrackPoint As New WorkflowTrackPoint()
    Dim workflowLocation As New WorkflowLocation()
    Dim workflowEvent As WorkflowEvent

    For Each workflowEvent In  [Enum].GetValues(GetType(WorkflowEvent))
        workflowLocation.Events.Add(workflowEvent)
    Next workflowEvent

    workflowTrackPoint.MatchingLocation = workflowLocation
    profile.WorkflowTrackPoints.Add(workflowTrackPoint)

    Return profile
End Function
```

The implementation for the ConsoleTrackingService class is now complete. Now you
need to implement the ConsoleTrackingChannel. The ConsoleTrackingChannel should
override the Send method that's defined by the TrackingChannel base class. The Send
method is called when the TrackingChannel should process a TrackingRecord, which
contains the details about that event that occurred. There are three specific classes that
derive from the TrackingRecord abstract base class and one specific class for each type of
TrackPoint (as shown in Figure 11.14).

In the case of this simple tracking service, cast the TrackingRecord into the appropriate
type and write the data from the TrackingRecord to the console. In addition to the Send
method, you also have to override the InstanceCompletedOrTerminated method, where
we will just write out a status message to the console.

```
Public Overrides Sub Send(ByVal record As TrackingRecord)
    Dim output As String = "[Console Tracking Service] "

    If TypeOf (record) Is ActivityTrackingRecord Then
        ' Cast the TrackingRecord to ActivityTrackingRecord
        Dim activityTrackingRecord As ActivityTrackingRecord = _
                                CType(record, ActivityTrackingRecord)

        ' Build the output string to write to the console
        output = output + "Activity Tracking Event: " _
```

```
                    + activityTrackingRecord.QualifiedId + " - " _
                    + activityTrackingRecord.Status.ToString()
    ElseIf TypeOf (record) Is WorkflowTrackingRecord Then
        ' Cast the TrackingRecord to a WorkflowTrackingRecord
        Dim workflowTrackingRecord As WorkflowTrackingRecord = _
                            CType(record, WorkflowTrackingRecord)

        ' Build the output string to write to the console
        output = output + "Workflow Tracking Event: " + "Workflow " _
                + " - " + workflowTrackingRecord.Status.ToString()
    End If

    ' Write the output string to the console
    System.Console.WriteLine(output)
End Sub

Public Overrides Sub InstanceCompletedOrTerminated()
    Dim output As String = "[Console Tracking Service] {0}"
    System.Console.WriteLine(output, "InstanceCompletedOrTerminated")
End Sub
```

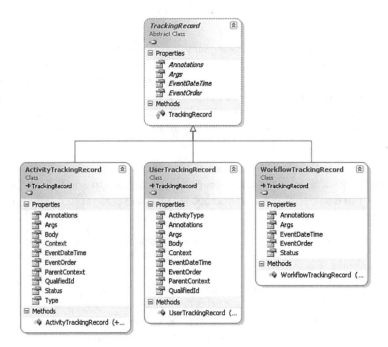

FIGURE 11.14   TrackingRecord, ActivityTrackingRecord, UserTrackingRecord, and WorkflowTrackingRecord classes.

Testing the Console Tracking Service

Finally, you're ready to test your `ConsoleTrackingService`. In this case you'll create a new application based on the Workflow Console Application Visual Studio 2005 template. The Workflow Console Application template provides a very simple workflow host. The following code defines the main method of the console application. To use the Console Tracking Service, simply modify the code in the main method to create a new instance of the `ConsoleTrackingService` class and add the new object to the `WorkflowRuntime` by calling the `AddService` method.

```
Class Program
    Shared WaitHandle As New AutoResetEvent(False)

    Shared Sub Main()
        Dim workflowRuntime As New WorkflowRuntime()

        Dim consoleTrackingService As New ConsoleTrackingService()
        workflowRuntime.AddService(consoleTrackingService)

        workflowRuntime.StartRuntime()
        AddHandler workflowRuntime.WorkflowCompleted, AddressOf OnWorkflowCompleted

        Dim type As System.Type = GetType(HostingExampleWorkflows.SimpleWorkflow1)
        workflowRuntime.StartWorkflow(type)
        Console.WriteLine("Workflow started...")

        WaitHandle.WaitOne()
        workflowRuntime.StopRuntime()
        Console.WriteLine("Press any key to close the console window")
        Console.Read()
    End Sub

    Shared Sub OnWorkflowCompleted(ByVal sender As Object, _
                            ByVal e As WorkflowCompletedEventArgs)
        WaitHandle.Set()
    End Sub
End Class
```

When you execute the `WorkflowConsoleApplication` you can now see that the `Workflow` and `ActivityTracking` events will be displayed in the console window (see Figure 11.15).

FIGURE 11.15   Console output from the `ConsoleTrackingService`.

Summary

In this chapter you learned how to code against the `System.Workflow.Runtime` APIs to host workflows in your application. You also learned how to take advantage of runtime services, including the `SqlStatePersistenceService`, the `SqlTrackingService`, and `TerminationTrackingService`. Finally, you learned how to develop a custom tracking service that writes out tracking data to the console window.

CHAPTER 12

Dynamic Update of Workflow

IN THIS CHAPTER

- Modifying a Workflow Instance
- Controlling Modifiability
- Planning for Changes— Open-Points

As incredibly useful as workflows are in helping to manage business processes, historically workflow technologies have suffered because of their static nature. After a workflow has been created, to change the workflow to reflect a new business rule, the workflow would need to be rebuilt (resaved or recompiled depending on the workflow technology used). The inability of a workflow to be fluid over time (as the business it helps to run often is) was a severe limitation of many workflow implementations. A workflow that can be modified during execution is known as an *adaptive workflow*. It can adapt over time because of changing requirements without having to be rebuilt.

You can imagine many situations where having the capability to modify a workflow dynamically would be advantageous. The change might be permanent to all instances of the workflow or temporary to just one running instance. In either case, that capability is readily expected from workflow products.

Windows Workflow Foundation is built to have this flexibility inherent in its model. With Windows Workflow Foundation, you can modify a running instance of a workflow, or dynamically create workflows and activities. You might never end up using the features this chapter covers, but when you do need them you will be very happy that they are there.

Modifying a Workflow Instance

Whenever you are going to modify a workflow instance you'll need an instance of the `System.Workflow.ComponentModel.WorkflowChanges` class (see Listing 12.1). This is the class that provides the functionality to add or remove activities from an already running workflow instance.

The steps you'll use to modify a workflow will be as follows:

1. Create an instance of the `WorkflowChanges` class.

2. Use the `TransientWorkflow` property to add and remove activities.

3. Apply the changes.

The exact code to accomplish those three tasks will vary depending on from where you are trying to update the workflow—inside the workflow itself, or outside the workflow (from the host).

LISTING 12.1   The `WorkflowChanges` Type

```
namespace System.Workflow.ComponentModel
{
    public sealed class WorkflowChanges : IDisposable
    {
        public static DependencyProperty WorkflowChangeActionsProperty;
        public WorkflowChanges(IRootActivity rootActivity);
        public IList<System.Reflection.Assembly> AdditionalAssemblyReferences _
            { get; }
        public bool Canceled { get; }
        public bool Saved { get; }
        public CompositeActivity TransientWorkflow { get; }
        public void ApplyTo(Activity activity);
        public void ApplyTo(DataContext companionObject);
        public void Cancel();
        public void Save();
    }
}
```

Modifying a Workflow from the Inside

Modifying a workflow from the inside means that the code that is using the `WorkflowChanges` object is inside of the workflow code itself (or inside of the workflow's `DataContext` class). Modifying a workflow from the inside is easier than modifying it from the outside. It is easier because to successfully modify a workflow, you must have fairly intimate knowledge of the workflow, its activities, and its current state. This is more likely to happen if the code is executing inside of the workflow itself.

Imagine a simple workflow like the one in Figure 12.1 that has nothing but a single `Code` activity in it (that has an ID of `AddActivity`).

FIGURE 12.1   A simple workflow before modification.

Imagine that you want to modify this simple workflow by adding another `Code` activity after the one that is declared at design-time. To accomplish this, you can add code to the event handler that executes based upon the design-time `Code` activity. Inside of this event handler method you create a new `Code` activity and add it to the currently executing workflow instance using the `WorkflowChanges` object to accomplish the task. You can see this code in Listing 12.2.

LISTING 12.2   Adding a New Activity to an Executing Workflow

```
Shared updated As Boolean = False
    Private Sub AddActivity(ByVal o As Object, ByVal e As EventArgs)
        If Not updated Then
            updated = True
            Using wc As New WorkflowChanges(Me)
                Dim c As New Code
                c.ID = "AddAnotherActivity"
                AddHandler c.ExecuteCode, AddressOf AddActivity
                wc.TransientWorkflow.Activities.Add(c)
                wc.ApplyTo(Me)
            End Using
        End If
        Console.WriteLine("Code Activity {0} Hit!", CType(sender, Code).ID)
    End Sub
```

You can see the output of running this workflow in Figure 12.2. Notice that the `Console.WriteLine` call is executed twice, whereas just from the compiled design of the workflow it should have only executed once. You've now successfully modified a workflow instance dynamically during its lifetime.

FIGURE 12.2   Output of dynamically modified workflow.

So how does this code work? Because you are adding new Code activity, and the activity's ExecuteCode delegate will point to the same method you are using to add the activity, you only want the code to execute once, so use a Boolean flag to control that (the update field, which is set to true as soon as the update begins to happen).

The interesting code is inside the If statement. This is a simple example, but it shows the basic flow of making changes to an executing workflow.

First create an instance of the WorkflowChanges type. Do this inside of a using block because WorkflowChanges implements IDisposable, and you want to make sure that its resources will be cleaned up—especially in the case of an exception. The constructor of the WorkflowChanges type takes an IRootActivity reference that represents the workflow you would like to change. Because you are inside of that workflow instance, you can pass the reference to the workflow object itself.

The TransientWorkflow property is where you will go to modify the workflow. It is a cloned version of the workflow you passed to the constructor, a cloned version that is read/write. With the cloned workflow you can add or remove activities. Changing activities isn't effective (more on this in the section named "Warning—Existing Activities Not Modifiable," later in this chapter).

In this example, create a new Code activity, set its necessary properties (in this case ID and the delegate for ExecuteCode), and then add it to the end of the workflow's activities by calling TransientWorkflow.Activities.Add. Then call ApplyTo on the WorkflowChanges instance, which persists the changes you made in memory only to this workflow instance. When the workflow's execution resumes, the workflow will execute this newly added activity, which in this case will cause the AddActivity method to be called again, but this time it will just output the string to the console.

When modifying a workflow, you need to be careful because if your changes aren't valid, the ApplyTo method will raise an exception (a WorkflowValidationFailedException). In production code it probably makes sense to wrap the call to ApplyTo in a try/catch block. See an example of this in Listing 12.3.

LISTING 12.3   Handling Exceptions from the `ApplyTo` Method

```
Try
                    wc.ApplyTo(Me)
                Catch ex As WorkflowValidationFailedException
                    Console.WriteLine("ApplyTo failed")
                    Dim msg As String
                    Dim er As ValidationError
                    For Each er In ex.Errors
                        msg = "Error: " & er.ErrorNumber & er.ErrorText
                        Console.WriteLine(msg)
                    Next
```

Again, the center point of the `WorkflowChanges` type is the
`TransientWorkflow.Activities` property. This is a read/write collection of the activities of
the workflow, so you can call any of the methods on this collection to remove or add
activities. This set of activities is cloned from the original version, but will replace the
original version if you call `ApplyTo`. You can see the useful methods on this collection
when modifying a workflow in Listing 12.4.

LISTING 12.4   `ActivityCollection`

```
namespace System.Workflow.ComponentModel
{
    public sealed class ActivityCollection :
 IList<Activity>, ICollection<Activity>, IEnumerable<Activity>, IList, ICollection,
IEnumerable
    {
        public int Count { get; } //Find out the number of activities
        public Activity this[int index] { get; set; }//Find or set an Activity _
            by index
        public Activity this[string key] { get; }//get an Activity by ID
        public event ActivityCollectionChangeEventHandler ListChanged;
        public void Add(Activity item);//adds an Activity at the end of the list
        public void Clear();//clears all Activities
        public bool Contains(Activity item);//determine if an Activity exists
        public IEnumerator<Activity> GetEnumerator();//enumerate all Activities
        public int IndexOf(Activity item);//find the index of a particular Activity
        public void Insert(int index, Activity item);//insert at a particular index
        public bool Remove(Activity item);//remove an Activity
        public void RemoveAt(int index);//remove by index
    }
}
```

12

The `TransientWorkflow` property is just a reference to a `CompositeActivity`. The `CompositeActivity` type has the `GetActivityByName` overloaded method (derived from `Activity`), which can be very useful when trying to find an activity during modification. You can see these in Listing 12.5.

LISTING 12.5   `TransientWorkflow` (`CompositeActivity`)

```
namespace System.Workflow.ComponentModel
{
    public class Activity : DependencyObject, IInitializeForRuntime
    {   //abbreviated for brevity
        //Find an activity if you have the name (ID)
        public Activity GetActivityByName(string activityQualifiedID);
        public Activity GetActivityByName(string activityQualifiedID,
                                          bool withInThisActivityOnly);

    }
}
```

Also note the `AdditionalAssemblyReferences` property on the `WorkflowChanges` type, which allows you to add additional assemblies that might contain the activities you are adding (or might be ones referenced by activities you are adding to a workflow instance).

By using the `WorkflowChanges` object and its properties and methods, you can take an existing workflow and add or remove activities at will, assuming that the workflow will be in a legal state. Take note however, that the ability to modify a workflow at runtime doesn't mean you get options unavailable at design-time. This just means any change you make at runtime would have to be able to be compiled if you were making the same change at design-time. For example, at design-time you can't have two activities with the same ID property value; likewise you can't add an activity using `ApplyTo` that would have the same ID as another activity in the workflow. These are essentially the same checks that are done at design-time.

Warning—Existing Activities Not Modifiable

When you modify a workflow, you are limited to adding or removing (or both) activities. Changing an existing activity in the workflow is not supported. Let's take our simple workflow from Figure 12.1, and try to modify the `Code` activity rather than add a new one. Assume that the `Code` activity's `ExecuteCode` delegate is linked to a method that will produce the output in Figure 12.3. This is just a simple `Console.WriteLine` call that prints out the string "`Static!`", indicating that the activity was statically created at compile time.

FIGURE 12.3 Output of a simple workflow.

Now get a hold of the Code activity before it executes and try to modify it in memory. See the ModifyCode1 method in Listing 12.6 (assume this code is executing in the workflow before the Code activity itself would have executed).

LISTING 12.6 Trying to Modify an Existing Activity

```
Private Sub code1_ExecuteCode(ByVal o As Object, ByVal e As EventArgs)
     Console.WriteLine("Static!")
  End Sub
  Private Sub Test(ByVal o As Object, ByVal e As EventArgs)
     Console.WriteLine("Dynamic!")
  End Sub
  Private Sub ModifyCode_ExecuteCode(ByVal sender As System.Object, ByVal e As
System.EventArgs)
     Using wc As New WorkflowChanges(Me)
        Dim c As Code = _
           CType(wc.TransientWorkflow.GetActivityByName("code1"), Code)
        AddHandler c.ExecuteCode, AddressOf Test
        wc.ApplyTo(Me)
     End Using
  End Sub
```

This code produces the exact same output as Figure 12.3. Adding an additional delegate to the ExecuteCode event has no effect—the change is ignored (although notice there aren't any exceptions thrown from ApplyTo).

If I add the following two lines of code (see Listing 12.7) the output changes to be what I want and expect (see Figure 12.4).

LISTING 12.7 Removing and Adding an Activity

```
  Private Sub ModifyCode_ExecuteCode(ByVal sender As System.Object, ByVal e As
System.EventArgs)
     Using wc As New WorkflowChanges(Me)
```

LISTING 12.7   Continued

```
        Dim c As Code = _
            CType(wc.TransientWorkflow.GetActivityByName("code1"), Code)
        AddHandler c.ExecuteCode, AddressOf Test
        wc.TransientWorkflow.Activities.Remove(c)
        wc.TransientWorkflow.Activities.Add(c)
        wc.ApplyTo(Me)
    End Using
End Sub
```

FIGURE 12.4   Output of a simple workflow modified.

You can see that we really didn't modify the activity while it was part of the workflow; we changed it, then removed it, and then added it back in to the workflow. The same activity instance can be reused, but in order for a change to be reflected in a workflow, the activity must be removed and then added; changing the activity object in memory has no effect. Only activities passed to the methods on the `TransientWorkflow.Activites` property will be noted as changes. Again, the changes that are noted are either adds or removes.

Modifying a Workflow from the Outside

What if your workflow wasn't designed with some dynamic purpose in mind, but you would still like to reach into its list of activities and make a change? It is possible to reach into a workflow from the outside and modify it, assuming you have access to the right information. This means a host can reach into a workflow that is executing and make modifications. Note that the same rules apply here in terms of what is a legal modification and what is considered an actual modification.

When you execute a workflow from a host by calling `WorkflowRuntime.StartWorkflow` you can get a reference to a `WorkflowInstance` type (see Chapter 11, "Hosting Workflows in Your Application," for more information about hosting workflows). You can use this `WorkflowInstance` to reach in and get the current `IRootActivity` you need to create a `WorkflowChanges` object. This really isn't the end of the story, however.

One issue you have to overcome when trying to modify a workflow from a host is determining when the workflow can be modified, and when such a modification will be effective. Usually your host isn't very informed as to when a particular activity is or has been executed, so trying to guess at what point a workflow change makes sense could produce fairly random results (imagine adding activity into the collection at a point that had already executed).

So somehow the host needs to know when the workflow is paused, or in a state where a modification can actually be effective.

One way to do this is if there is a Suspend activity in the workflow. The host can subscribe to the WorkflowRuntime.WorkflowSuspended event. When the Suspend activity hits, the WorkflowRuntime will fire this event. The host, in its event handler method, can then modify the workflow. Let's take the same example I used earlier where I added a new delegate for a Code activity, and make that modification happen from the host instead of from inside of the Workflow.

You can see the code for this in Listing 12.8.

LISTING 12.8 Removing and Adding an Activity from the Host

```
Imports System
Imports System.Collections.Generic
Imports System.Text
Imports System.Threading
Imports System.Workflow.Runtime
Imports System.Workflow.ComponentModel
Imports System.Workflow.Runtime.Hosting
Imports System.Workflow.Activities


Module OutsideModifyWF
    Class Program
        Shared WaitHandle As New AutoResetEvent(False)

        Shared Sub Main()
            'fire up the engine
            Dim workflowRuntime As New WorkflowRuntime()
            workflowRuntime.StartRuntime()

            AddHandler workflowRuntime.WorkflowCompleted, _
                AddressOf OnWorkflowCompleted
            AddHandler workflowRuntime.WorkflowSuspended, _
                AddressOf ChangeWorkflow
            'load workflow type
            Dim type As System.Type = GetType(Workflow1)
```

LISTING 12.8   Continued

```vb
        workflowRuntime.StartWorkflow(type)


        WaitHandle.WaitOne()

        workflowRuntime.StopRuntime()
    End Sub
    Shared _updated As Boolean = False
    Shared Sub ChangeWorkflow(ByVal o As Object, _
        ByVal e As WorkflowSuspendedEventArgs)
        'Note the change has to happen after the event
        'returns since the Workflow doesn't actually stop
        'until after this event handler returns
        'doing this avoids a race condition and
        'and an exception
        Dim wc As WaitCallback
        wc = New WaitCallback(AddressOf DoUpdate)
        Dim wo As Object
        wo = e.WorkflowInstance
        ThreadPool.QueueUserWorkItem(wc, wo)
    End Sub
    Shared Sub DoUpdate(ByVal state As Object)
        Dim wi As WorkflowInstance = CType(state, WorkflowInstance)
        If Not _updated Then

            _updated = True
            Dim ra As IRootActivity
            ra = wi.GetWorkflowDefinition()
            Using wc As New WorkflowChanges(ra)
                Dim a As Activity
                Dim tw As Activity
                tw = wc.TransientWorkflow
                a = tw.GetActivityByName("code1")
                Dim c As Code = CType(a, Code)
                AddHandler c.ExecuteCode, AddressOf Test
                wc.TransientWorkflow.Activities.Remove(c)
                wc.TransientWorkflow.Activities.Add(c)
                wi.ApplyWorkflowChanges(wc)
            End Using
        End If
        wi.Resume()
    End Sub
    Shared Sub Test(ByVal o As Object, ByVal e As EventArgs)
```

LISTING 12.8   Continued

```
        Console.WriteLine("Modified Workflow from Host!")
    End Sub
    Shared Sub OnWorkflowCompleted(ByVal sender As Object, _
        ByVal e As WorkflowCompletedEventArgs)
        WaitHandle.Set()
    End Sub

  End Class
End Module
```

The differences between this code and the "inside" code are subtle. First, getting a reference to the workflow is different. In the "inside" method you could just use the "this" reference. From the host, you get a reference to the running workflow by going to the `WorkflowInstance.GetWorkflowDefinition` method (this assumes that you've kept a live refernce to the `WorkflowInstance` you retrieved from the `StartWorkflow` method). This returns an `IRootActivity` reference that you can use to construct the `WorkflowChanges` object.

The code that adds or removes activities from the workflow stays the same. But the code that changes is the line that causes `WorkflowChanges.ApplyTo` to be called. In the "inside" version you could just call `ApplyTo` directly. `ApplyTo` takes either an `Activity` type or a `DataContext` type. In this "outside" version you don't have a reference to either of those objects, but you do have a reference to the `WorkflowInstance` object. It has a method named `WorkflowInstance.ApplyWorkflowChanges`. So `ApplyWorkflowChanges` is used as the mechanism to cause the workflow changes to persist when you are using `WorkflowChanges` from outside of the workflow instance itself.

Controlling Modifiability

Despite the fact that having an adaptive workflow is useful, you might not want your workflow to be modified at runtime. Also, you might want your workflow to be modifiable only under certain conditions.

All workflow instances are modifiable by default, but all have a `DynamicUpdateCondition` property. When a workflow change is being attempted, the `WorkflowChanges` instance checks the property. If this property is null or the `Condition` returns true, the workflow instance can be modified. This means if you fail to set the `DynamicUpdateCondition` for your workflow, it will be modifiable. If your `Condition` returns false, an exception will be thrown and the workflow will not be modified and the changes will be lost.

The two built-in classes that derive from `Condition` are `CodeCondition` and `CodeDomCondition`. Again it is often the case that a workflow can be modifiable at certain times and not others. If your workflow has that kind of requirement, you'll need to set the `DynamicUpdateCondition` property and then set up the `Condition` activity correctly to return true or false depending on your workflow state.

To select your `DynamicUpdateCondition`, go to the workflow designer and select properties on the workflow itself. The `DynamicUpdateCondition` has a combo box in the property grid, which shows you the options you can select. Once you select your option, you must set the `Condition` property. You get the `Condition` property by expanding the `DynamicUpdateCondition` property in the properties grid. See Figure 12.5.

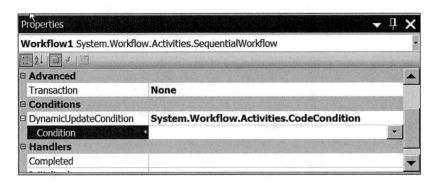

FIGURE 12.5   `DynamicUpdateCondition` property.

If you've selected a `CodeCondition`, you can either type in a method name, or select an appropriate method from the combo box. If the method specified returns true, the dynamic update can happen. If the method returns false, the dynamic update fails with an `InvalidOperationException`, which you may want to add as a possible exception to catch from the `ApplyTo` method.

With the `CodeCondition` you can execute code (check a property perhaps) to see whether the workflow instance is in a state where a modification can occur. If not, return false from the method. See an example in Listing 12.9.

LISTING 12.9   Removing and Adding an Activity from the Host

```
Dim _updateable As Boolean = True
Private Function Update(ByVal o As System.Object, _
    ByVal e As System.EventArgs) As System.Boolean
    Return True
End Function
```

The `CodeDomCondition` allows you to have a more fluid way of defining the condition, but the effect is the same; if the `CodeDomCondition` returns true, modification is possible, otherwise an exception will occur. Remember again that if you do not set the `DynamicUpdateCondition` it will be set to null, which means y our workflow will be updatable.

Planning for Changes—Open-Points

Although you can see it's possible to take an existing workflow and modify it from the outside even when the workflow itself was never designed to accept changes, it might not be a good design idea. First, the mechanism for doing so can be difficult (if not impossible) if the workflow itself isn't developed to know about the possible change(s). Trying to modify an existing workflow that isn't expecting a change can result in unexpected behavior and random errors, and is fraught with potential race conditions, none of which are very attractive.

It is possible (and probably preferable) to design a workflow to accept changes. Although the Suspend shape gave you a way in, it isn't really a very pleasing design. Adding Suspend activities just to have extensibility points doesn't really make much sense in a production workflow. Modifying the workflow from the host in general doesn't make much sense because of the dangers involved; designing the workflow to make the changes itself in a safe, extensible way is a much better design.

To have a workflow that can accept changes at runtime, you need to design it with extensibility in mind. When you have a workflow design that demands plugability or flexibility, you'll (hopefully) know at design-time where you want the extensibility point(s) to be. In workflow terminology these points are called open-points and can be an effective design technique to create a workflow that can give you the best of both worlds—design-time stability but runtime flexibility.

Let's take a slightly more complicated workflow than the simple ones you've been looking at in this chapter. Imagine a workflow to model what happens to a patient during a visit to a hospital. The patient has to be admitted, and then some treatment must be applied to the patient. In midtreatment the physician might change the diagnosis and want the patient to be run through some completely different treatment. New treatments and diagnoses are discovered everyday, so the system would need to be both flexible and extensible. A workflow to model a patient's flow through a hospital stay would have to be dynamic in terms of the activities that the workflow would go through. The workflow would also have to be extensible in that new activities could be added to the system to accommodate the changes in medical technology.

For this example let's not bite off the whole apple; let's just take a patient through being admitted to the hospital, through a single treatment, and then discharged (obviously a more complicated long-running workflow would be needed to fully model this in a real-world application).

Figure 12.6 shows the simple UI of this workflow application. The user can enter a patient's name, and then click the Admit button. After the patient has been admitted, the user can pick a treatment from the combo box (which is really a list of activities that the workflow can be extended with) and then click the Treat button. Once the treatment activity is finished, the patient is discharged.

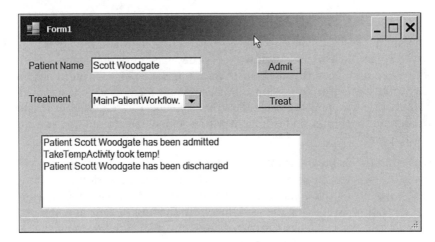

FIGURE 12.6   Patient workflow UI.

Next let's look at the workflow and then dissect it to see how it all works. The workflow is visible in Figure 12.7.

This workflow makes heavy use of Data Activities (see Chapter 6, "Using Web Services," for more information about Data Activities) to communicate between the workflow and the host (which is built into the Windows Form UI layer). When a patient is initially admitted via the UI, the workflow starts, but immediately uses the UpdateData activity to fire an event notification notifying interested subscribers in that event. Inside of the sequence there is a WaitForData activity. This uses an ObjectDataSource, which is linked to a field of type PatientData, which is the type that the host passes to this WaitForData activity and the type that the workflow passes out via the UpdateData activities. Part of the PatientData type is a property named Treatment, which is a string that indicates what activity type should be loaded into the sequence with the ID of TreatSequence. This is the open-point build into this workflow.

Because the WorkflowChanges model is so flexible, a predefined activity like a sequence isn't absolutely necessary (you could just not have any activity in the "place" where you want to add dynamic activities) but having a placeholder makes the design of the work-flow easier to understand (and to maintain). So any container activity will work—for this workflow, use a sequence.

After a workflow instance has been initialized, it sits and waits on the WaitForData activity, so when a treatment is picked from the combo box in the UI, the host sends a DataObject message to the workflow (via the DataSourceService) and the workflow then continues. The next activity picks up the treatment value that has been passed in and uses it to dynamically load an activity type and add it to the TreatmentSequence's list of activities. The workflow then continues, causing the newly added activity to execute, and then the patient is discharged. You can see the code that dynamically adds an activity in Listing 12.10 (this is the method that gets called by the Code activity, which executes right after the WaitForData activity).

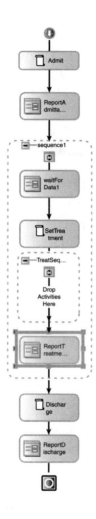

FIGURE 12.7   Patient workflow.

LISTING 12.10   Modifying the Extensible Workflow

```
Private Sub SetTreatmentActivity(ByVal sender As System.Object, ByVal e As _
    System.EventArgs)
    'get the type
    Dim t As Type = Type.GetType(_patient.Treatment)
    'create the activity instance
    Dim a As Activity
    a = CType(t.Assembly.CreateInstance(t.FullName), Activity)
    'the activities in this design need a PatientData instance
    'so they all have a Patient property of that Type
    Dim prop As DependencyProperty
    prop = DependencyProperty.FromName("Patient", t)
```

LISTING 12.10　Continued

```
    'Bind that parameter to this workflow's PatientData field
    Dim bind As New ActivityBind()
    bind.ID = "/Workflow"
    bind.Path = "_patient"
    a.SetBinding(prop, bind)
    'change the workflow
    Using wc As New WorkflowChanges(Me)

        'get the sequence "open-point"
        Dim ca As CompositeActivity
        ca = wc.TransientWorkflow()
        Dim s As Sequence
        s = CType(ca.GetActivityByName("TreatSequence"), Sequence)
        s.Activities.Clear()
        'add the Activity
        s.Activities.Add(a)
        'save the changes
        wc.ApplyTo(Me)

    End Using
End Sub
```

Again the purpose of this design is to build into the workflow a place where new activities can be dynamically loaded. There are a number of ways to accomplish this, but having a predefined open space for adding activities makes adapting the workflow much easier.

Summary

In this chapter you saw that although Windows Workflow Foundation is based on a compiled workflow model; it is built from the ground up to support adaptive changes. Using the WorkflowChanges object, you are able to modify a running workflow by adding or removing activities. By designing your workflow well, you can build very robust, adaptive workflow systems.

Index

recursive composition of states, 223-225

Reflection (System.Reflection.Assembly), 235-236

rehydrating

description of of, 54

WorkflowInstance, 247-248

repeat patterns (state machines), 227

Replicator activity

APIs, 157

configuring, 154

description of, 54

overview, 153-154

sample workflow, 154-157

UntilCondition, 154

reports (workflow), 80

ReviewComplete (Set State activity), 222

rework patterns, 207, 227

root activities

state machines, 216-217

types of, 137

Rules (runtime layer), 10

RuleSet (Policy activity), 164

externalizing, 171

forward chaining, 169-170

halt and update functions, 170

maximum execution count, 171

prioritizing, 168-169

runtime architecture (Windows Workflow Foundation)

description of, 229-230

System.Workflow.Runtime assembly, 231

runtime layer (architecture engine), 10

runtime services

adding, 243-244

custom runtime services, 257-258

default services, 243

limitations, 242

purpose of, 184

S

SayHello, 40

scenarios (workflow), 5

Scheduler (runtime layer), 10

Scope activity, 58-59

SelectData, 92, 96

Sequence activity, 48-49

Sequential Workflow Library, 197-201

sequential workflow model (workflow model layer)

description of, 10

example activity, 16-18

Sequential Workflow template, 13

sequential workflows, 207-208

server administrators, 69

Service Oriented Architecture, 119. *See also* web services

Service Request Management Systems, 187, 197

Service.asmx, 134

session web services, 126-127

SessionID property, 126

T

W

X - Y - Z